A THOUSAND PAPER CUTS

SIGN, STORAGE, TRANSMISSION

A series edited by Jonathan Sterne and Lisa Gitelman

A THOUSAND PAPER CUTS

US EMPIRE AND THE BUREAUCRATIC LIFE OF WAR

Anjali Nath

DUKE UNIVERSITY PRESS | *Durham and London* | 2025

© 2025 Duke University Press

All rights reserved

Project Editor: Bird Williams

Designed by Dave Rainey

Typeset in Arno Pro and Zuume by Copperline Books

Library of Congress Cataloging-in-Publication Data

Names: Nath, Anjali, [date] author.

Title: A thousand paper cuts : US Empire and the bureaucratic life
of war / Anjali Nath.

Other titles: Sign, storage, transmission.

Description: Durham : Duke University Press, 2025. | Series: Sign,
storage, transmission | Includes bibliographical references and index.

Identifiers: LCCN 2025013308 (print)

LCCN 2025013309 (ebook)

ISBN 9781478032854 (paperback)

ISBN 9781478029410 (hardcover)

ISBN 9781478061601 (ebook)

Subjects: LCSH: United States. Freedom of Information Act. | Freedom of
information—United States. | Government information—United States. |
Government information—Censorship—United States. | Transparency
(Ethics) in government—United States. | Official secrets—United States. |
Visual communication—Political aspects—United States.

Classification: LCC KF5753 .N38 2025 (print) | LCC KF5753 (ebook) |
DDC 342.7308/53—dc23/eng/20250415

LC record available at https://lccn.loc.gov/2025013308

LC ebook record available at https://lccn.loc.gov/2025013309

Cover art: Courtesy of Bahar Behbahani.

for mom

CONTENTS

I believe the United States is nothing but a *paper tiger* . . . outwardly a tiger,
[America] is made of paper, unable to withstand the wind and the rain.
—MAO TSE-TUNG, "U.S. Imperialism Is a Paper Tiger"

On February 22, 2017, an intern at the Department of Homeland Security sent an
email up the chain to their supervising analyst for a first-level review of a document referred to in the subject line as simply the "Race Paper." The analyst responded with a laudatory note a few days later, couching editorial comments on
the draft with enthusiasm for the project: "As you can see, there's a lot to chew on
here. I honestly think this is going to turn out to be a really solid paper (no, I'm
not blowing smoke up your asses)."[1] The intern attended to the edits with their
cowriter, and shot the document back with a request to talk through the new
draft. "I'll come by in a sec," the analyst replied, attaching a file named "RaceDTIA
_1st levelsecondlook.docx," and ending the email exchange with what one might
reasonably infer was a cubicle visit to their supervisee.

   This banal, bureaucratic exchange would be forgettable if not for a few men-
acing peculiarities: the location of the exchange (the Internal Threats Division
of the Office of Intelligence and Analysis); the process by which the emails arrived in the public sphere (a request for public records issued through the Freedom of Information Act); and, most ominously, the appearance of the "Race

Paper" itself (a nine-page attachment, completely blacked out from margin to margin, censored beyond comprehension). In other words, this otherwise un-remarkable email exchange presented the only window into this "Race Paper," which appears (from context) to be a government-requisitioned position paper on race-based surveillance and monitoring of social movements in the United States. As of the writing of this book, the "Race Paper" remains fully redacted, its title and contents withheld from the public.[2]

Activists composed this public records request that unearthed the "Race Paper" in the midst of popular uprisings against police violence, calling on nearly a dozen federal offices to release "records detailing policies and actions involving the monitoring and surveillance of public protests surrounding police violence, policing reform, racial justice, and the Black Lives Matter movement."[3] The request, drafted by the media activist organization Color of Change (CoC) and longtime civil rights organization Center for Constitutional Rights (CCR), pinpointed the Federal Bureau of Investigation and the Department of Homeland Security and their affiliate departments and programs, in an attempt to return a surveilling gaze at a repressive state whose watchful eyes were a constant presence.[4] Activists and abolitionists engaged in mobilizations precipitated by the murders of Trayvon Martin, Michael Brown, and other victims of racist violence had long known their movements were being surveilled and infiltrated. Journalists and civil rights organizations confirmed these suspicions, mining government and private security firm documents that they had procured through litigation alongside those voluntarily released by agencies themselves.[5] The government had been using military-grade technologies and militarized counterinsurgent strategies against the racial justice movement, drawing on federally funded "counterterrorism" programs to monitor the activities and whereabouts of protesters and to intimidate them. CoC and CCR's public records request letter contextualized their demands by writing their concerns about these surveillance activities in detail.

The Internal Threats Division produced hundreds of papers in response to this public records request, including the email and its mysterious blacked-out nine-page "Race Paper" attachment. The CCR and CoC took particular pause at this release. "Considering the documents are all fully black[ed] out," they wrote in a briefing guide on the case, "we are thus left to speculate, as to why DHS would prepare a document it refers to only as the 'Race Paper' and then closely guard its contents, even to the point of concealing its actual title and a basic

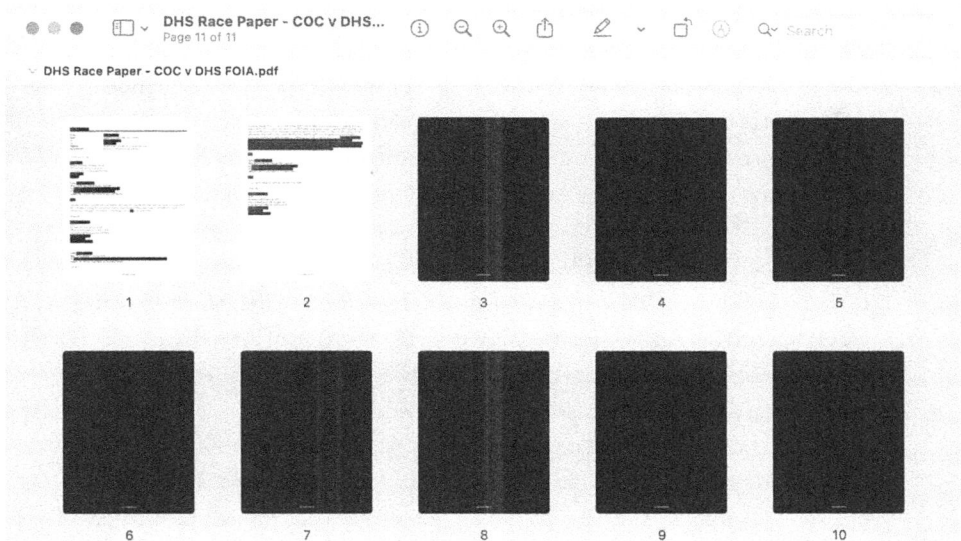

I.1 Contact sheet of Department of Homeland Security "Race Paper" PDF disclosure, released under the Freedom of Information Act in 2019 under the *Color of Change v. Department of Homeland Security and Federal Bureau of Investigation* legal case.

description."[6] Running atop the left edge of each blacked-out page of the fully censored "Race Paper" was a cluster of red letters and numbers: "(b)(5),(b)(3)." The code referred to the specific legally permissible exemptions to the disclosure of government documents under the Freedom of Information Act. Reading the margins, exclusions, and censor's mark was practically limiting, yet speculatively profound. Even the name *Race Paper* gestured toward a form of knowledge more grandiose than its surveillant utility, pointing toward the idea that paper itself might form a racial and imperial infrastructure. Let us begin with paper, as the most basic unit of a surveillant, archiving, war-making police state.

This book is an attempt to make sense of not just of this correspondence but also the mechanism by which one might write a letter to the state demanding to see its files. What is the political, intellectual, and media history whereby papers can be requested for public viewing, only to be censored or denied? Why does the Freedom of Information Act—or any other public records act—exist? By which process are formerly classified documents censored—or, as the censoring of paper records is known, redacted? Further, what are the visual politics of such redacted documents, living in the public sphere as *images* that invite shock and speculative awe? Rather than a singular event, the "Race Paper" episode is but one in a repeating pattern in which people struggle to wrest papers from the state, to variable outcomes. From the paper trails of the FBI's infamous Counterintelligence Program (COINTELPRO) to the dark archives of US covert actions in the Global South, to whistleblower document exposés like those spearheaded by Daniel Ellsberg or Edward Snowden, the struggle to access informational files is stitched to a shadow archive. Moreover, the aesthetic of the redacted motifs that emerge from such repetitive encounters echo across a variety of social and political spaces of contestation.

My fascination with the entanglements of paper and power began in the midst of the War on Terror, during a period of suffering that was both spectacular in its imagery and patently hidden from view. I sought to understand, precisely, the visual politics at work in the security state, in an attempt to make sense of an emergent configuration of power that was at once familiar and disorienting. Like others, I found myself drawn to the aesthetic dimensions of redaction as they appeared in the numerous "Torture Memos," leaked and released in censored form during the presidency of George W. Bush. This cache of legal memos and correspondence mapped a real-time project of dispossession and disappearance, and the flimsy attempt to justify unlawful detention and cruel and unusual punishment. But their redacted appearance mirrored their patchy appearance in the public sphere, as the spectacle of their censored release belied a sinister regulation on sight into the labyrinth of US military detention centers and black sites. These years of post-9/11 endless war generated an experientially paradoxical relationship to visuality. On one hand, the possibility of seeing and being seen was everywhere; images of planes crashing endlessly into New York City skyscrapers looped endlessly to the point of ubiquity, and flak-jacketed embedded reporting emerged as the new media standard of journalism. Yet at the same time, the War on Terror proliferated in shadows, far from public eyes, with explicit declaration from Vice President Dick Cheney that the imperial machine would covertly operate in such a "dark side." There was an ironic public acknowledgment, in other words, of the role that secrecy would play in the imperial war. As lawyers and civil rights groups sought information about the secretive operations taking place in this clandestine, postmodern, networked theater of permanent war, the *look* of redaction became an attendant and incessant ghastly presence.

Censorship was so enmeshed in the project of rendition (and the War on Terror in general) that it became impossible to disentangle the aesthetics of redaction from the practices of state violence. One contention of this book is that the redacted document—and the aesthetic of redaction—must be understood as a particular kind of militarized view, in relation to other militarized views: aerial views, the actuarial gaze, the infographic and data visualization, soldier-produced videos and police bodycams, biometric views, spectacular views, and more.[7] The redacted document lives as an image within an economy of ever-present, easily tradable images, what Susan Sontag once critically, and presciently, appraised as an attempt at the *imprisonment* of reality in the image-form.[8] Yet the censored document is also information, emerging from a bureaucratic apparatus that manages and disseminates paper in both digital and print forms. Another idea of this book is that a cultural history of information can also be a visual study in imperial forms of knowledge. The ideals of transparency, the implementation of public access laws like FOIA, and dialectics of concealment and disclosure must be relationally positioned to other forms of knowing and the impossibility of seeing in totality.

Rob Nixon, elaborating on the visual dimension of nuclear colonialism and other forms of what he terms "slow violence" perpetrated against the wretched of the earth asks: "How do we both make slow violence visible yet also challenge the privileging of the visible?"[9] Secret nuclear testing, in fact, provided the backdrop for key precedent-setting legal cases under the Freedom of Information Act in its early years, as communities fought to make visible government documents to index the harms of nuclear proliferation on their communities. The political practice of transparency emerges from a structural opposition between what Nicholas Mirzoeff has called "the Right to Look," and the limits of the beheld object to illustrate the violence of actuality.[10] Yet government documents do not tell us what they profess to, precisely because of the authority they represent. This can be one starting point, but certainly not an end.

A Thousand Paper Cuts dwells in this dialectical contradiction of visual objects—papers, documents—as produced out of racialized and uneven encounters, managed by imperial information regimes yet nevertheless made meaningful through political struggles to seize them. This book arcs around a cultural history of FOIA. I begin with a broad discussion of transparency to situate the Freedom of Information Act within an intellectual landscape of the Cold War. I do so in order to place declassified documents and their aesthetics within a political and social history that emerges from the contradictions of capitalism in its Cold War form. From there, I examine activist contestations to imperialism through FOIA, the aesthetic dimensions of the redacted document and the lifeworlds they conjure, and conclude with a reflection on the place of redaction art within a militarized landscape. The structure of the book foregrounds my investment in tethering the now-ubiquitous redacted aesthetic back to the political and cultural conditions that made it possible.

FREEDOM OF INFORMATION AND IMPERIALISM

The Freedom of Information Act (FOIA) was passed in 1966, amid global movements against colonialism and racism, and in a newly nuclearized world both discursively and materially split in three through violence. FOIA emerged from these world-breaking and -remaking phenomena, as a tempered response to the kinds of secret archives that proliferated in the tense shadows of the Cold War, advancing "transparency" as a natural extension of American exceptionalism. Within certain parameters, the law allowed everyday people to request information from the federal government, with the assumption that documents should be presumptively accessible to the general public. The law thus reversed previous operating norms, thereby forcing the government to prove why a document should be withheld, rather than evaluating the legitimacy of a person's request for information. It is worth emphasizing that historically, FOIA is inextricable from this security bureaucracy that was exponentially producing more and more pages of classified material as the Cold War dragged on. Surveillance files collected in the midst of a McCarthyite campaign against the left were innumerably voluminous. Critical studies of surveillance must reckon with the central role that documents play in the making of the security state as critical infrastructure of the intelligence world. Paper is the grist of state violence.

Though FOIA is not presently the only law to govern the disclosure of paper, many pieces of legislation were authored *after* FOIA, modeled in tandem with, in likeness of, and in response to the law. Since 1966, all US states have adopted open records laws, and in 1974 the federal government passed the Privacy Act, which addressed access to files of individuals. Document withholding, censorship, and redaction occur under these numerous laws, and within the theater of the court or in legal proceedings between different agencies. However, FOIA remains the most important and best-known piece of transparency legislation in America, one around which people organized, and one, as well, that has its own aesthetic and political cultures that were precedent setting. FOIA in many ways has been an unlikely and unexpected, if not ironic, protagonist in struggles against US state violence.

Since 1966, FOIA has been amended numerous times and its parameters debated both in the courts and in the public sphere. FOIA's purview includes federal documents, but there exist nine exemptions, nine categories of information that are not required to be released, and three exclusions that are also not required to be released.[11] These exemptions cover national security, trade secrets, personnel files, personal privacy, and privileged communications, but they are hardly straightforward. For instance, in 2015 Nate Jones, director of the FOIA Project of the National Security Archive, testified in Congress about the specific overuse of Exemption Five (privileged communication), which he argued was being unfairly marshalled to "censor embarrassing or inconvenient information that should be released."[12] The National Security Archive, an incredible physical and virtual repository of government documents founded in 1985 by transparency advocates, had by Jones's account more than fifty thousand FOIA requests in their history, and figure prominently in historic, legal, and ethical conversations around government document accessibility. Jones and other critics underscored that Exemption Five, delineating possible exemptions of inter- and intraoffice memoranda, had been used as pretext to preemptively withhold information that might paint the requisitioned agency in a bad light, but not information that was inherently sensitive or otherwise excludable in some way.[13] These contested parameters of nondisclosure exist within a political struggle over information access.

My critique of transparency resonates with Chandan Reddy's elaborations of the intimacies between imperial notions of *freedom* and the attendant regimes of violence that such a notion welcomes. As Reddy writes of the United States, "Every effective expression of universal freedom arrives with the materially produced network of repressive and ideological institutions whose provisional unity is the basis of the state's claim to a monopoly violence." In other words, a serious examination of FOIA must account for precisely the kinds of imperial pathways and ideas that made it possible. Reddy insists that "freedom with violence" summons how "socially and institutionally produced forms of emancipation remain regulatively and constitutively tied to the nation-state form."[14]

The *Freedom* of Information Act is ethically, discursively, and materially tied to the violence of the state, paradoxically as a seeming defense against such violence yet also an ancillary of it. As I explore in chapter 1, some of the vociferous supporters of transparency legislation were often silent about the United States and its participation in racialized and anticommunist violence and, in other contexts, participated in its forward imperial march.[15]

Nevertheless, FOIA has become an indispensable tool in the writing of critical histories of the state, its surveillant practices, and its histories of abuse and neglect. And in its first years it presented a new horizon of possibility. For instance, in 1974, a young Cedric Robinson, while at his first tenure-track job at SUNY Binghamton, issued a FOIA request for the history of the Communist Party in South Africa. At the time FOIA, still relatively new, was in the process of being amended and had debuted in the public sphere as a tool by which to challenge the authority of state power.[16] Robinson's request produced a few responsive documents, though, as most were simply publications or broadcasts that the CIA had on file, not their own internal memoranda. Still, I highlight Robinson's use of the then-new law to indicate a broader desire to make a nascent FOIA useful for critical scholarly inquiry. There was a curiosity about the kind of work FOIA might do in the service of social justice movements and students of left history. Noting the importance of the new law, the American Historical Association at the time had a Freedom of Information Committee, one that included members like feminist scholar Blanche Wiesen Cook, who advocated for the political and methodological necessity of document access in writing women's histories and history from below.[17] Many of these members would shortly thereafter be involved with a political organization, the Fund for Open Information and Accountability, Inc. (FOIA Inc.), who were protagonists in the world of radical transparency activism I detail in chapter 2. Athan Theoharis and Angus MacKenzie were some of the earliest chroniclers of FOIA's significance, though MacKenzie's work in particular remains relatively forgotten.[18] These historians simultaneously advocated for the importance of FOIA for radical histories and while working with activists in New York City (primarily) to challenge workplace conditions, police violence, and counterintelligence more broadly through transparency laws.

In the same period, Columbia University professor Sigmund Diamond submitted a FOIA request to obtain his file from the FBI based on his experiences as a student at Harvard. While a graduate student (and later administrative

Jile DC-1

14 NOV 1974

Professor Cedric Robinson
Department of Afro-American Studies
State University of New York at
 Binghamton
Binghamton, New York   13901

Dear Professor Robinson:

The results of the search of Agency files for unclassified data on the history of the Communist party in the
Republic of South Africa are enclosed. The data include.

    a. Two foreign broadcasts on the party that
provide some insight into the development and history
of the party.

    b. A JPRS translation of an interview in Czecho-
slovakia of Yusuf Muhammad Dadoo, Chairman of the
Communist party of South Africa.

    c. A short reading list of recent books and
governmental studies on the South African Communist
party that might be of value in developing your
course.

I have also reproduced the frontispiece of the
journal, *The African Communist*, which is distributed
by Inkululeko Publications, 39 Goodge Street, London,
W.1. This journal may be available in your university
library. If not, the reproduced title page gives you
information on subscription costs and how you may order
the journal.

For your information the Agency releases unclassified research and reference aids to the public through
the Document Expediting (DOCEX) Project of the Library
of Congress. DOCEX provides its subscribers with governmental publications not available at the issuing agency or
the Government Printing Office. Your university is a
participating member of DOCEX. We have not published
any reference or research aids to date on your subject
but you may find it useful to check with the library on
a periodic basis to review Agency research aids that are
released through DOCEX.

Sincerely,

/s/ Angus MacLean Thuermer
Angus MacLean Thuermer
Assistant to the Director

Enclosures

I.2   Letter to Professor Cedric Robinson from Angus MacLean Thuermer, November 14, 1974; released by the CIA on July 7, 2005.

worker) at Harvard in the 1950s, McGeorge Bundy, dean of the Faculty of Arts and Sciences, had asked about Diamond's associations with the Communist Party. Diamond's FOIA, filed in 1977, led to documentation revealing Harvard University's close ties with US intelligence agencies on the part of administrators, students, and staff during the Second Red Scare, which he detailed in the 1992 book *Compromised Campus: The Collaboration of Universities with the Intelligence Community, 1945–1955*.[19] Diamond's book inaugurated a specific kind of inquiry into the collaborations between institutions of higher education and the intelligence world. Most notably, Diamond's use of FOIA to uncover on-campus abuse inspired anthropologist David Price's exacting trilogy of books detailing the history of anthropology's ties to the national security state.[20]

In both the academic and trade press, entire books have been dedicated to reprinting the FBI files of particular individuals and communities. For instance, *Che Guevara and the FBI: The U.S. Political Police Dossier on the Latin American Revolutionary*, edited by radical lawyers Michael Ratner and Michael Steven Smith, contained over a hundred surveillance documents from the FBI and CIA on Guevara. For students of ethnic studies, *The Cointelpro Papers: Documents from the FBI's Secret Wars Against Dissent in the United States*, edited by Jim Vanderwall and Ward Churchill, since its publication in 1990 by the leftist, cooperatively run South End Press, has been an indispensable sourcebook for those looking for primary texts on US government infiltration and spying on activist groups from the early Cold War period through the 1970s.[21] The files of James Baldwin, Martin Luther King Jr., and Malcolm X, among others, have been published as standalone books.[22] As I account for in chapter 2, in the 1970s and 1980s, the efforts to secure such files emerged from within activist and community spaces, as everyday people as well as social movement lawyers sought to bring public scrutiny to secret documents. Before the possibility of electronic file-sharing, these sourcebooks, filled with the primary texts of imperial power, were themselves a political endeavor, as exemplified by texts like Christy Macy and Susan Kaplan's book *Documents: A Shocking Collection of Memoranda, Letters, and Telexes from the Secret Files of the American Intelligence Community*, published in 1980 on behalf of the Center for National Security Studies. These sorts of publications, both past and present, reproduce papers with an indexical fidelity to the originals, in order to create broader community access to the primary sources that archive state repression. More recently, MIT Press has partnered with the information activist organization MuckRock on a series of books—*Activists Under Surveillance, Scientists Under Surveillance,* and *Writers Under Surveillance*—that curate a set of documents relating to the security files of specific figures.

In addition to such annotated collections of the security archive's primary texts, declassified and redacted documents by necessity figure centrally in writing the histories of state power, racialized communities, and activism on the left, particularly in accounts that oppose the brutality of state violence.[23] Recent works focused on the long traces of American war in the Pacific, scrutinize the document in their thorough accounting of racialized violence. For instance, Ma Vang's work on Hmong refugee lives and epistemologies, insists on critically reckoning with the work of redaction in the security archives of the United States' so-called secret war in Laos. She argues that a focus on missing things in the archives reveals the structural particularity of secrecy in the making of US imperialism, as such exclusions manifest in Hmong life alongside the document productions of resettlement case files, CIA ID cards, and the like.[24] Monica Kim attends to another weaponization of paper in the Korean War. She highlights the dual aerial bombardments of paper and napalm over Korean landscapes to illuminate a broader intervention: "Paper was also a weapon of war," she writes.[25] While attending to the formerly secret interrogation archives of the US Counterintelligence Corps (released through FOIA) and other official government documentation, Kim carefully considers the circulation of such papers, the designs for more paper production that interrogation itself compelled, and the way oral histories and against-the-grain readings might more fully capture such weaponizations of paper.[26] Kim highlights the centrality of these newly FOIA released documents in the theorizing of this paper infrastructure. Such recent accountings of the paper archive point to the specific character of such pulp productions in the making of imperial history.

The continued struggle over the memory and meaning of social movements in the 1960s and 1970s, and their subsequent decimation, is inextricable from the life of secret government documents, and their use has not been without controversy. When Bay Area journalist Seth Rosenfeld published *Subversives: The FBI's War on Student Radicals, and Reagan's Rise to Power* in 2013, his book alleged that that Japanese American activist Richard Aoki—known for his participation with a then-incipient Black Panther Party—was a likely FBI informant. Rosenfeld's discovery hinged on an excavation of FOIA files that spanned over thirty years, 300,000 documents, and several FOIA cases in court.[27] Reading around redactions and through unique FBI codes, Rosenberg argued that Aoki (who he argues was known as "T-2" in the files) had been recruited by the FBI in the 1950s. He released 221 pages from a FOIA disclosure alongside his assertions, after his claim angered community activists and those who admired Aoki's legacy.[28] Fred Ho—Asian American activist, musician, and close comrade of Aoki—came to the immediate public defense of his deceased friend, arguing in two op-eds that these disclosures had been misrepresented.[29] In a line-by-line rereading of the most controversial passages from the files Rosenfeld had procured, Ho argues that *Subversives* willfully misconstrues the true history of Asian American radical activism by projecting falsehood into redacted spaces and accepting the veracity of the FBI's account:

> I read each page of the mostly redacted 221 pages of the files that the FBI released to Seth Rosenfeld on the subject of Richard Aoki (and many multiple names with varying versions of first, middle and surnames, including the supposed code name Richard Ford). The only thing that I believe can be confirmed by these heavily redacted files is that the FBI *believed* it had an informant. The files begin in the early 1960s and go to the fall of 1977. No files seem to exist after 1977, so any allegation or intimation of on-going contact with the FBI is non-existent. Let's for the sake of argument assume that the FBI "had their man" (as Rosenfeld concludes) in one Richard Aoki. In their vetting of Aoki, they do a background check including the possibility that Aoki might even be a "plant," the FBI word for an infiltrator into the FBI! There is no conclusion or methodology revealed as to how they vetted that question of Aoki possibly being such a "plant." We read page after page of repetitive bureaucratic corroboration that Aoki is indeed a quality informant. Of course, due to the redactions, nothing is revealed as how valuable was his information and service to "the Bureau."[30]

Ho's defense hinged on a rereading of documents, most of which were produced in the moment in which Aoki lived. Regardless of Aoki's guilt or innocence, Ho's argument illustrates to a palpable suspicion of state paper that complicates readings of redacted documents. Further, it points to the ironic centrality of FOIA in the writing of the radical history of twentieth-century America. This is a history, as I show, that may have been challenged by the very people who supported the legislation in the first place.

Indeed, encounters with FOIA are so notable in their irregularity that journalists and academics alike often comment on the bizarre experience of requesting and receiving (or not receiving documents), and strategies for requesting and interpreting these materials.[31] Simone Browne opens *Dark Matters: On the Surveillance of Blackness*, a book that reshaped the landscape of surveillance studies through an exacting history of racialized ways of looking, with a brief vignette about FOIA. Browne submitted a FOIA request for Frantz Fanon's file to the FBI, which they produced only minimally responsive documents. Browne attributes the scanty response to the ability of a surveillant state to disappear evidence.[32] (File destruction is a routine exercise of power; the transparency activists of the 1970s and 1980s I discuss in chapter 2 galvanized against such destruction of FBI and police papers.) Browne's book addresses how surveillant technologies are inextricably and historically tied with the policing of Black life, but the focus of her opening vignette resonates with how FOIA shapes a politics of knowing, seeing, and looking back. Labor historian William Pratt's 1992 article "Using FBI Records in Writing Regional Labor History" reflects on the writing of radical history in the American Midwest through the security archive. Pratt's article provides an account of his experiences using FOIA that is also intended as a methodological guide for left scholarship. Gaps in the record, Pratt notes, follow the strategic and regional interests of the FBI; for instance, he was able to find records regarding communist and farmer-labor organizing in Montana before 1940, whereas the Bureau had little analogous material on the Dakotas in the same period. In Pratt's account, the FBI's quarterly reports on regional communist organizing alongside their surveillance files were rich in biographical data and useful for mapping political communities, though they often provided inaccurate, misleading, or incomplete information. For this reason, he concludes: "It cannot be stressed too strongly: FBI materials, useful as they may be, are only one kind of source, and the historian who utilizes them to the neglect of more conventional materials acts at his or her peril."[33]

Despite the obvious contradictions of using such documentation to map a people's history, the Freedom of Information Act has nevertheless played a key role in the material politics of knowledge production. How do we approach this contradiction? Files were, of course, filled with lies, speculations, and observations inflected through a racist, sexist, homophobic frame. In her canonical feminist analysis, "Sex and Death in the Rational World of Defense Intellectuals," Carol Cohn illuminates the bizarre, untethered, and sexually inflected languages developed in the militarized context as experienced during her time participant-observing a defense institute.[34] Defense intellectuals, she argues, rely on sanitized language, sexual metaphor, and acronym, to discuss the intricacies of war without summoning its consequences: from *clean bombs* to *surgical strikes* to *peacekeeping missiles*, to the language of thrust, penetration, and virginity. It is this language that lives on the pages of secret reports on nuclearization and warfare, where a structured militarized thinking distances the weapon from its existential purpose to kill or maim. In the papers that proliferate in the security archive, it is *this* writing that rewrites the world, its people, and its resources in an imperial form.

Yet the contents of the government file can also produce oddly vivid portraits, or those which can be meaningful for their strange pattern of counterrevolutionary lies and unlikely observations. Teishan Latner's work closely examined the FBI files of Veneceremos Brigade, the most significant and long-lasting Cuban solidarity organization in United States. He reveals how despite the attempts to criminalize the Veneceremos Brigade, the material documented in the voluminous twenty-three thousand pages of surveillance files defies the logic of the archive. That is, "files on the Venceremos Brigade illustrate the manner in which counternarratives can surface even within the body of the state's archives on grassroots political movements, narratives that are potent enough to challenge the power of the state's evidence deployed against them."[35] Latner details how literary analyses of radical material, information drawn from the public domain, the presence of anti-imperial voices, and even the material accounted for through direct surveillance resists the intent to criminalize and discredit the organization.[36] Yet another example of the surveillance archive's peculiarity emerges from William Maxwell's chronicle of the FBI's spying on Black modernist writers. Through an extensive FOIA search, Maxwell unexpectedly found that the Bureau not only focused on the biographical sketches and physical whereabouts of writers but also engaged in literary criticism and close study of Black writing.[37] That is, the files show a relentless denigration and pursuit of the authors, and a simultaneous parsing of their words and texts.

This is not to privilege the government document but, rather, in the words of Orisanmi Burton, to "analyze [them] as hostile sources through a rebellious and disloyal interpretive paradigm."[38] The work of Burton and others scholars working with counterinsurgent archives attends to the structuring conditions of the paper, just as much as their content: Were they dropped as aerial warfare from the sky? Where and how do these files exist? Can their existence illuminate a physical map of counterinsurgency? How does their vocabulary reveal a racialized and sexual politics to the state? What do their omissions, classifications, and gaps reveal about the exertions of the state? Of course, histories of US government surveillance against dissidents live not only in documentary records but also in the embodied memories of everyday people who have long lived under—and resisted—US racialized violence and surveillance.[39] In his work on the Attica Rebellion, Burton offers an approach to the carceral archive through a method he terms "archival war," a "simultaneous reading of carceral and Black radical sources" that recognizes and amplifies the inherent animus between the security archive and its subjects.[40] The struggle over papers and documents is made meaningful within this context: not as a disembodied and authoritative look but, rather, as a particular view from a violent state that is best understood through social movement and in the context of community struggle.[41] The *race paper* account is so compelling precisely because it makes visible a familiar pattern of brute suppression and mundane violence, and the conscription of paper qua paper in an imperial project. These nine completely redacted pages distill into a chilling shorthand what we know, *what we've always known*, about the machinations of the imperial state.

PAPER AND POWER

A censored sheet, blacked out and edited, is a paper *cut*. The soft fleshy bits of a finger that wrestle with documents develop improbably painful *paper cuts*. In Viet Nguyen's novel *The Sympathizer*, a protagonist Vietnamese spy embedded in the landscape of Southern California, laments his boring filing job in an academic Department of Oriental Studies, noting that "these things . . . amounted to *death by a thousand paper cuts*" (emphasis mine).[42] An intimacy exists between the cut (or censored) paper and the power of paper to cut, wound, kill. Martin Espada, civil rights lawyer and poet, penned a piece titled "Who Burns for the Perfection of Paper," a first-person reflection on working in a legal pad printing as a teenager. On the workshop floor after hours of work, "hands would slide along suddenly sharp paper, and gather slits thinner than the crevices," as critical steps of assembling the legal pads were done gloveless.[43] Espada's poem culminates in a final stanza in which the invisibilized labor of paper manufacture surges through the present:

Ten years later, in law school,
I knew that every legal pad
was glued with the sting of hidden cuts,
that every open lawbook
was a pair of hands
upturned and burning.

Espada's poem brings the politics of paper to light in at least two ways: First, the poem draws the reader into the embodied, material world necessarily mobilized to produce paper as a commodity under capitalism. A related second dimension to Espada's poem is the gesture toward an always already-present subaltern story written into a text or an object—this sense that paper itself might have a counterhistory, or might point toward a history from below. *Every legal pad was glued with the sting of hidden cuts.* In her exploration of neoliberal subject-making, Imani Perry draws on Espada's poem to underscore the extractive nature of the global economy, wherein even objects like paper, thought of only as mediating technologies, can illustrate the violence of the world-system. Paper is itself a product of capitalist production, at least the papers on which the American Cold War was composed. The industrial production of paper invented the possibility of printing such voluminous reams. It is not without irony that inscription of histories and ideas happen on such a commodity. "Like the word, it [paper] is the surface on which life and death are written," Perry writes.[44]

The redaction of paper—like a jump cut in cinema—lays bare an editorial process that creates discordant visual objects. Visual cuts assert authoritatively the limits on sight imposed by the state. In popular culture, censored paper is a constant, yet rarely commented on, recurring motif: the partially redacted document sent in a manila envelope to a plucky journalist; the secret file casually tossed across the desk of a corrupt government official; the PDF cache scoured by a rogue intelligence officer using stolen login credentials. Beyond just the appearance of paper-as-prop, manifold films and TV series revolve around the politics of secrecy and whistleblowing, centering paper as an actor in the social and material world. A number of recent political thrillers are based on real stories of whistleblowing, and hinge on the exposé of internal memoranda and other secret documents to public news outlets. For instance, Gavin Hood's *Official Secrets* (2019), a British drama starring Keira Knightley, is about the exposure of British intelligence plans to secretly manipulate the UN Security Council into supporting war on Iraq in 2003. Based on the true story of Katherine Gun, a translator for the Government Communications Headquarters, the story follows the government's prosecution of Gun under the Official Secrets Act; in early scenes, the viewer, with bated breath, watches Knightley—in her role as Gun—transform into a whistleblower at work. She copies and pastes a secret memo into a Word document, saves the file to a zip drive, and anxiously saunters into the copy room to print the material surreptitiously. Similarly, Steven Spielberg's *The Post* (2017) dramatizes the publication of the Pentagon Papers in print news, begins with a reenactment of Daniel Ellsberg's photocopying of the pages, including close-ups of hands and documents illuminated as if copied: the material practice of cutting off top secret demarcations on these Xerox copies.

Beyond the cinematic motif of the document, real FOIA requests have revealed real-life collusions between Hollywood and the military, the former providing platform for the latter as a broad part of a propaganda apparatus. For instance, the CIA consulted on Kathryn Bigelow's film *Zero Dark Thirty* (2012), a gritty film glorifying the covert operation to assassinate Osama Bin Laden, as did the Marines on the sci-fi blockbuster *Avatar* (2009).[45] *Zero Dark Thirty*, publicized with redacted billboards and advertisements, made intense uses of shadows and negative space to conjure censored materials. Secret papers thematically and semiotically appear in cinematic story worlds, and they can also tell us about the relationship between the entertainment industry and military.

There is also, in this book, a relationship being sketched between the paper document and the documentary film; or, to be more precise, the book in some ways has sprung forth from the tensions between (and similarities among) the document and the documentary. These tensions and relations flash up throughout this work: in the use of a documentary titled *The Intelligence Network* (1978) produced by the Campaign for Political Rights as an organizing tool for FOIA activism to liberate and demand access to government paper; in the visual summoning of redacted documents within War on Terror detention documentaries as spectacles of state violence; in the destruction of the paper trail leading to the infamous CIA torture videos; and in the eerie, thrilling, and beautiful autoethnographic film *The Feeling of Being Watched* (2018), on Assia Boundaoui's fight to access the thousands of FBI surveillance files on her Arab American community in Chicago. This is not to say we should speak of cinema and paper together, nor as extensions of one another. Rather, when we consider both as media which attempt to translate an actuality, their mutually tenuous relationships to the evidentiary becomes clear.[46] The documents this book covers are largely those penned by the government that justify, catalogue, and organize the bureaucracy of national security. On the other hand, documentary films, particularly those I attend to in this work, largely present critiques of the state, and the disclosure of information is woven into their narrative form. In other words, documentary accountings, in both senses of the word, mobilize the evidentiary to display and circulate information in a public/counterpublic sphere.

My approach to thinking about the evidentiary nature of documents, and the public sphere within which they circulate, borrows from the critical work of scholars like Cait McKinney, who, in *Information Activism: A Queer History of Lesbian Media Technologies*, illuminates the collective political labors of compiling and sharing material within queer and feminist spaces. McKinney's frame resonates with the work of transparency advocates who used and shared materials in hopes of reclaiming freedom of information for liberatory ends: "Information work gives ground to nascent counterpublics by establishing new terms of reference and building shared infrastructures for encountering information."[47] Their work on feminist information-sharing networks emphasizes how a document is an object of material struggle that both informs and creates what Nancy Fraser termed "subaltern counterpublics."[48]

A document is, of course, a site of information and disinformation, and an authoritative performance of what is considered information at all. Further, a document is a visual object and an elemental unit of subject-making under state power. To possess documents affords particular kinds of rights, as the brutal realities of an undocumented life reveal. In her eponymous 1951 essay *What Is Documentation?*, Suzanne Briet asked the question nearly a decade and a half before Andre Bazin published "What Is Cinema?" in *Cahiers du Cinema*. Briet argued for both a discursive and social answer to her question, highlighting that documents might only be understood in comparative relation to other documents, and moreover that documentation as such should be understood as interdocumentary: "intimately tied to the life of a team of workers or scientists or scholars," and creatively produced "through the juxtaposition, selection, and comparison of documents and the production of auxiliary documents."[49] These auxiliary documents, in the case of the security archives in addition to the standard accompanying identifying information, might include the Vaughn Index or other documentation specific to the FOIA litigation, as I discuss in chapter 1. But Briet, writing for a social interpretation of the document as a "new cultural technique," in the aftermath of World War II, pushed back against the emergent new scientific secrecy regimes. "Secret documentation," she argued, "is an insult inflicted upon documentation."[50] While this book does not argue that secret archives are an aberrant formation, Briet's response nonetheless sheds light on the conceptual and material force that secret documents had, even in the very beginnings of the Cold War. In other words, they must be understood as centrally part of postwar American bureaucracy, even if as a constitutive other, a secret-sharer if you will, that constitutes the public sphere.

Before I continue, I offer a rough distillation of these terms for the reader: Paper is the grist of violence, of racialized state violence, of violence in the form of capital accumulation. Paper has a material and social history. As midcentury media theorist Harold Innis reminds us, paper should be understood as a space-time media that lends itself to large, centralized authorities and a system of imperial expansion.[51] That is, the portability of paper and the possibility of its inscription itself epitomizes the endlessly bloated and self-proliferating nature of imperialism. Paper is the precondition for the document which, following Briet, exists only discursively and intertextually. Even in the digital age, our desires for the paper remain, or the expectations for what it means to possess and produce documents in the context of the state.[52] The document exists in relation to other documents as a network of authorizing statements that records, produces, and performs information.[53] Inherently, the document occurs in an organizing infrastructure of files, indexes, and archives; an ecosystem which gives meaning to the document in the social and political world. Racial capitalism authorizes itself through the file (the land becomes property, the person becomes a slave, a prisoner, a worker, a landlord) and rewrites the world through an incoherent and sometimes clandestine frame (the security archive, the carceral archive, the defense industry, the intelligence world). Of course these transformations could not happen without the gun, the missile, or the soldier, but it is the paper that authorizes them. Out of this ecosystem, regulation of the contents of information becomes meaningful, the state asserts power with a confidential stamp on a file, the ideas of the so-called intelligence community dwell. Out of this ecosystem, media like "the rap sheet" cohere, or the possibility of a person as "undocumented." David Graeber elaborates this media theory: "Police are bureaucrats with weapons."[54]

Of course, there are tactical distinctions in the work of the police, intelligence agencies, and the military. I do not intend to flatten these. But Graeber expands an important dimension; the rise of midcentury bureaucracies must be linked with the practice of policing. Police work involves enforcing code and law through paperwork. Filling out, pushing, and authorizing forms for death, burglary, assault present a far greater proportion of policework than acknowledged, particularly as they interface with other large bureaucratic institutions like stage agencies or insurance companies.[55] Policing is largely paperwork, and even the violent abuses of policing often emerge as moments of bureaucratic enforcement. *License and registration, please*; or, *Can I see some identification?* For Graeber, the idea of the faceless disembodied bureaucrat does not adequately capture bureaucratic enforcement under capitalism; instead, we must think about the union between the muscle of the state and its regimes of information. It is *this* that produces the force of law.

In this book I use the terms *security archives* or *secret documents*, but without naturalizing their existence across an information landscape. These papers are not simply records of violence; their existence, proliferation, and organization is itself a form of violence. They should not exist: Their existence testifies to the crushing, well-capitalized tactics of a security state and a bureaucracy fashioned around the organization and production of militarized, surveillant, and policing power. It is within the context of this security bureaucracy that secrecy and transparency become key political practices. If paper is a basic, inherent media of the imperial state, the circulation of paper makes political meaning. Circulation, for security archives, always already implies noncirculation: secrecy. A dialectic of secrecy and transparency, of disclosure and nondisclosure is inherent to the power of the security file. It is this *dialectic* that is important, as it produces the possibilities and actualities of state violence as *state* violence.

Indeed, studying the histories of these papers, and of bureaucratic organization more broadly, presents an opportunity to "unlearn imperialism," as Ariella Azoulay suggests.[56] Recent work on the history of paper and files sheds light on the ideological and cultural modalities that produce and organize paperwork.[57] Through the vertical filing cabinet, as Craig Robertson shows, one might glean an entire history of capitalist ideas of hierarchy, efficiency, and the feminization of organizing labor.[58] Though the physical organization of government files is not the focus of this book, it is significant that the architecture of the archive reveals the logics and labors of capital accumulation and militarized knowledge. For instance, FOIA activists of both present and past often share their law-use skills as an act of solidarity and capacity building. Activists demystify the organizational structure of policing and intelligence units to increase the efficacy of requests, as I discuss in chapter 2. These tactics points to the way the seemingly mundane organizational logics and practices can illuminate the contours of state power. A powerful example of this can be found in the historical work of Kirsten Weld, who reveals how after the US-backed coup against Jacobo Arbenz Guzmán in Guatemala, the American government materially supported the "modernization" of police files through information management training programs (including modernizing individual surveillance files, property records, police reports, use of notecards) and the physical import of vertical filing cabinets to house them.[59] The surveillance, disappearance, and murders of left activists in Guatemala City during the decades-long civil war were a direct result of the seemingly benign new filing systems that had been implemented.

For compelling reasons, critics of transparency and the punitively structured surveillant gaze have turned toward Édouard Glissant's assertion of "the right to opacity," as a counterpoint to naive celebrations of transparency.[60] As a tool of the state, transparency is but a ruse that endlessly promises a rights-bearing subject while in reality the state wages permanent wars, unhindered, and punitively discards the lives of most. In this way, the idea of *opacity* as a *right* suggests that lifeworlds that exist beyond the "extractive viewpoint," to draw from Macarena Gómez-Barris, are sites of fugitive possibility, political solidary, and a different kind of futurity.[61] To be sure, the political and aesthetic interventions through a frame that disavows transparency are delightfully plenty; opacity can lead us toward a capacious, unruly, ungovernable understanding of life and our relations to each other.[62] My argument, while distinct from this line of critique, runs parallel to it. In suggesting an intellectual and aesthetic approach to transparency, this book seeks not to salvage it from liberal forms of governmentality but, rather, to think dialectically and locate it within a contested political terrain. The kiln of the state fires the possibilities of opacity into the tactics of disappearance, surveillance, clandestine operations. But the hands of the people can also transmute transparency from regulatory mechanism of the state into something else. In other words, what possibilities can the transparency / secrecy dialectic produce? The histories of anti-imperialism and antifascism clearly also demonstrate the unruliness of transparency, which extends beyond what opacity can conceptually account for. The seizure and reappropriation of government documents for various political ends has been a common if not an inherent theme: from the Egyptian Revolution of 2011 to the struggles over land in contemporary

I.3   Egyptian revolutionaries go through State Security Police reports, amid bags of shredded documents, in an underground garage on March 5, 2011. Photo courtesy of Hossam El-Hamalawy.

Paraguay, from the movements to wrest counterinsurgency files from American "intelligence" agencies to the high-profile prosecution of military whistleblowers.[63] Indeed, is there a state without papers? Or a law without documents? A revolution without the seizure of files, the storming of the embassy or the intelligence building? Or a modern military without secrets?[64] Secrecy and transparency are concepts, discourses, and ideas, not normative states of being, made meaningful through a fundamental contradiction between labor and capital, oppressed and oppressor, colonized and colonizer. I understand paper as a material battleground that emerges from such antagonisms.

A PAPER TIGER

In the early days of the Cold War, Mao Tse-tung famously proclaimed the United States and its atomic bombs to be no serious threat. He commented, "I believe the United States is nothing but a *paper tiger*," adding to his earlier contention that "outwardly a tiger, [America] is made of paper, unable to withstand the wind and the rain."[65] From the perch of the present, sifting through the volumes of decaying, frayed, and photocopied paperwork produced in the offices of the Cold War, Mao's words paradoxically ring true, though in a different register. Paperwork crafted the Cold War state, as bureaucracy, in turn, crafted a paper tiger, as curious researchers who request government documents, dwell on their redactions, and ponder the secrets they reveal can corroborate. The Cold War, indeed, produced this paper tiger, this paper bureaucracy: classified memos detailing clandestine operations, files and filing systems to document subversives, and complex systems of classification to determine which eyes could see which files. Cold War blocs were built from reams of pressed pulp.

This book—itself now an artifact of print culture—is an attempt to think through paper politics with Mao's unintentionally astute observations in mind. That is, the repressive state and its lawfare hinges on the production of particular papers, some of which are classified, some of which are not. *A Thousand Paper Cuts* draws from this rereading of Mao's words in staging the key interventions into the history of military bureaucracy, and the visual politics of transparency. Militarization produces both particular files and particular subjects, two phenomena that are profoundly interconnected. The book arcs around the cultural history of FOIA, beginning with a broad discussion of transparency within the intellectual landscape of the Cold War, and from there examines activist contestations to imperialism through FOIA, the aesthetic dimensions of redacted documents and the lifeworlds they build, and concludes with a reflection on the place of redaction art within a militarized landscape. The structure of the book foregrounds my investment in tethering the now-ubiquitous redacted aesthetic back to the political and cultural conditions that made it possible.

Chapter 1, "Secrecy Is for Losers: Freedom of Information and Cold War Politics," examines the cultural history of freedom of information in America. On the Fourth of July in 1966 and with no reporters present, Lyndon Johnson quietly signed into law the most powerful piece of information legislation in American history, the Freedom of Information Act. FOIA was a response to a particular transnational American formation, a paranoid Cold War politics that mobilized state secrecy and produced copious amounts of documents, most of which were classified. Using a critical ethnic studies lens, I analyze the history of three key figures who were prominent protagonists of transparency: John Moss, the plucky and somewhat obscure congressman from Sacramento who was the driving force behind FOIA, Senator Daniel Patrick Moynihan, who wrote prolifically about transparency after the end of the Cold War, and the sociologist

Edward Shils, the canonical modernization theorist who wrote one of the first texts on American secrecy during the Cold War. Though these men represented varying political ideologies, each of their calls for transparency emerged from profound anxieties about communism and a racialized logic of the good citizen-subject. These politicians and intellectuals saw no contradiction between the denuded brutality of American counterinsurgency at home and abroad and calls for an end to government secrecy. In his passionate defense of transparency and his advocacy for a more robust implementation of FOIA, Moynihan summoned the Soviet gulags and the specter of Stalinism as his foil. "Secrecy," he argued, "is for losers." In other words, transparency *toward* a more perfect union, not *against* the racialized practices of a settler colonial and imperial republic. This chapter engages against-the-grain readings of archival papers, published primary sources, and legislative sources, alongside news articles that were published at the time to trace a counterhistory of FOIA.

Despite FOIA's deeply patriotic genesis, subversives and activists of all varieties seized the opportunity to request documents from the state that might provide evidence of their persecution. Chapter 2, "How to Free Information: Counterinsurgency and Radical Transparency," deepens a critical understanding of transparency through the work of radical transparency advocates in the period immediately after FOIA's passage. I examine this ethos of countersurveillance in the 1970s and 1980s through the histories of three organizations—the Center for Political Rights (CPR), the Center for National Security Studies (CNSS), and the Fund for Open Access and Accountability, Inc. (FOIA Inc.)—that sought to challenge the American imperial state. Unlike the earliest advocates of FOIA, for these leftists, radical transparency was a primarily critique of American exceptionalism, rather than a defense of it.[66] I trace these organizations through their prolific publications based on the declassified documents they were able to procure. While it may be tempting to situate FOIA as foil to document stealing, whistleblowing, and other unsanctioned acts of radical transparency, the historical record reveals that FOIA was but one in a continuum of tools. During this era, disparate parties wrote urgently to various agencies to request documentation that would help explain the political phenomena they saw unfolding around them: from imprisoned people to celebrities, from anti-nuclear activists to members of the Black Panther Party. While chapter 1 reveals how transparency embodied liberal American exceptionalism, chapter 2 asks what a radical praxis of transparency looked like for activists in the 1970s? I argue that this ethos of countersurveillance exemplifies a layered visual politics, thick with contradiction and struggles over the politics of seeing and sight.[67]

In chapter 3, "On Redacted Documents and the Visual Politics of Transparency," I suggest an aesthetic and materialist analysis of document redaction. During the presidency of George W. Bush, increased secrecy and noncompliance with FOIA requests allowed the Rendition, Detention, and Interrogation (RDI) program to function with systematic efficiency. Often, Torture Memos and other documents related to detention that were procured through FOIA requests were produced extraordinarily redacted and nearly unreadable. Though challenges to militarized imprisonment often attempt to "make visible" unseen practices, the "transparency" of these documents does not actually enunciate the detainee's social and experiential worlds. Instead, the visual politics of redaction offer a point of entry that allow us to read these documents as more than simply the failure of transparency. I examine how redacted spaces—typically censored with black-and-white boxes—are visual images that often paradoxically signal the innate impossibilities of recording and witnessing violence; borrowing from Edward Said, I argue that we paradoxically find a "contrapuntal" aesthetic to redaction. I examine materials produced around the imprisonment of Zayn al-Abidin Muhammad Husayn (commonly known as Abu Zubaydah) in US black sites: one of the infamous Torture Memos from 2002 legally justifying torture and documents detailing the secret destruction of ninety-two CIA detainee interrogation videos in 2005. I reconsider the evidentiary status of the interrogation tape as well as the corresponding claims against their destruction. I argue that by focusing on hidden yet spectacular acts of violence, the mundane and originary violence of detention becomes naturalized as part of the security landscape. My analysis centers around documents produced and released in accordance with the ACLU v. Department of Defense court case, presided over by Judge Alvin Hellerstein, and the corresponding FOIA request.

From the aesthetic dimensions of censorship, I turn in the final chapter, "Paper and the Art of Censorship," to contemporary redaction art and the stakes of transparency in our state of permanent war. I situate this art in the longer history of contestations around transparency, asking how these new emergent art practices might articulate contemporary political, visual stakes in government transparency. Redaction art crystallizes in relation to the digital age, corresponding to an increase in document dumps and online activism. Censored aesthetics have become particularly legible in an era of digital file transfer and are used by artists for varying political or conceptual reasons. Broadly, I trace how redacted documents are used by artists in one of two ways—either to explore personal and community memories of histories that have been willfully denied or obscured, or to express liberal shock that fails to fully account for the imperial tableau they represent. I consider the possibilities of redacted documents in the telling of personal, intimate histories as refracted through the broader state technology of information classification. By examining Sadie Barnette's work on the FBI file of her father while he was active in the Black Panthers, Voluspa Jarpa's installations of CIA documents detailing the excesses of Operation Condor in Chile, Bahar Behbahani's *Garden Coup* series, and Jenny Holzer's *Redaction Paintings*, among others, I show how subjective renderings of bureaucratic documents can reveal the inherent tensions in FOIA as a government technology itself.

A *Thousand Paper Cuts* ends with a brief epilogue reflecting on the redacted memoirs of Mohamedou Ould Slahi, who from 2001 until October 2016 was detained in Guantánamo Bay Naval Base (GTMO). In the first years of his fifteen-year imprisonment, the Mauritanian-born Slahi taught himself English and meticulously wrote a 466-page account of his capture and detention with pen and paper, which was classified for many years. Two public versions of *Guantánamo Diary* have been published to date: the original version (2015), edited by the writer Larry Siems, which maintains the heavy redactions even in its published form; and a "restored" version of the memoir in which Slahi and Siems worked together to fill in the missing parts. In this "restored" publication, the original redactions remain as gray highlights through which Slahi's recollections of the redacted parts appear. I consider what lessons *Guantánamo Diary* might present for thinking about the dialectics of secrecy and transparency, and the overall reckonings with these questions that must happen within a radical frame.

Paper is political. From the politics of being documented to the kind of bureaucratic warfare enacted on poor and marginalized people in America through mandated paperwork, to the secret surveillance files against activists, to the administrative violence of state documents for transgender and gender-nonconforming people, paper mediates and makes the world.[68] We each have voluminous files that follow us. Consumer advocate Ralph Nader wrote in a 1971 essay that "it is the rare American who does not live in the shadow of his dossier" and that "the law and technology have provided the 'dossier industry' with powerful tools to obtain and use information against people in an unjust way—whether knowingly or negligently. The defenseless citizen now requires specific rights to defend against and deter such invasions of privacy."[69] Nader, unbelievably, was not writing about the FBI file. His essay, "The Dossier Invades the Home," centered on secret credit files, which he explicitly likened in their invasiveness to that of the secretly assembled intelligence dossier. Though the erosion of privacy that Nader then bemoaned is now a foregone conclusion, his outrage illustrates the endless invention of the file form in a way that mirrors the security state and in the service of power. Nearly every measure of living exists in file form somewhere, hidden or public in varying degrees. *A Thousand Paper Cuts* offers a way of thinking about political struggle, imperial ideas, and aesthetic practices through the story of the document.

Secrecy is for losers. For people who don't know how important information really is. The Soviet Union realized this too late. —DANIEL P. MOYNIHAN, *Secrecy*

In 1967, the essay "I'm Glad the c.i.a. Is 'Immoral'" ran in the *Saturday Evening Post*. The titillating piece was written by Thomas W. Braden, CIA operative, columnist, and, later, host of the CNN talk show *Crossfire*. Braden's blunt defense at first reads as burlesque, an apologia for clandestine and unethical tactics deployed by American intelligence agencies recently exposed in the short-lived but high-impact *Ramparts* magazine and covered by the *New York Times* and other major news outlets. *Ramparts*, a sleek, vanguard publication for an irreverent New Left, had revealed that the CIA was deeply involved in the noncommunist left. Their exposé showed the CIA as exerting influence within a litany of unlikely spheres. Their activities ranged from funding student organizations and interfering with student organizing, to supporting a variety of social and cultural organizations including, most famously, the Congress for Cultural Freedom, an anticommunist group that supported writers and artists working within a narrowly conceived vision of individual freedom to stem the tide of communist dreams.[1] The *Ramparts* story ushered in the first public scandal for the then-twenty-year-old organization, and it was the first of several similar exposés on

CIA activities.[2] *Ramparts* continued to publish critical pieces about intelligence work over the next few issues, and next month's magazine cover visually referenced the new secrecy/transparency dialectic that had come to characterize that moment. A man's face, obscured by shadows, emerged against a white background. White text lay distorted across his features, reading "When I joined the 'Company' I expected to be involved in a battle of wits between professionals of the opposition. It wasn't until they taught me to kill civilians and to recruit foreign students to spy on their own country that I realized what the CIA was all about. Of course I had to quit." The contrasting black-and-white design, foreshadowing the redacted aesthetics dominating later decades, captured the sentiment that the politics of looking and obfuscating were central to the Cold War.

Braden's article, published a month later, was a direct riposte to *Ramparts* in particular, even as the story transited across all the mainstream outlets. His article ran with an accompanying image nearly inverse that in *Ramparts*: His profile, well-lit and unobstructed by shadows, faced the laudatory title of his article, smiling as if directly at the words *immoral* and CIA. In the piece Braden, comments on a secret program that funded the American Federation of Labor (AFL) against radical communist dockworkers in the Mediterranean. He wrote, "On the desk in front of me as I write these lines is a creased and faded yellow paper. It bears the following inscription in pencil: 'Received from Warren G. Haskins, $15,000. (signed) Norris A. Grambo.' I went in search of this paper on the day the newspapers disclosed the 'scandal' of the Central Intelligence Agency's connections with American students and labor leaders. It was a wistful search, and when it ended, I found myself feeling sad."[3] Braden offered *Haskins* as his own code name, and *Grambo* as that of Irving Brown, a CIA operative and member of the AFL.[4] Brown and Braden together built the "Mediterranean Committee," an organized group assembled to squash communist labor objections to Europe's import of American weapons through the post–World War II Marshall Plan.[5] These scraps of paper documented the money that moved muscle in the violent suppression of worker protests against America's conscripting of Europe in its ascendance as a global military superpower in the postwar era.[6] Frayed pulp in hand, Braden waxed nostalgic about this time with the CIA: "I looked at the yellow paper [and] I sat sadly amidst the dust of old papers, and after a time I decided something. I decided that if ever I knew a truth in my life, I knew the truth of the cold war, and I knew what the Central Intelligence Agency did in the cold war, and never have I read such a concatenation of inane, misinformed twaddle as I have now been reading about the CIA."

The remainder of his article argues that the CIA's actions during the then-ongoing Cold War were heroic, not duplicitous. In her important history of the cultural Cold War, Francis Stonor Saunders explains another dimension to Braden's article: In defending the CIA, Braden revealed previously secret details about their programs that otherwise would have been unknown within the public sphere.[7] I begin with this anecdote to highlight certain tensions and call forth other conspicuous absences. First, Braden's account underscores a fetishism of paper and of empirical fact. His search for nearly lost scraps of paper advances the argument that *paper* constitutes *proof*. Yet his relation to this paper is entirely subjective, emotional, almost sentimental. The receipt he unearths reveals precious little about the circumstances of its drafting, yet the paper's existence in the world suggests the discrete and objective fact of a shadow world. Braden had himself been involved with the CCF and the shadowy, clandestine activities of the incipient intelligence agency. Second, Braden's article points to the dialectical and productive relationship between secrecy and publicity; between documents and published accounts; between secret scraps of paper and meanings obscured by code. The prior year, in 1966, President Johnson had signed into American law the Freedom of Information Act (FOIA), the product of a decade of legislative activism by a junior congressman from California, John Moss. Braden's musings on a secret scrap of paper and his clandestine memories were published precisely at a moment of rupture, of public reckoning with the collective papers produced by these very shadow worlds.

Third, even as Braden performs transparency by revealing a formerly secret paper, the meaning of such transparency is elided for the port workers bullied and beaten by AFL thugs. Without irony, a paper that proves America physically bullied and beat communists for resisting the ascendance of US military imperialism is cast in his account as a sentimental and patriotic artifact. The anecdote highlights how transparency's strange and strategic mobilization in the service of imperial power can cast aside the social worlds and lived histories of marginalized people and those who dare to challenge empire.

This chapter reads relations of power within American transparency, which is itself a militarized history that rests on racial and imperial cultural discourses, even if not always perceptibly so. To obtain a government document before the Freedom of Information Act was passed, one had to navigate a convoluted sys-

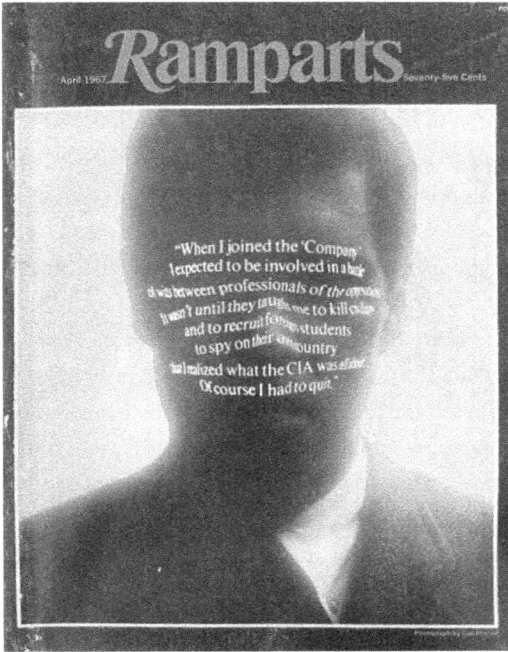

1.1   Cover of *Ramparts* magazine, April 1967.

tem of procedures to prove the relevance of their public records request to the queried agency. This often involved agency-specific regulations, as lawyer Harold Cross detailed in his 1953 legal reference book *The People's Right to Know*, which was commissioned by the American Society for Newspaper Editors (ASNE). The right-to-know movement had its roots in journalists who sought access to state papers, and accounts of FOIA stress the centrality of ASNE and Cross's efforts in advancing a progressive agenda. But this is not the whole story. To be sure, advocates for the right-to-know argued that the emergence of a secret bureaucracy alongside the ascendance of intelligence-gathering practices created the conditions for the abuse of power. Yet the language of transparency was entirely tethered to American exceptionalism, and inextricable from racial and imperial politics in its formative years.

In what follows I trace three key figures in the history of the Freedom of Information Act: John Moss, the plucky congressman from Sacramento who was the driving force behind FOIA; sociologist Edward Shils, the canonical modernization theorist who wrote one of the first texts on American secrecy during the Cold War; and Senator Daniel Patrick Moynihan, who wrote prolifically about transparency after the fall of the Soviet Union. Though these men represented varying political ideologies, each of their calls for transparency emerged from profound anxieties about communism and a racialized logic of the good citizen-subject. Who did this transparency serve? Who did it make visible? Whose rights were intended to be defended? These politicians and intellectuals saw no contradiction between the denuded brutality of American counterinsurgency at home and abroad, on the one hand, and calls for an end to government secrecy, on the other. For them, bringing paper into the public sphere represented a necessary defense of American ideals, which they argued were being eroded in the tense shadows of the Cold War.

My ensuing account is chronological. The first section illuminates debates around secrecy and security in the years leading up to 1966, focusing on the work of Shils and Congressman Moss as emerging from ideas steeped in racialized and anticommunist leanings. From there, I discuss the period between 1966 and 1974, delving into the metaphoric murky waters of FOIA implementation as played out in the literal murky waters of a militarized Cold War Pacific Ocean. I conclude by examining FOIA in the aftermath of the Cold War primarily through the work of Moynihan, who wrote prolifically about the relationships between secrecy, transparency, and American exceptionalism through the prism of normative American white masculinity. Rather than taking them at face value, I read archival papers, published primary sources, and legislative sources against their grain, alongside news articles that were published at the time, to produce a counterhistory of FOIA. When we thus read the margins, the implicit assumptions, the tandem writings, and the historical context, the racial and imperial underpinnings of transparency become clear.

My central claim—that transparency as a discourse must be understood through critiques of empiricism and rationalism—builds on the work of ethnic studies and anti-imperialist critique. Studies of power and difference have long been concerned with the politics of sight and the character of transparency in general. In her influential text, "Mama's Baby, Papa's Maybe," Hortense Spillers eviscerates Moynihan's racist report, "The Negro Family: The Case for National

Action," by taking the reader through white supremacy's long historical making. Writing on the American grammars of seeing, she shows how even highly visual markers of brutality, wounds on the bodies of Black people, are rendered incomprehensible. Violence against persons made captive is rendered on "flesh" rather than "bodies"—a syntactic dismembering as wounds are discussed anatomically, outside conceptualizations of Black subjectivity. This racial scopic regime through looking, writing, and naming cements itself. She writes, "These undecipherable markings on the captive body render a kind of hieroglyphics of the flesh whose severe disjunctures come to be *hidden to the cultural seeing by skin color*."[8] More recently, Simone Browne, in her now-essential study of the anti-Black and racial origins of surveillance, writes, "Surveillance of Blackness [is] often unperceivable within the study of surveillance, all the while Blackness being that nonnameable matter that matters the racialized disciplinary society."[9] These Black feminist interventions into the grammars of seeing—and, by extension, the ethics of transparency—critique the American administration of life.

Taken together, Browne and Spillers write American anti-Blackness back into the grammars of language and seeing, reading race within forms that implicitly produce power relations, though not with explicit reference. In *transparency*, at first glance race seems to be imperceptible, but on closer look it is inextricable from the ordering of sight that produces differential subjects. A different elaboration of this point might be gleaned through Rey Chow's observation that it is precisely a racialized view of the Chinese language as inscrutable (or falsely ideographic) against which Jacques Derrida famously articulated the basic claims of deconstruction. Assessing deconstruction's racial dimensions, Chow argues for a specificity of the visual: "Although stereotypes are not necessarily visual in the physical sense, the act of stereotyping is always implicated in visuality by virtue of the fact the other is transformed into a (sur)face, a sheer exterior deprived of historical depth."[10] The implication of the visual in the politics of race is not simply in the instantiations of racial caricature but is also in the politics of seeing surfaces more broadly: bodies, documents, and texts. There are important distinctions in the visual-racial formations, and I do not mean to suggest an equivalence between readings of American grammars of race and the Eurocentrism of deconstruction, nor between anti-Blackness and Sinophobia. Rather, there are relationships between incomprehensibility (or inscrutability) and transparency that hinge on visual articulations and a racialized optic.

Film and photography scholars have long argued that the illusion of verisimilitude possible in the inverted refraction of light allowed not only racist images but also a racial infrastructure of film shooting and processing that favored white skin. FOIA, like a piece of charcoal or a camera, is a tool of rendering visible. This tool of reproduction is also one of regulation. In this chapter, I reveal how transparency as a discourse is caught up with these racialized and imperial politics of reproduction. The visual politics of transparency are haunted by many questions: What is the color of transparency? Is the transparent medium that which something can pass through, unfiltered? Is it understood against that which is murky? Or is it the blank canvas of white against which color is articulated? And, conversely, against which bodies were these ideas of transparency developed? Transparency, born out of a militarized Cold War context, cannot be disentangled from the racialization of the Third World, a fear of the communist left, and a desire to leverage the visual to preserve American exceptionalism. In what follows, I offer a diametric account of transparency's emergence, as traced through a racial state.

TRANSPARENCY JUXTAPOSED WITH RED

In his opening salvo for the 1967 essay "Color, the Universal Intellectual Community, and the Afro-Asian Intellectual," University of Chicago sociologist Edward Shils presented a visual tautology that he must have thought was quite clever: "Color is just color. It is a physical spectroscopic fact."[11] From this abstract visual quality that is *color*, Shils posits a facile and cosmetic query about the nature of racial formation: "The mind is not at work in it, and it is not a social relationship. It is inherently meaningless. Why, then, has this inherently meaningless property of man come to assume such great importance in the self image of human beings?"[12] Shils continued on, mapping, predictably, a teleology of Western progress against the culturally backward peoples of the world. Intellectuals, for Shils, surely existed in the Third World, but in his view they were trapped between tradition and their own inferiority complex when presented with the advances, so-called, of the West. In an earlier piece he wrote, "They [Indian intellectuals] are ashamed their country is not a 'modern country,' that its institutions are not abreast of the institutions of Great Britain and 'the modern world.' They feel their literature is on the whole inferior to the foreign literature which they read, that Indian science does not stand in the forefront of world science."[13] These *colored* intellectuals, in Shils's view, were pitiable.

Shils's own whiteness, or the symbolic whiteness of modernity, needed not to be called forth; the juxtaposition between *white* and *colored* is unequivocal even if referred to obliquely.

In his work on the symbolic dimensions of whiteness, visual studies scholar Richard Dyer illuminates the metonymic power of color as race. Dyer's schema unpacks color as hue, skin, and symbol, calling into focus the production of whiteness as both a specific ideal and universal category of humanity. White, conceptualized simultaneously as color and as the absence of color, "forms part of a system of thought and affect whereby white people are both particular and nothing in particular." Or, as legal scholar Cheryl Harris puts it, "Whiteness . . . is a ghost that has haunted the political and legal domains," something that is spectral and felt but whose power derives partly from its naturalization within the American landscape of American capitalism.[14] Shils apprehended color as merely chimeric in its hold over social relations, but refracting his metonym through Dyer reveals its rhetorical deployment to further the superiority of white against color.[15] Shils's writings on Third World intellectuals are within the broad aims of his significant contributions to center-periphery theory, an attendant cultural discourse to the claims of midcentury modernization theorists.[16] Whites in the West weren't biologically superior, they argued; rather, their scientific advances and liberal cultural plurality made them so: The West was an advancing "center," the center of the world. To Shils and his interlocutors, that these advances were forged in the colonial fire remained insignificant, as did the dialectical historical production of dispossession. For instance, in an essay from 1966 on Lebanon, Shils naively suggested that the young nation-state and its citizens adopt a culture of civility to combat political rifts stemming between "communities of belief and primordial attachment," obfuscating the role of foreign rule in creating Lebanon as a modern sectarian state.[17] Stuart Hall said of Shils's "Center and Periphery" theory that it fetishized cultural plurality "as if cultural relations function outside of the impact of economic relations, of social structures, and especially power." Hall noted that Shils accordingly "produce[d] a concept of culture which is evacuated."[18]

Alongside the reduction of race to color and the dismissal of color as merely hue, Shils wrote apropos another set of visual politics: transparency. In 1956, a decade before FOIA's passage, Shils published *The Torment of Secrecy: The Background and Consequences of American Security Policies*, a rejoinder to the United States' growing security bureaucracy and secret surveillance programs that proliferated during the Second Red Scare. Shils was cautiously critical of the rise of espionage networks and secret forms of governance, even as he was suspicious of dissenting Americans and ethnic minorities in their loyalties to the United States. In other words, secrecy's *torment* in Shils's view emerged from the tension between the need to protect America from the world and from un-American values. *The Torment of Secrecy* lay foundations for a critique of secrecy in governance, albeit one that was American exceptionalist in character. Commenting on the physical and ideological dimensions of protecting secrets, he wrote:

> One of the reasons there is so much disturbance around the protection of secrets is that it is so extraordinarily difficult to do it well. In the first place security policy, in so far as it is not merely physical security, is directed towards the future. It is not a matter of putting a guard at a given place and preventing documents from being removed. It is rather a matter of entrusting documents to a person whose *probability of disobeying the security rules* must be estimated. The estimate must be made on the basis of very poor and fragmentary data of uncertain reliability in accordance with the principles of interpretation which are extraordinarily primitive at best, which have never been formulated and which perhaps can never be adequately formulated.... The confusion of loyalty and security-reliability adds to the unmanageability of the task.[19]

In Shils's vivid portrait, the torment of secrecy emerges from both the physical securitization of paper, and a quantitative probability of human loyalty. This was a vulgar but illuminating reduction of ideology to a metric of subversion —an early precursor, perhaps, to the soft biopower that defines our age of algorithmic governance and the securitization of valorized life.[20] Shils moves from this discussion to one about the parameters of loyalty, which, he argues, is fundamentally about a crisis of Americanism. Drawing a distinction from England, he argues, "In America, being American is not a primordial fact attendant on residence [but rather defined] by the extent to which he acts and feels and thinks in a way that is American."[21] Shils explicitly argues that such structures of feelings encompass an investment in the assimilation of ideology (individualism, capitalism) and the assimilation of culture (speaking English, abandoning ethnic affiliation, etc.).[22] Xenophobia, he notes, is an unfortunate consequence of the American experiment, but remarkably, his discussion of ethnic difference myopically focuses on the European immigrant identity at the exclusion of nonwhite peoples. Shils's "possessive investment in whiteness" demonstrates his ultimate view of white ethnic assimilation into the category *American*.[23] Other than in passing reference, he does not mention non-European populations in the United States, as if Black, Native, and other populations were entirely inconsequential to discussions of xenophobia or ethnic difference. In this sense, he unpacks questions of loyalty and social difference within the shifting parameters of whiteness, which have an unstated but direct claim to the security state.

Much of Shils's book situates the debates around secrecy explicitly in such terms, summoning the creed of individualism and its constitutive other, assimilation, to argue for the uniquely American burden and contradictions of securitization for the United States as an emergent hegemonic power in the aftermath of World War II. Shils's ideas were not produced in isolation, of course: Shils was part of a cadre of intellectuals writing about the unique cultural and intellectual merit of "The West" overall and the United States in particular. More to the point, Shils was himself heavily involved with the Congress for Cultural Freedom (CCF), the CIA-funded organization established to promote the superiority of American capitalist ideas and attendant cultural discourses (and defended by Thomas Braden, as mentioned in the beginning of this chapter). Shil's remarks about the inferiority of African and Asian intellectuals is set against the backdrop of the CCF's work to promote liberal, individualist ideas of freedom worldwide in the context of the Cold War, as the CCF funded journals throughout the world, including in the Global South.[24] By one account, it was Shils's explicit insistence that Third World writing was uniquely important for this imperial project that prompted a shift in the CCF's priorities and entrance into the world of African literature.[25] In this view, we can read his writings about secrecy against the ironies of his own involvement with the CIA-funded CCF and the distorted, imperial demands of his writing.[26]

Shils's work had long and wide-ranging impacts on how secrecy was discussed by scholars and political figures. Some forty years later, after the breakup of the Soviet Union, Daniel Patrick Moynihan would cite Shils's work in his campaign against secret bureaucracy, which he believed to be a vestigial artifact of the Cold War. Moynihan drew inspiration from Shils's work, so much so that he worked with Shils's estate to republish the out-of-print *Torment of Secrecy* in 1996 accompanied by a new introduction he penned. In his reflections on the work, Moynihan honed in on Shils's distinction between "functional security" and "symbolic secrecy," the former being necessary and the later a performance of compulsory loyalty, an affront to the ideas of individual choice and American moral superiority that Moynihan and Shils shared.[27] I discuss Moynihan's stakes in transparency more fully later in this chapter. Another conservative intellectual who drew from Shils was the American political scientist Samuel Huntington—infamously known for his racist "Clash of Civilizations" thesis, which Edward Said astutely described as a "belligerent kind of thought" and which reductively presupposed an ahistorical unity to and binary opposition between categories like "the West" and "Islam."[28] In Huntington's book *American Politics: The Promise of Disharmony*, he argues that the emergence of America as a hegemonic actor on a global stage occasioned a misdirected antistate politics. In doing so, he draws from Shils's work in *The Torment of Secrecy* to suggest that the American ideal of open government paradoxically creates possibility for "conspiracy theory" and critiques of the military industrial complex, not the fact of America's imperial endeavors worldwide.[29] Huntington would later sit on the committee spearheaded by Moynihan to assess the efficacy of FOIA after the end of the Cold War.

The modern cultural politics of secrecy sprang forth from the advent of nuclear weaponry, which has itself always encompassed the visual dialectic between secrecy and publicity. Shils was an early member of the *Bulletin of Atomic Science* (BAS), a journal founded by former scientists of the Manhattan Project troubled by the destructive outcome that the secrecy of nuclear science had made possible.[30] Nuclear science and the scientists who advanced the field struggled with questions of transparency and opacity that emerged from the development of nuclear weapons in two ways: first, the ethical implications of developing nuclear science in secret and the sharing of scientific knowledge within the broader scientific community; and second, the politics of sight as they emerge from the explosive collision of particles. In the first regard, many scientists involved with BAS (and the correlated Federation of American Scientists) found themselves at odds with the postwar efforts to legislate atomic science into a secret, national domain, exemplified by the passage of the Atomic Energy Act of 1946, in which the restrictive category of the document *born secret* was inaugurated.[31] To the latter point, Akira Lippit, in his work on the visual politics of radioactive light writes, "The atomic blast . . . brought forth a spectacle of invisibility, a scene that vanishes at the instance of its appearance only to linger forever in the visual world as an irreducible trace of visuality."[32] Though

Lippit was writing about the specific dialectic between the explosion, irradiated light, and its materially present—yet invisible—trace, the atomic bomb existentially points to a nuclear visuality. From the militarized point at which the unseeable (invisible) converged with the idea of making seen (transparency), a nuclear horizon emerged in postwar America, that was intrinsically *born secret*.

Alongside the rise of atomic secrecy arrived a concomitant paranoia against scientists, particularly those of foreign extraction. In the wake of the devastations at Hiroshima and Nagasaki, atomic scientists organized to challenge the military's presumptive right to atomic science; to this end, they had opposed the Atomic Energy Act (AEA), which in its initial incarnation had all but given the growing field to state oversight and application.[33] Many of these scientists were founding members of BAS and were correspondingly targeted for their contestation of the military's presumptive right to atomic science.[34] The initial 1945 proposal of the AEA allowed for the near complete military control over the intellectual project. A number of people, particularly those in the BAS, wrote against this provision.[35] An amended version of the bill passed in 1946. Not long thereafter, two bills would pass that would have subsequent impacts on the ability for foreign scientists to gain entrance into the United States: the Internal Security Act of 1950 and the McCarran-Walter Act of 1952.

Shils lambasted this paranoia against foreign scientists—Europeans—in a 1954 issue of the BAS titled "American Visa Policy and Foreign Scientists" that Shils himself both edited and contributed to.[36] The issue contains contributions from numerous European scientists, from Albert Einstein to Michael Polanyi. In his contribution, Shils assured the reader that these whites were decidedly anticommunist and had come to the United States only for the free exchange of unclassified scientific information.[37] He clarified the ideological stakes in denying their entry: "The refusal of a visa to an educated European applicant not only raises doubts in his mind about America's devotion to freedom of thought and about the calm sanity of its foreign policy as a whole, it also causes him great and often costly inconvenience."[38] Strikingly, while Shils directed his critique toward restrictive visa policies for European scientists, the acts he cites created and solidified racial and imperial discourses of racially desirable immigrants and intolerable political discourse.[39]

His critique is not without further irony. In 1953, in the midst of a rising anticommunist panic, Shils targeted German Jewish refugee and Marxist theorist Theodor Adorno for his left politics, so much so that Adorno feared for his status in the United States and his ability to obtain a passport.[40] It was precisely Shils's blatant contempt for communists and the "colored" peripheries that motivated his critique of the bureaucracy that prevented European scientists from getting visas amid an emerging Cold War. In 1952, the BAS published his defense of the European scientists with the title "America's Paper Curtain."[41]

Three years later, Representative John Moss echoed Shils's formation in asking Congress, "Is there a paper curtain in Washington?"[42] Moss was elected as a representative from the California Central Valley region in 1953 to advocate for public accountability and citizen privacy. His address to Congress signaled the beginning of a decade-long battle to pass right-to-know legislation. Both in these comments and more broadly, Moss excoriated the "slapp[ing] of a confidential stamp" on papers that might potentially embarrass the US government. When speaking in public, as captured in a photograph from 1957, Moss would use paper as a prop, displaying superfluous classification and declassification notations to precisely signify this point: The paper, in its materiality and visual excess, was proof that the system was not working. As Moss gazes at the paper, the photograph insistently asks: Is paper's excess itself the crisis? Like his contemporary Edward Shils in the 1950s, Moss's ideas emerged from a structure of Cold War feelings about American capitalism in terms of an ontological anxiety about the survival of white bourgeois society and the state infrastructures built to protect it. In his cultural history of transparency, Michael Schudson argues that in this period, Moss "readily appealed to the language of the Cold War" but "used Cold War language to oppose the secrecy that the Cold War had itself promoted."[43] Moss's numerous characterizations of American bureaucratic secrecy as a *paper curtain* invoked Winston Churchill's famous description of the Soviet Union as an *iron curtain*. Moss's rhetorical gesture reflected a profound investment in the narrative of American exceptionalism, the same kind of naive view that would suggest civil rights struggles at the time were just contradictions that needed to be resolved, not epistemic foundations of citizenship that undo the notion of "the free world."

Prior to his time in Congress, Moss, a liberal Democrat, fought for consumer protections in California against Pacific Gas and Electric, a major utility company with a near monopoly in this region, and for other liberal causes. During the Second Red Scare, Moss faced accusations of being a communist at community townhalls and in the local press. Moss retold one such incident:

1.2 Rep. John E. Moss (D-CA) displays some of the secrecy stamps that appear on classified government documents, March 6, 1958. Library of Congress.

An old gentleman out in Elk Grove branded me as a communist. I was asked about this at a meeting. . . . I said, "Well maybe I am. Let me tell you the kind I feel I am. I love to own property. I want to get ahead. I want to make money. I want to be free of any political influence that isn't absolutely necessary. I want my children to have a great many opportunities. I want to be able to go out and start a business of my own if I want to and risk my own capital without having someone poking a finger at me and saying 'you can't do that.' And if I want to go someplace, I want to be able to go there. Now if that's a communist, I guess I'm guilty."[44]

Interestingly, Moss's response did not denounce communism, as a rebuff to the panicked proclamations of loyalty that the Second Red Scare compelled. However, his critique of big business hardly opened more robust critique of capitalism and the production of wealth. Moss believed the *real* threat to American capitalist democracy was not the ideological spread of communism but, rather, an erosion of its liberal values vis-à-vis a creeping authoritarian regime of secrecy. In other words, his proclamation "Let me tell you the kind of communist I am," was followed by a declaration of love for an idealized American liberal capitalism, represented by the idea that freedom meant American capitalist democracy and that, in Michel Foucault's words, this society must be defended.[45] To this point, when Moss recounted his reasoning for advocating for FOIA in an oral history, he offered this condemnation of the overreach of the US security state:

> One of the reasons I finally got the Freedom of Information committee going was because of the charges that developed in 1953, the early days of the [President Dwight D. Eisenhower] administration, about the great number of federal employees being discharged as security risks. When I finally learned what a security risk was under federal laws, I discovered it was anyone who might go out and play around with young ladies, drink too much, or do any number of things that had nothing to with his job performance. And when I wanted to get more information on it, of course, I wasn't able to get the information because they had it classified. That's when I decided I wanted to know what the hell they were classifying and why and what good it was serving.[46]

Moss's retrospective denunciation of the US security bureaucracy on the one hand rightfully points to a moral policing that "security" discourse enables. On the other hand, his critique centered around a gendered and racialized subject: white, masculine, and presumed heterosexual. In Moss's view, that "anyone who might play around with young girls" or "drink too much" might have "his job unfairly" taken away represented a particular limit of acceptability. I need not recount what other events were happening at the time, including the CIA-backed coup against Iranian Prime Minister Mossadegh, a growing struggle against the violent regime of American apartheid, and a culture of intersectional sexism that sanctioned the subjugation of women from varying social classes and ethnic backgrounds. That is to say, visible at the surface were numerous abhorrent actions of the US security state, yet the idea that a security bureaucracy might turn against its own ideal citizen-subjects is what Moss cited late in life as the exemplar of government excess.[47] Only after the punitively visual logic of surveillance grew so large that it encompassed white men did it cause alarm in this liberal register. In other words, *transparency* was meant to save *white*, as color, an ideology, and a subject.

Based on these encounters with red panic, Moss took up the "right-to-know" cause, as it had been dubbed by journalists at the time who expressed increasing frustration at the growing security apparatus. By several accounts, Moss's turn to freedom of information originates with a 1954 conversation with Cross.[48] In 1953, Harold Cross, lawyer for the American Society of Newspaper Editors (ASNE), published the aforementioned reference book *The People's Right to Know: Legal Access to Public Records and Proceedings*. Cross's report detailed document access statues and functional practices for journalists across a variety of levels: municipal, state, and federal, both judicial and nonjudicial.[49] In its range and scope, Cross's report was by all accounts singular in its description of freedom of information in America.[50] The report was foundational to the growing right-to-know movement. Within the first paragraph he locates the American newspaper within a capitalist mode of production: "The newspaper gathers together tangible and intangible raw materials from the earth's four corners; it employs labor, manufactures and delivers a tangible—and singularly sensitive and provocative—product, uses capital, receives and grants credit, and pays taxes."[51] Within the same introductory section, Cross cautions against a growing secrecy regime, noting "the backwash of world trends towards secrecy in government," and "habits of secrecy and censorship flowing from war."[52] Though Cross did not deliberate further over American enterprise in the rest of his text, one might read Cross's report against the grain and observe a retrenched commitment to American capitalism that discursively frames his treatise on public records in the midst of a creeping Cold War.

Of the numerous materials he examined, Cross's most significant contribution was to map the dimensions of the Administrative Procedures Act (APA), legislation passed in 1946 that was meant to expand disclosure of information to the public. The APA reacted against the proliferation of federal administrative agencies addressing social welfare under the New Deal. Conservatives sought to mitigate administrative power by creating more regulation to agency rulemaking and adjudication. The APA also expanded guidelines about the disclosure of information to the public. Paperwork review, while not the singular focus of the APA, was thus one maneuver in a broader conservative pushback against the administrative state.[53] Information scholar Lotte Feinberg has highlighted the ironic consequences of the APA: "Although one intent of the APA was to make agency records available to the public," she writes, "the statutory language, such as releasing records to 'persons properly and directly concerned,' turned it from being an access to a withholding statute."[54] Cross argued that this phrase — "persons properly and directly concerned" — led to a particular ambiguity for the press, whose work hinged on matters concerned to governance.[55]

Despite Cross's meticulous accounting of information's freedoms at the start of the Cold War, however, the ASNE had a long history of collaboration with state officials around secret information. The ASNE officially hosted secret off-the-record briefings with high-ranking officials and military officers until the early 1950s, when the hypocrisy between ASNE's off-the-record sessions and the public records demands articulated by their newly formed Freedom of Information Subcommittee became too great.[56] Undoubtedly, Cross's ASNE-commissioned report had a dramatic impact on American politics, most strikingly through the work of Moss. In advocating for clarity on the disclosure regulations within the APA specifically and increased transparency in government generally, Moss positioned himself as defending a particular kind of populist but individualist Americanist scrutiny of state and corporation. But a longer view of transparency in America illuminates the political calculations made by journalists and lawmakers that refute the narrative of transparency as a maneuver toward democracy, fought for by activists, journalists, and people's politicians. Instead, the one constant in the right-to-know struggles remains a rearticulation of America's exceptional status in the world without confronting American grammars of race and capitalism.

Building on the momentum of the journalist-led right-to-know movement, Congressman Moss formed the House Government Information Subcommittee, at which he asked both Cross and the chairman of ASNE's Freedom of Information Committee to testify.[57] Moss advocated for transparency legislation for ten years before it gained traction in the House through a circuitous path. In the end, FOIA 's passage would be marked by two ironies. First, one cosponsor of the bill that became FOIA was Congressman Donald Rumsfeld, who later served as secretary of defense in a Bush administration that was notoriously defined by a regime of information classification and wholesale redactions of the War on Terror's shadowy archives.[58] Second, Lyndon Johnson signed FOIA into law on July 4, 1966, as an amendment to the APA, with no reporters present. Ironically, the most powerful piece of information legislation in American history was signed in proverbial shadows.[59] Since 1966, FOIA has been amended multiple times and continually contested in the courts. The history of FOIA's passage and the subsequent struggle over its meaning and implementation shows that transparency is a floating signifier, regularly raised by competing political positions, none of which neatly break down into a schema that equates transparency with democracy and, thus, secrecy with authoritarianism.

MURKINESS OF THE SEA

Even as the principle of freedom of information became codified in American law, there was profound unclarity around the parameters of application, the process of release, and the regulatory mechanisms to ensure its function. New laws and their meanings are inevitably shaped through interpretation and precedent. As requesters failed to procure the documents they demanded from agencies, they turned to litigation to enforce and clarify the full extent of FOIA. Though Moss would continue to play a role in advocating for FOIA, the courts became a significant battleground. In the decade following 1966, and in a period coinciding with very public, highly mediated conversations around the transparency, several very significant legal cases shaped the Freedom of Information Act.[60] Precisely from this murkiness, in other words, came into being new patterned responses and new forms of classification that continue to guide legal understandings of transparency's limit. As a consequence, by 1974 FOIA would be amended. One year later, in the midst of public clashes over the secret operations and secret documents, the Church Committee convened, a public reckoning (or performance, depending how you look at it) with the work of transparency.

But of course, in the legal refining of the state mechanism of transparency, we can examine a dual valence or perhaps an equivocality in the common use of the verb *classify*. There exist two interrelated but distinct uses. First, of course, *to classify* means "to assign category." In his genealogy of natural history in *The Order of Things*, Foucault excavates the semiotic history of classification as it emerged in the field. Natural history, he writes, "introduce[s] the possibility of a constant order into a totality of representations. It constitutes a whole domain of empiricism as at the same time *describable* and *orderable*."[61] Classification thus materializes from the broader history of category, which conjures a racial history, as it is indelible from the application of a scientific epistemology to the study of human difference. Classification, as a scientific modality, is inextricable from the history of race, racial taxonomies, a colonial ordering of the world. *To classify* can also mean not just "to arrange for view" but also, rather, "to obscure, hide from view, and take out of circulation": for instance, "The document has been classified."

The *Oxford English Dictionary* traces the latter use of *classified* as "secret" to an article from 1940 that mentioned a "highly classified secret in the Air Force."[62] At the dawn of the new era of secrecy, a unique lexicon emerged from the development of atomic science, the normalization of aerial bombing, and the technologies of military imperialism more broadly. In some ways, we can think of secrecy during the Cold War as serving two distinct purposes. On the one hand, of course, secrecy was practically employed to conceal the development of potent advances in weaponry and to keep intelligence-gathering networks effective. On the other, secrecy in the form of clandestine operations and proxy wars allowed for the discursive production of America's assured moral narrative during the Cold War. This secrecy—in concert with the racist inability to conceive of "proxy wars" in the Third World as real war—allowed for American political theorists to ponder whether this this period might just be "The Great Peace."[63] Thus this new sense of classification (of a secret variety) made possible an American Cold War governmentally that hinged on the aesthetics of the liberal state.

What Foucault did not elaborate is that science also gave birth to this other meaning of classification, albeit routed through the military industrial complex. As many have documented, the birth of the state secret was coeval with the arrival of the nuclear era and advances in military science. Indeed, the first FOIA case deliberated in the Supreme Court concerned the release of documents detailing secret underground nuclear explosions in Alaska in 1971. The case, *Mink v. the Environmental Protection Agency*, was originally filed in federal court in 1971 before the tests occurred and made its way to the Supreme Court in 1973. Congresswoman Patsy Mink sought information from governmental agencies that had assessed implications of the Atomic Energy's Commission's proposed secret tests, code-named Cannikin, in the Alaskan archipelago on Amchitka, one of the Aleutian Islands that bends out into the Pacific. Cannikin had many long-lasting health ramifications for the workers who were involved in it as well as the Indigenous communities living nearby. Amchitka, notably, was at the center of two Supreme Court cases: an attempt to get an injunction against the testing, and an attempt to access documents. This case is exemplary of what Rob Nixon has argued is the visual politics of "slow violence," where the harm of militarized violence can escape optic registers of the spectacular and instead show up in other metrics, like illness clusters or degradation. The practice of document classification all but cements a narrow field of vision.

Of the litany of cases that invoked the newly passed FOIA, I turn to two cases that expounded the praxis of classification. The first of these, *Vaughn v. Rosen*, pushed back against the murky territory of FOIA denial. Robert Vaughn sought information about the US Civil Service Commission for research on the potential retrenchment of a spoils system. Vaughn's career touched numerous areas within public interest law: civil service, employment protection, whistleblowing, administrative transparency. In the early 1970s, at the behest of activist Ralph Nader and on behalf of Public Citizen, the organization that Nader had founded in 1971, Vaughn searched for answers from the commission regarding its preferential and discriminatory hiring practices. Through his work, Nader had already found himself at odds with several government agencies over FOIA. During a speech at the American Society for Public Administration Conference in 1970 he denounced what he termed the government's "contamination ploy"—inserting bits of classified documents into a file to claim that the entire file is exempt from release—while simultaneously announcing the launch of the US Civil Service Commission study.[64] That same year, Nader also published a critical assessment of FOIA's implementation for the *Harvard Civil Rights–Civil Liberties Law Review* that delineated the schema of FOIA denial and identified the main pretexts deployed by various government agencies to impede the law's effectiveness. He wrote:

> After three months of exploring the frontiers of the Freedom of Information policy of several federal agencies, with one hundred students working in study groups coordinated by the writer, I have reached a disturbing conclusion: government officials at all levels in many of these agencies have systematically and routinely violated both the purpose and specific provisions of the law. These violations have become so regular and cynical that they seriously block citizen understanding and participation in government. Thus the Act, designed to provide citizens with tools of disclosure, has been forged into a shield against citizen access.[65]

Between 1967 and 1969, Nader and these civic-minded law students (who became popularly known as "Nader's Raiders") collectively found not only systemic "agency avoidance techniques," as he called them, within the government but also a dual system of information release for individuals and special interest groups.[66] Among numerous irregularities, Nader argued that special interest groups and companies had benefited the most from FOIA's passage. Not only did they have the means to litigate under FOIA, but as the main constituencies of the queried agencies, a preferential information-release policy emerged that favored them.[67] Vaughn worked in tandem with Nader's broad efforts at a kind of liberal transparency and accountability. His research on civil services was later published for the Public Interest Research Group as *The Spoiled System: A Call for Civil Service Reform*.[68] Though the agency had been compliant in other matters, Vaughn was met with resistance when requesting the "Evaluation of Personnel Management" Reports from the Bureau of Personnel, a wing of the Civil Service Commission.[69]

Though Vaughn was targeting abuses of power through the tedium of civil service employment records, the implications that emerged from the litigation to release the documents were profound. Despite not being granted access to the documents, the court opined that requesters should have a right to know what they are being denied, "formulating a system of itemizing and indexing that would correlate statements made in the Government's refusal justification with the actual portions of the document."[70] This system became known as the Vaughn Index, now a standard component of FOIA litigation. This may be accompanied by a narrative Vaughn Declaration, requiring the respondent to narrativize the absences. We might understand the Vaughn Index and Declaration in the broad spirit of FOIA, a bureaucratically legitimated attempt to trace the outlines of the unseeable, the effects of which still shape the statecraft of making visible. In 2009, for instance, Leon Panetta was compelled to submit a twenty-four-page Vaughn Declaration, regarding documentation of the CIA's destroyed videotapes of interrogation, which I discuss further in chapter 3. We might think about the Vaughn Index as reiterating a bureaucratic mode of visuality, one that demands accountability through productive visibility. The Vaughn Index produces a silhouetted transparency by indexing and describing the secret, while still maintaining an aporia, and in doing so, it entrenches transparency law as a system of knowledge production.

If *Vaughn v. Rosen* demanded that the state account for its obfuscations, another case would challenge this demand with as much murkiness as the sea from which it emerged. On March 1, 1968, a Soviet submarine armed with nuclear ballistic missiles sank to 16,500 feet below the Pacific Ocean's surface, just 1,560 miles away from Hawai'i.[71] Hawai'i had been colonized just seventy-five years earlier and had been conscripted into statehood for less than a decade. The wreck's Pacific location was indicative of an entire militarized network of maritime seafaring vessels, an aquatic front of the Cold War. The accident happened quietly in the ocean's umbras, the vessel plunged into the shadow world of intelligence as it arrived deep at the bottom of the sea. Undiscovered by the Soviet military, the wreckage of K-129 submarine, as it was known, enticed the American intelligence world into a secret discovery mission. The mission was funded with the capital of the American businessman and war profiteer Howard Hughes, who by at least one account was a sexual abuser and by others was a racist.[72] Hughes put up the money for Global Marine Inc., a company known for deep-sea mining vessels, and the *Hughes Glomar Explorer* was built. Hughes's fame contributed to the CIA's cover story about the mission.

The word *Glomar* (a contraction of Global Marine, Inc.) was emblazoned on the side of the seafaring vessel that was bound for the South Pacific. The secret CIA expedition, known as Project Azorian, operated under the cover story that the ship would mine manganese nodules from the ocean floor. The *Glomar* was able to raise the K-129 submarine, but as the ship got close to the surface, it partially broke off. An account of the operation, a self-congratulatory internal CIA report titled "Project Azorian: The Story of the Hughes Glomar Explorer," was declassified in 2010.[73] Despite the hubris bursting through the still moderately redacted Project Azorian report, the mission to rescue the ship was not entirely successful, as most of the ship was still left at sea. Before the declassification in 2010, however, the story had come to light in fragmented news pieces. Investigative reporter Harriet Ann Phillippi filed a FOIA request with the CIA in 1975 about the expedition. Rather than release redacted documents—or deny the request—the agency pioneered a new approach: refusing to comment directly on the existence of such documents. In the corresponding court case, *Phillippi v. the C.I.A.*, they argued that "in the interest of national security, involvement by the US Government in the activities which are the subject matter of your request can *neither be confirmed nor denied*" (emphasis mine).[74]

Thus was born the oft-invoked opaque phrase "neither confirm nor deny," which gestures, though perhaps fittingly in its opacity, to a terraqueous history. As a bureaucratic mechanism meant to manage the world built and described by paper, the legal "Glomar exemption," as it came to be known, surfaces from Pacific waters. The obscurity of deep waters literally shaped the visual field in which the K-129 submarine was lost and, later, secretly found. The meaning of

1.3 Schematic drawing of the *Hughes Glomar Explorer*, from the formerly secret CIA in-house report "Project Azorian: The Story of the Hughes Glomar Explorer" (1985).

this oceanic murkiness, of course, comes into being through the efforts to exert sovereignty and gain position within the seafront: what Campling and Colás call a "terraqueous territoriality." Scholars of racial capitalism and its attendant military apparatuses in increasingly consider the space of the sea, the shifting human relationship to the sea, and the interplay between land and water in the making of the modern world.[75] In that journey's wake, the word *Glomar* became synonymous with the murky predicate *neither confirm nor deny*, a FOIA equivocation genealogically linked to maritime power. The *Glomar* denial has become a floating signifier for the ability of the US government to operate with impunity and autonomy. Its ubiquity has lent itself to parody, even by the phrase's regular users. In 2014, when the CIA joined Twitter, it rebranded the *Glomar* exception with an attempt at irony: "We can neither confirm nor deny that this is our first tweet."[76]

The story of the *Hughes Glomar Explorer* ends in 2015, when, after being repurposed for decades as an oil rig, it was sold off to become scrap materials to an unknown, unannounced buyer. Recycled bits of this ship, whose name is now inextricable from a history of state equivocation, may well make up manifold new infrastructures, vessels, and commodities that we will never know. The *Glomar* ship's legacy was both an unwitting legal contribution the state's field of vision and a material contribution to logistics industry salvage.[77]

DISCLOSURES AFTER THE HAMMER AND SICKLE

In 1992, during the first official visit by CIA officials to Moscow in the aftermath of the Cold War, a formerly classified videotape from the *Hughes Glomar Explorer* was produced and presented to Russian President Boris Yeltsin.[78] Bodies of six Soviet naval officers had been recovered from the helm of the sunken submarine that the *Glomar* managed to raise to the surface of the water. The video captured the burial ceremony for these recovered seamen, pixelated moving images of the crew playing the American and Soviet national anthems while returning the bodies to the sea.[79] Yeltsin had earlier presented files relating to Soviet participation in the 1983 bombing of a South Korean airliner. New overtures toward transparency symbolically were meant to place the Cold War in the past tense. In other words, at the so-called end of history, it was precisely an accounting of the very material of history-making, or the state document, that occupied and framed new state relationships. Such "declassified diplomacy," as Peter Kornbluh from the National Security Archive called it, constituted—and continues to constitute—a symbolic gift economy that trades in transparency.[80] Between the end of the Cold War and the beginning of the War on Terror, cloak-and-dagger statecraft ceased to have rhetorical weight, but the new art of declassified diplomacy was meant to cement the United States' authority as global hegemon by making the bipolar geopolitical contest that characterized the Cold War a historical artifact.

After the fall the Soviet Union and near the end of his career, Senator Daniel Patrick Moynihan pivoted his work and attention to the politics of transparency and covert action in the new era. He introduced the "End of the Cold War Act of 1991," which called for the dissolution of the CIA, whose basic functions would be taken up by the secretary of state.[81] Declaring a victory of capitalism over communism, he addressed the Senate with a reflection on the necessity of covert action and the shadow world of intelligence: "The time has come to ask, with the Cold War over, can we purge the vestiges of this struggle from *our laws, our bureaucracy and, most importantly, from our way of thinking*?" (emphasis mine). Though some initially considered Moynihan's bill a symbolic act, he reintroduced it in 1995 and continued to advocate for transparency until he passed away in 2003.[82] A major point of Moynihan's argument was that the culture of secrecy made America less secure, as faulty intelligence prevailed. The United States, he argued, had spent money on unnecessary military technologies based on what turned out to be inaccurate assessments of Soviet capabilities. In the Senate during the same period, Moynihan also denounced the nature of President George H. W. Bush's military actions, which he characterized as unilateral rather than coalitional and thus as a holdover from the Cold War. He positioned his bill as a challenge to the "Cold War mentality" that he argued was "woven through all of our institutions."[83]

But how do these late-career critiques of the CIA and government secrecy comport with Moynihan's long-standing service and labors in the intellectual and political apparatus of imperial white supremacy? Indeed, Moynihan's name is tethered in history to his infamously sexist and racist report "The Negro Family: The Case for National Action" (1965), which set forth a sociological defamation of Black families and Black kinship, as framed against a violent fiction of the white heteronormative family ideal.[84] Hortense Spillers, in the same essay I cited at the beginning of this chapter, parses the anti-Black grammars and lexicon that the Moynihan Report draws on, revealing the report as a material and discursive continuation of an American racial frame.[85] In 1969, as the Bronx was burning, Moynihan suggested in a memo to Nixon a policy of "benign neglect" directed at Black New Yorkers. One argument raised in defense of Moynihan's "benign neglect" comments was that the memo he had drafted to Nixon was private, not meant for public eyes, and in being leaked, it was taken out of context.[86] And in 1975, as US ambassador to the UN he vigorously defended the Israeli state project, insisting at the United Nations, against the majority of the General Assembly, that Zionism is *not* racism. Moynihan apparently made nothing of the contradiction between the naked brutality of American counter-insurgency—both at home and abroad—and the calls for an end to government secrecy. In other words, an assessment of Moynihan's life work renders palpable who, within his cosmology, could be full subjects (and agents) of transparency, and who would be rendered as racially other through a seemingly transparent gaze, yet *hidden to the cultural seeing by skin color.*

Moynihan's preoccupation with post–Cold War transparency and denaturing the CIA was not a departure from his earlier defenses of American exceptionalism but, rather, a direct outgrowth of his years as diplomat in India. In

1973, Moynihan began his two-year tenure as US ambassador to India, and was a founding member of the Non-Aligned Movement and regular critic of US imperialism on the international stage. Though tensions between the United States and India stemmed from inherent conflicts between the imperial designs of the global hegemon and the postcolonial ambitions of a Third World state publicly conducting its first nuclear tests at the time, Moynihan's encounters with the CIA in India convinced him that their attempts at covert action could and would backfire.[87] After the CIA-backed coup against Chilean President Salvador Allende on September 11, 1973, Prime Minister Indira Gandhi was certain she was the next target on the CIA's list, a concern that Moynihan was made aware of.[88] The 1967 *Ramparts* magazine revelations, mentioned at the outset of this chapter, rippled out beyond Braden's CIA apologist article; in India, concerns over US covert actions occupied journalists and politicians alike.[89] Moynihan far preferred the veneer of hegemonic benevolence, opting for soft-power solutions—like negotiating grain debt forgiveness for India—to warm up relations.

Moynihan's letters from the time express his frustration with Henry Kissinger specifically, and the CIA and US intelligence apparatus in general, for their muddled approach to US-India relations. But woven into these letters, between his annoyance at US intelligence, is an account of how profoundly the Orientalist writings of intellectuals like Edward Shils impacted him. For instance, among other books, Moynihan brought with him Shils's *The Intellectuals and the Powers* on a beach trip to Kovalum in 1974.[90] In a letter drafted just a month later while traveling the Rajasthani countryside, he reflects on the Indian socialist J. P. Narayan, noting, "Reading Shils on 'Asian Intellectuals.' Of whom Jayaprakash Narayan is surely one."[91] Ironically, Narayan himself was associated with the CIA-backed Congress for Cultural Freedom, the same liberal anticommunist organization that Shils had outed himself for being involved with. Shils's writings shaped the lens through which Moynihan absorbed India, and the CIA's long shadow perennially lurked over Moynihan's time in India. In his essay "The United States in Opposition," penned just after he returned to the United States from India, Moynihan opens with a quote from Shils before launching into an ethnocentric tirade against the United Nations. Arguing that America and Israel were unfairly persecuted by an empowered Third World, Moynihan summons India as an example of a misguided modernity.[92] In his study of Moynihan, the historian Paul McGarr argues, "It is within the pages of *Secrecy* that we are reminded, almost as an aside, that the genesis of Moynihan's interest in the linkages between intelligence operations, secrecy and diplomacy were first distilled not in the cool, marble chambers of Capitol Hill, but in the fierce political heat of India."[93]

Beginning in 1994, for a period of two years, Moynihan spearheaded the Commission on Government Secrecy, assembling a "bipartisan" committee that would review classification practices at the end of the Cold War. The commission was composed of government officials who worked in the areas of defense and intelligence (including a retired CIA director and the former director of the National Reconnaissance Office, who was responsible for declassifying its existence in 1992) and others representing the defense industry, journalism, policy, and academia. Samuel Huntington, of then-contemporary "clash of civilizations" thesis fame, was among the appointees. The Senate majority leader appointed Moynihan as chair of the commission. When the commission published its findings in 1997, within the report's was an eighty-six-page entire academic treatise titled "Secrecy: A Brief Account of the American Experience."[94] The piece, appendix A of the report, would later turn into Moynihan's full-length solo-authored manuscript bearing almost the same name. Notably, Moynihan's writings for the Commission on Government Secrecy extensively cite Shils's *Torment of Secrecy*.

Like those of his inspiration, Shils, Moynihan's understandings of secrecy were both explicitly and implicitly refracted through a lifetime of ill-conceived writings on race and ethnicity. In appendix A, Moynihan meditates at length on what he refers to variously as the "ethnic element," "ethnic terms," and "ethnic dimensions." He specifically addresses these "ethnic dimensions," because "a recurrent pattern of these crises [espionage, attacks] is the involvement of ethnic groups, often first-generation immigrants who have retained strong attachments to their ancestral homes and, not infrequently, to political movements that were prominent at the time of immigration." Though he is also quick to decry "prejudice" and "fear" that accompanies these crises, he pointed out that "the secrets came about largely because there was a perceived threat." "Loyalty," he notes, "would be the arbiter of security."[95] Moynihan's addendum to the congressional report reflects on the histories of German Americans, Japanese Americans, and Punjabi-Californians, and the rise of the anti-imperialist Ghadar Party. Later in the addendum, Moynihan argued that secrecy "responds . . . to the fear of conspiracy, regularly and consistently associated with one or another ethnic or religious group *within* American society." He then argued that "it should be obvious that our Muslim citizens are now especially vulnerable."[96] The racial and ethnic other, as a potential subversive within the United States, underwrote his ideology of transparency. Not long after the commission released its report, Moynihan published a monograph with the same title *Secrecy: An American Experience*, which drew from his writings for the commission confirmed this view. "Espionage," he wrote in the preface, "is almost invariably associated with diaspora politics."[97]

The masculinist, Orientalist, and racist bravado that is particular to Moynihan's writing here also reflects the politics of seeing and unseeing that is characteristic of American imperial visuality. In his passionate defense of transparency, and advocacy for a more robust implementation of the Freedom of Information Act, Moynihan summoned suspicions of the nonwhite world and the specter of communism as his foil. In this way he summoned an Americanism distinct in rhetoric from, yet resonant with, that which Moss raised in the wake of the Red Scare. Both calls for transparency, Moynihan's in the 1990s and Moss's in the 1950s, emerged from America's anticommunist paranoia. Moynihan believed transparency meant cooperation between government agencies, academics, and the private sector, and thereby clear, rational, informed discourse which, in his view, the information age would make even more crucial.[98] But as I have shown, this patriotic call for open government was underwritten by a racial and imperial gaze, by the grandiosity of the perceived victor. In the book published in 1998 from the commission's findings, Moynihan wrote, "Secrecy is for losers. For people who don't know how important information really is. The Soviet Union realized this too late."[99]

CONCLUSION

Ideas about political transparency in America were neither shaped in a vacuum nor born from egalitarian experiments with democracy. Rather, transparency was shaped in discourse and policy by the postwar emergence of American empire in the nuclear age and the concomitant regimes of racialized knowledge/power that the new hegemon compelled. For its legislative champions, transparency was understood as a tactical advantage against bureaucratic inefficiencies and government factionalism. The ideology of freedom of information could not be separated from the techniques of wielding political power within most elite segments of society. To return to the question posed at the beginning of the chapter: For its supporters in government, transparency was eminently tethered to white men and whiteness, in both conspicuous and obscured ways.

Today, liberal transparency advocates bemoan FOIA's improper functioning as a machine that needs fixing. It should be dispassionate, rational, perfunctory, not subjective. The intense subjectivity, some advocates argue, can obscure the purpose and potential of FOIA. Of course, FOIA is part of an arsenal of attempts to countersurveil the state, which I assess in the next chapter. What I am suggesting here is not that FOIA is irrecoverably tethered to the imperial machine but that in the use and deployment of FOIA within an activist sphere, our contemporary political imaginaries might stand to gain from dwelling in its contradictions.

As I've attempted to show here, transparency is not inherently a radical project. To use a visual metaphor, it was the product of a racial myopia, an inability and unwillingness to conceptualize what Simone Browne has named "dark matter," the structuring matter of the universe that remains imperceptible to the scientific eye. FOIA is tied irreducibly to the material world: first, to its own emergence from piles of pulp, fashioned into reams of paper; and second, to the role of paper in describing and shaping American empire. FOIA thus must be understood within racial and imperial architectures of seeing and making visible; the trace of American militarism in even the most seemingly mundane aspects of life. In other words, to turn back to the words of Spillers, transparency cannot inherently reveal that which is *hidden to the cultural seeing by skin color*.

I have retethered FOIA to the unfolding story of American capitalism and American imperialism. As the record of Moss's life and that of the broader history of bureaucracy in America reveal, FOIA emerges from a Cold War context as a reaction to the proliferation of documents and the rapid expansion of state secrets and intelligence-gathering practices. While people of all persuasions use FOIA to better understand the arcana of statecraft that structures their political world, a central contradiction remains: FOIA was meant to preserve American capitalist democracy, even as it has exposed the terrors on which this imperial and racial project hinge.

In addition to John Moss, who in some ways stands apart for the other figures I've discussed here, many of the other characters who show up in the state discourse around transparency are familiar to students of American imperialism and ethnic studies: Samuel Huntington, Francis Fukuyama, Daniel Patrick Moynihan, Edward Shils, and Donald Rumsfeld. This is not to suggest that they agreed on the specifics of transparency or the kinds of ways disclosures should be used. Clearly, they all had varying kinds of investments in the American security state. But this is precisely what is interesting: Each of them, believing in the project of America, was invested in a rational, optical discourse that rested on a dialectical connection between secrecy and transparency. Transparency as a utopic project for its theorists and executors presumed the exclusion of evidentiary claims against the state from the nonwhite peoples of the world. But as I show in the next chapter, transparency and its legislative avatar, FOIA, are not overly determined in political meaning.

In 1982, Ronald Reagan proposed serious curtailments to the Freedom of Information Act. Moss, along with the activists whom I discuss in the next chapter, challenged Reagan's attacks on transparency and whipped up support to defend the law. Rumsfeld, responding to Moss's requests for support, defended Reagan's proposal, arguing that it should be "adjusted to fit the realities that are now more apparent."[100] Rumsfeld's changing position on FOIA might be extrapolated more broadly to a political sphere in which transparency was not in itself an ethical stance but, rather, a convenient one wielded too often as a sanctimonious weapon in the war that is the American imperial.

This is nothing but an ill-founded propaganda campaign to justify government efforts to isolate, harass and repress supporters of progressive causes throughout the U.S. Targets of these attacks have been and will likely continue to be Black and other third world activists, trade unionists, opponents of war, nuclear power, and nuclear weapons, and women's movement and gay activists. Accordingly we will fight against any further changes in FOIA that will cover up government spying and we call upon all other freedom-loving people to oppose such changes.
—GRAND JURY PROJECT, "Part of a Threat to Liberation Struggles"

On January 26, 1979, a letter addressed to Stansfield Turner, director of the Central Intelligence Agency (CIA), was dropped in the mail in Washington, DC. "Dear Admiral Turner," it read, "we invite you* to attend a special 'preview' of 'The Intelligence Network.'" The asterisk clarified that the invitation extended to any member of the CIA, in the event that Director Turner was otherwise occupied. The film would screen on February 13 at the Folger Theater on Capitol Hill. It was by invitation only. Commissioned by the Campaign for Political Rights (CPR), the documentary attempted to turn a watchful gaze back onto the surveilling state. "Based on information obtained through Freedom of Information requests, citizens' lawsuits and Congressional investigations," the CPR declared, "'The Intelligence Network' reveals past and current abuses of local, state, and federal intelligence agencies." The letter was printed on CPR letterhead, which, as is visible on the left side of the stationery, was a consortium of about fifty organizations ranging in scope and purpose, from the Black Panther Party to the Puerto Rican Socialist Party to the American Civil Liberties Union, the Middle East Research and Information Project, and even the Church of Scientology. CPR's national coordinator, Peggy Shaker, signed the letter, along with Robert Borosage of the Institute for Policy Studies (IPS) and Morton Halperin of the Center for the National Security Studies (CNSS). Shaker, Borosage, and Halperin concluded their letter to the CIA with a final overture: "We hope you will join us to view this film."[1]

Dozens of similar invitations arrived in the mailboxes of members of the intelligence community: those working in the Federal Bureau of Investigation (FBI), National Security Agency (NSA), State Department, and more.[2] Though accounts suggest that Stansfield Turner did not show up, the event drew a motley crew of activists, reporters, officials, and at least one self-identified employee of the FBI.[3] The *Washington Post* reported, "The ACLU, Quakers, ADA, Nader's people, the abortion rights people, the Institute for Policy Studies people all steam[ed] up the windows at Folger Theater yesterday afternoon." The *Post* even noted the impact of the shadow world on the event's atmosphere: "There was even a guy loping around in work boots and a backpack." The thirty-five-minute documentary, commissioned by the CPR, illuminated stories of government spying, harassment, and intimidation in the United States and beyond. The film prominently featured the testimony of Isabel Letelier, the widow of exiled Chilean Minister of Foreign Affairs Orlando Letelier, who was assassinated in Washington, DC, in 1976 at the behest of Augusto Pinochet; the story of Fred Hampton, member of the Black Panther Party, murdered in 1969 by the police in his own bedroom; and numerous other interviews with people surveilled for their dissent and protest activities. None of this information, of course, would be new to the intelligence agencies. But this special screening, planned before the film's public release, attempted to address the surveillers with an unaverted gaze.

I first encountered CPR's letter of invitation to Director Turner on the CIA's digital archive of declassified documents. At the bottom of the PDF, typewritten text reveals that the invite and a corresponding info packet were declassified by the CIA in 2004. The packet included the film's promotional materials as well as a number of other books, pamphlets, and visual texts curated by CPR to disseminate "information about surveillance and harassment for political reasons by U.S. Governmental Agencies."[4] I begin this chapter with CPR's invite as exemplary of a layered visual politics, thick with contradiction over the politics of seeing and sight. The letter itself indexes several simultaneous visual dynamics, the most dramatic of which, of course, was that its authors intended to flip the script on surveillance. The invite was a performative gesture, returning the CIA's monitoring of leftist activity with a countersurveillant gaze: *You watch us, we watch you.* That CPR produced a film in the expository mode of documentary cinema underscores a subversive politics of looking and seeing that must be understood within its historical context. A dialectic between secrecy and transparency permeated the political and social life of the era.

As mainstream political debates over freedom of information hinged on which eyes might appropriately view varying documents, a confrontational politics of transparency emerged from the left. New laws are made meaningful through their use, as it is the struggles over them that create precedent and practice. FOIA was no exception; the years soon after its passage were marked by world historical upheavals and framed by this struggle to seize files and demand information from the state.[5] The work of Ralph Nader and his peers (discussed in the previous chapter) demonstrated how FOIA remained largely ineffectual subsequent to its passage in 1966. Nader and his Raiders (as they became known) sought FOIA reform through activist demands and citizen oversight. Others took more radical approaches to government transparency. Some confrontations resulted in subversive encounters with the security state, as many rejected the authoritarian idea of property (and propriety) that governed how documents were classified. Offices were broken into, documents stolen. Files were snuck out of their cabinets, surreptitiously copied, then released to the public. Articles were prolifically published in left newsletters and magazines on government surveillance and clandestine operations. In 1971, the infamous Pentagon Papers leaked, which presented a meticulous imperial account of US intervention in Southeast Asia that Daniel Ellsberg stole from the RAND Corporation, his employer. Following Lisa Gitelman's illuminating discussion of the Pentagon Papers, both the history of the surveillant bureaucracy and, crucially, the history of challenges to it were bound up in the medium of xerographic reproduction.[6] That is to say, the ideology of transparency was inextricable from the material conditions that enabled replication and circulation of a file.

But one of the most significant contributions to the genesis of a confrontational politics of transparency might be traced to the night of March 8, 1971. During the "Fight of the Century," a match between world heavyweight boxers Muhammad Ali and Joe Frazier, a secret group calling themselves the Citizens' Commission to Investigate the FBI broke into an FBI office in Media, Pennsylvania. The Citizens' Commission stole over a thousand documents—all the files in the office; they stuffed them in suitcases and scuttled away by getaway car.[7] After reviewing their content in a secure farmhouse outside the area, the group sent the papers to media outlets for publication. The files detailed widespread surveillance and infiltration operations against social justice movements in the United States and were filled with memos, letters, and other transmissions. The media papers were revelatory on multiple fronts: They hinted at the profundity of the surveillance and counterinsurgency operations against Americans challenging the government. They exposed how FBI agents recruited assets at universities and libraries throughout the country, sowed dissent between and among activists, spied on students and library-goers. A fuller accounting of this surveillance operation would not become clear until much later, after an interested journalist followed clues from the break-in.[8]

The subject line of one small routing slip in the cache read "COINTELPRO—NEW LEFT."[9] At the time, the code was incomprehensible outside the FBI. It was only through FOIA litigation brought against the FBI by reporter Carl Stern that the COINTELPRO files were released in 1973. This campaign was known as the Counter Intelligence Program (hence COINTELPRO), and the declassified documents revealed the extent to which the program had infiltrated and repressed communities of color and activists in America. The members of the Citizens' Commission had no further activities as a group and kept their identities secret for over forty years. But the unveiling of COINTELPRO in this manner would have profound impacts on transparency organizing. The break-in revealed a curious and perplexing memo, which was a meaningless transmission on its own in the public sphere but, when refracted through the medium of FOIA, exposed the secret paper network in which it had a great deal of meaning. This was radical transparency by any means. To write about and publish previously classified government documents was, at this point, a liberation of paper and a smashing of state narrative.

One of the first publications from the Media papers, as they were fittingly and uncannily known, was assembled by the magazine *Win: Peace and Freedom Through Non Violent Action*. In 1972 they printed an issue titled "The Complete Collection of Political Documents Ripped-Off from the F.B.I. Office in Media, P.A., March 8, 1971." *Win* was published with the support of the War Resisters League, a pacifist antimilitarization organization. They had received the documents directly from Citizens' Commission, who had unsuccessfully tried to find a mainstream publisher for all of them. Though some documents had been drawn on by the press, at least half had not been addressed at all. Certainly, copies of the original documents were not available to the public in any capacity. The *Win* issue was printed exactly a year after the FBI office break-in and comprised a typeset dossier of original materials, condensed to fit 271 documents into 82 pages of the magazine.

In the opening pages, *Win* lay out a full-size picture of FBI workers cataloguing fingerprints from 1943—hundreds of workers hunched over fingerprint cards on shared tables, their faces and features blending into the shadows of the magazine's xerographic medium, visible mostly by the whites of their dress shirts.[10] A media history of surveillance and its human labors can be gleaned from this image. *Win* includes the original letter from the Citizens' Commission to Investigate the FBI, followed by a guide to reading the documents. The two-page spread directs the reader to an FBI memo and points out numerical codes and agency lingo delineating filing and categorization systems for papers, populations, and agents. The spread was meant to instruct the reader in precisely how to read a document, critical to the project of liberating the information captured on these pages. *Win*'s publication can be seen as a precursor to the left magazines and pamphlets that would publish formerly classified documents. It is worth reiterating that this publication preceded Stern's COINTELPRO FOIA release. No one yet knew what COINTELPRO fully signified, but they did know that the documents contained significant information that needed to be shared. At the time of its publication the *Win* issue propelled an urgent call for radical transparency, to bring attention to an unfolding story. Complete obfuscation around widespread government surveillance is what had compelled a small cadre to burgle the FBI office in the first place.

Papers, the creation of them, and the struggle to access them were tethered to the zeitgeist of the era, spanning decolonization and the rise of neoliberalism. Consider, for instance, the document theft that happened at the 1972 break-in at the Democratic National Convention's headquarters. The break-in and its subsequent cover-up commenced the Watergate scandal, a story that in its unfolding revealed widespread clandestine and surveillant activities sanctioned by the Nixon administration. But we might understand this story within a landscape already profoundly politicized over questions of access and restrictions to information. In 1974, an amendment to FOIA was passed. Then, in 1975, Senator Frank Church convened a committee (known as the Church Committee) to investigate intelligence abuses that had been leaked in the public sphere, to mixed results. The period between the FOIA's passage and amendment also marked the height of the Vietnam War. The regulation of paper within a war bureaucracy became a flashpoint for activism. While a number of significant radical histories draw from the declassified archives, few specifically examine the labors to liberate these papers. Most accounts of this moment take the fight against the secret machinations of the state as matter-of-fact. However, the contours of a secrecy-transparency dialectic are brought into clearer focus by the work of activists who confronted covert action, as critiques of US imperialism and domestic warfare illuminated the struggle to seize paper. In other words, the making of this archive is a part of this radical history.

The COINTELPRO revelations in particular provided a specific and potent flashpoint for this radical demand for transparency. Whereas the Watergate scandal revealed corruption within political ranks, people on the ground felt the injurious impact of COINTELPRO directly. Dirty battles to consolidate electoral political power—no matter how unethical—did not compare with the widespread impact of surveillance, harassment, and infiltration on the lives of entire communities.[11] In other words, though Watergate (and Nixon's disgraced name) live on within the public sphere, the activist and community organizations that energized transparency activism did so because of a concern for the suppression of dissent and the destruction of the left. FOIA itself thus became a point of convergence for activists: as both an oculus or place from which to peer and perceive and an underdog's tool to whittle away at the edifices of secrecy. FOIA, in its inchoate and as yet undefined form, provided an unexpected political possibility. People drafted how-to FOIA guides to request their own FBI files, alternative presses procured and published declassified documents. Entire newsletters were dedicated to revealing—through the craft of declassification—the statecraft that classification built. Cait McKinney's account of analogous queer and feminist media practices in the same moment describes this work as "information activism," arguing that information-sharing networks were themselves sites of subaltern organizing.[12] A web of letters connected activists across space as people wrote to organizations requesting how-to FOIA guides and alternative documentaries, drafted letters demanding FOIA files, and shared stories by pen about surveillance. This account maps the media activism that comprised this alternative paper network.

For the CPR and other similar organizations, the utopian promise of FOIA worked in step with the ethos of whistleblowing, alternative self-publishing, and document theft. In other words, a more radical sense of transparency emerged at this moment not from the anticommunism central to the creation of FOIA but from the opposite: a critique of American imperialism and state repression against insurgency at home and abroad. Radical transparency was a critique of American exceptionalism rather than a defense of it. While it may be tempting to situate FOIA as foil to document stealing, whistleblowing, and other radical, unsanctioned acts of transparency, the historical record would suggest otherwise. FOIA was one in a continuum of tools that leftists used to give official confirmation to what they saw happening to their communities, comrades, and the broader world: for instance, the publication *Counterspy*, which was lambasted for "outing" American spies abroad, used FOIA documents in many of their articles in addition to publishing classified information based on government leaks.

Other publications emerging from heavily policed communities of color often used FOIA documents not as revelation of secret actions but as confirmation of the repression they had experienced. In 1974, *Jihad News*, the publication of the African People's Party (a reconstituted version of the Black Marxist organization Revolutionary Action Movement), published a short article titled "Sabotage": "A disclosure by the FBI in early March confirmed *what everybody had known all along*—J. Edgar Hoover and his henchmen used every weapon at their disposal (and many beyond legal constraints) to attempt to sabotage the drive for Black liberation of the late 60s and early 70s" (emphasis mine).[13] Detailing the techniques of government subterfuge, the article points to FOIA: "Departmental memos came to light as a result of a suit won by NBC reporter Carl Stern under the 1967 Freedom of Information Act. The released records were heavily censored to blot out names of most organizations and persons who were targets of the program. *But in the Black community, few people had any difficulty filling in the blanks*" (emphasis mine).[14]

Accompanying the short article were pictures of Amilcar Cabral, Malcolm X, and Patrice Lumumba, "African leaders . . . struck down at the hands of imperialist and fascist saboteurs," meant to illuminate the open secret of political assassination and covert action. For the author, the disclosure's redactions were not muffled gaps; rather, they were loud aporias that announced their own violence. Such accounts point to the intimate reception of these documents within subaltern counterpublics, where redactions were not scandals but confirmations of life lived under surveillance and state violence.

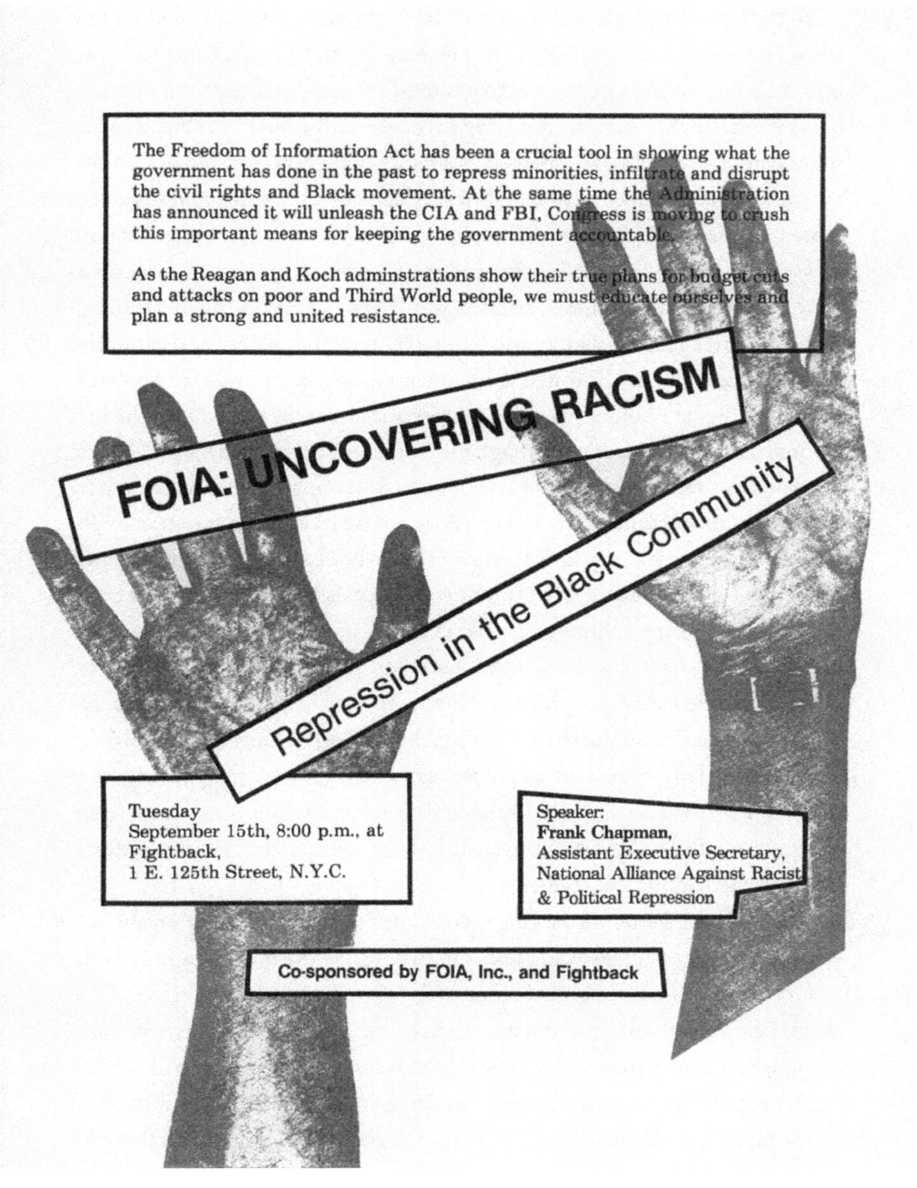

The Freedom of Information Act has been a crucial tool in showing what the government has done in the past to repress minorities, infiltrate and disrupt the civil rights and Black movement. At the same time the Administration has announced it will unleash the CIA and FBI, Congress is moving to crush this important means for keeping the government accountable.

As the Reagan and Koch adminstrations show their true plans for budget cuts and attacks on poor and Third World people, we must educate ourselves and plan a strong and united resistance.

FOIA: UNCOVERING RACISM

Repression in the Black Community

Tuesday
September 15th, 8:00 p.m., at
Fightback,
1 E. 125th Street, N.Y.C.

Speaker:
Frank Chapman,
Assistant Executive Secretary,
National Alliance Against Racist
& Political Repression

Co-sponsored by FOIA, Inc., and Fightback

2.1 Flyer for event "FOIA: Uncovering Racism, Repression in the Black Community," hosted by the National Alliance Against Racist and Political Repression, cosponsored by FOIA Inc., and Fightback. NCARL Papers, M92-045, box 7, file "FOIA."

In the last chapter I argued that FOIA emerged from a set of Cold War tensions and a white liberal impulse to preserve the state. In this chapter, however, I show how transparency activists used FOIA to challenge the exigency of state overreach, if not, at times, the existence of the imperial state itself. In other words, even as FOIA emerged as a mode of power/knowledge administrating a Foucauldian governmentality in American life, many requesters were more than managed citizen-subjects who accepted the authority of the state and its logic. These are the interwoven stories of those agitating around transparency, like the Campaign for Political Rights, FOIA Inc., the National Coalition Against Repressive Legislation, and the resultant media tactics, legal cases, and activist entanglements. Through these organizations, individuals, and publications, I examine this ethos of countersurveillance from the period after the 1975 Church Committee hearings through the first term of the presidency of Ronald Reagan, who seriously curtailed use of FOIA and implemented wide-ranging restrictions on document access. I consider the creation and promotion of *The Intelligence Network* alongside other materials—books, pamphlets, magazines, and letters—that CPR and others produced as expressions within a visual economy defined by censorship and the secret life of paper. CPR published a regular newsletter, *Organizing Notes*, which focused on stories of government harassment and surveillance alongside developments in transparency activism. The account of transparency activism I present here is by necessity a media history, as organizing hinged on a visual politics expressed through the production of media, understood capaciously. Papers and classified archives were, respectively, contested media and infrastructures. And what is transparency if not a contestation over mediations and media?

As much as I center on varying media stories as entangled within antisurveillance organizing, however, I also aim to describe the broad ethos of countersurveillance, of which cultural productions played one part. That is to say, this chapter draws forth stories of documentaries, newsletters, and papers, while also bringing to the fore stories of activists, academics, and lawyers who illuminate the broad politics of radical transparency. I began this chapter with a discussion of *The Intelligence Network* to contextualize the other kinds of tactics that CPR undertook to challenge the security state. I discuss CPR alongside peer activist and media organizations working to demand transparency from the state: the Center for National Security Studies (CNSS), the National Coalition Against Repressive Legislation (NCARL), the Fund for Open Access and Accountability Incorporated (FOIA Inc.), and the Institute for Policy Studies. As I argued in the previous chapter, protransparency establishment rhetoric often willfully ignored the visible detriment of American violence against Black people and other people of the Third World. While transparency activists certainly engaged how surveillance specifically targeted communities of color, some organizers' continued attachments to patriotic ideals prevented them from producing a program of countersurveillance that adequately confronted the racial state.

What this chapter illustrates is that information—and paper—are terrains of struggle and political mobilizing. Indeed, radical transparency activists demanded to see the state specifically to refuse its nefarious mobilization of sight and surveillance. This is not a negation of what Glissant called for as 'the *right to opacity*' but, rather, another dimension of it, which encompasses *both* the right to demand information and the right to withhold it. One particularly illustrative example of this might be gleaned from the case *Wilkinson v. FBI*. Frank Wilkinson was a member of the Communist Party (and perhaps best known for his problematic involvement in the destruction of the Chavez Ravine community).[15] In 1980 Wilkinson, along with other named plaintiffs, filed a case against the FBI to contest and gain information about the long-standing surveillance that they knew had been waged against them. The litigation played out in multiple court battles over six years, which involved extensive and protracted FOIA litigation to determine the scope of the surveillance against Wilkinson and, ultimately, to release the documents. After the case closed in 1987 and a 132,000-page dossier compiled on him came to light, Wilkinson bemoaned not having litigated further and added, "Without question, thousands of likeminded, socially concerned individuals and organizations who were under similar political surveillance and disruption as were we, have *still* not availed themselves of the protective source of information under the FOIA."[16]

Wilkinson's case opened onto another tactical battle over the right to see and the possession of paper. In the 1970s, NCARL had donated papers to the Wisconsin Historical Society (WHS), as they were known as a repository for activist papers. The WHS already housed the papers of Anne and Carl Braden, who were social and economic justice organizers. The Bradens, along with Wilkinson, had cofounded the organization that became NCARL, which challenged the House Un-American Activities Committee (HUAC) and conspiracy thinking during the Red Scare. In the deed of acquisition to their papers, the Bradens had specified that the collection remain on restricted access, viewable by permission only. During the course of the protracted *Wilkinson v. FBI* case, as a counterattack and reaction against the insistent FOIA demands to release Wilkinson's surveillance file, the FBI demanded access to the Braden Papers through the process of discovery. The legal case tested the extent to which the donor's access restrictions would be respected, and ultimately extended even to ongoing oral history tapes Wilkinson was recording with an archivist at UCLA.[17] The distillation was that the countersurveillant impulse of Wilkinson's demand to open the files was countered by the FBI's surveillant demand to see archival papers they had no good reason to access. To add another layer of complexity, in later additions to the now-public Braden Papers, some of the documents from the *Wilkinson v. FBI* case and the subsequent Braden release have now been added to the collection.[18]

This illustration emerges from the Wisconsin Historical Society, the archive from which I drew some materials for this chapter: the Anne and Carl Braden Papers, the NCARL Papers, and the papers of the Campaign for Political Rights. While in Madison, I sifted through the photocopied pages inscribed with both state abuses and challenges to them. An aura emanated from them. These annals vibrated with traces of those who had sought to wage a war against the imperial, racial state with letters, photocopies, and films. To frame this in another way: Following media theorist Marshall McLuhan, we might think of these paper transmissions, not simply the content within them, as the message.[19] Apart from the centrality of these papers in the history of transparency activism, they were something beyond a record of rebellion against a surveilling state. These papers themselves were, in fact, a rebellion.

HOW TO FREE INFORMATION

The documentary film *The Intelligence Network* was prefaced by a far more unassuming, but nevertheless powerful, countersurveillant genre: the how-to instructional FOIA guide. After the Church Commission, activists saw the newly amended FOIA as a tool that might counter government spying. People wanted access to the information that intelligence and law enforcement agencies had collected and weaponized against them; organizations and individuals learned how to write FOIA requests, where to send the requests, and how to appeal request denials. Many activist organizations shared these newly acquired skills by issuing and circulating how-to FOIA guides that instructed readers in all manner of requests. The Fund for Open Access and Accountability, Inc. (FOIA Inc.), founded in 1976, published *Are You Now or Have You Ever Been in the FBI? How to Secure and Interpret Your FBI Files*, in 1981, one section of which they self-published as a booklet, *Getting FBI Files: An Activist Handbook*. The guides were based on their own experiences with FOIA as participants in the campaign to support Ethel and Julius Rosenberg, convicted of spying for the Soviet Union. The Rosenbergs' children, Robert Meerpol and Michael Meerpol, actively sought information about the surveillance of—and charges against—their parents, and eventually won 300,000 documents from government agencies, including the FBI.[20]

How-to FOIA guides encouraged a correspondent's insurrection against a surveillant bureaucracy. The FOIA Inc. guides, for instance, included not only sample letters but also details about FBI classification codes acquired through long-standing work on the Meerpol case and helping numerous FOIA suits for other causes.[21] Even FOIA Inc.'s logo—a chain being broken—embodied this radical relationship to FOIA. *Freedom* of information, though born from Cold War imperial sentiments, had materialized in a moment of great political struggle within the United States and beyond. This demand and mandate were interpreted within the broad liberatory engagements with the idea of *freedom* itself. Asian American studies scholar Glenn Omatsu reflected on a version of FOIA Inc.'s how-to guide in a 1988 issue of *Amerasia Journal*. After detailing the step-by-step request information that the reader might learn from the manual, he asked, "Just how important is the Freedom of Information Act for Asian Americans? In a recent special issue of *Amerasia* on Japanese American history, information cited in three articles was obtained through the Freedom of Information Act."[22] Besides, he continued, the right to know was "fundamental" and should be "defended."

A centerfold map of America in *Getting FBI Files: An Activist Handbook* instructs the reader where appropriate FBI field offices are located. Ann Mari Buitrago, research director of FOIA Inc., noted that their own guide to the FBI Central Records System index was more detailed and helpful than that published in the federal registrar, which she attributes to their extensive use of FOIA.[23] Appendix 5 in the manual lists over two hundred classifications in the CRS (including obsolete ones), and appendix 6 included lists of other special indexes and the field offices where the corresponding files might be located. The significance of FOIA Inc.'s efforts to catalogue should not be lost; they produced the sorting and classification tools by which FOIA was made meaningful to the public and, accordingly, built the infrastructure of the law itself. This endeavor was scholarly in its methods (indeed, Buitrago had a PhD in political science), and political in its intent. Index classifications would tell the FBI specifically where to look within their own files: countersurveillance qua surveillance, mobilizing the minutiae of the FBI's very own ordering system to challenge the Bureau's authority.

How-to pamphlets were central to this early moment of democratization around the use of FOIA, as well as the shaping of its meaning within the public sphere. In journalist Penn Kimball's autobiographical book *The File*, he details decades of government surveillance and the use of FOIA to gain access to his record. He makes clear that he would not have been able to access his file if not for the encounter with ACLU pamphlets on using FOIA. "Knowing little about such matters, I obtained a couple of pamphlets issued by the American Civil Liberties Union that explained the standard procedures for obtaining information in the government's possession. One dealt with access to the broad fund of information government records; a second focused on access to personal record on file in federal agencies. The Freedom of Information Act and Privacy Act."[24] Kimball, himself a journalist, learned the practice of requesting information from these pamphlets. These self-published how-to guides—printed, Xeroxed papers—were integral to proliferating FOIA as a countersurveillant tool; in other words, papers were insurgent weapons waged against already weaponized reams of pulp. Instructional guides, letters, and other documents contested paper militarism.

The instructional FOIA guides and other FOIA media circulations expounded FOIA as a people's tool. One aspect of these guides was to elaborate the exemptions to FOIA and how they might be unfairly used to thwart requests. For instance, in the Center for National Security Studies (CNSS) publication *Using the Freedom of Information Act: A Step by Step Guide*, the authors list all nine of the official exemptions (as well as exemptions to the Privacy Act), explain them in simple terms, and finally offer practical suggestions for appeal in the case that FOIA exemptions are unduly invoked. The twenty-page guide encouraged would-be requesters to not be dissuaded by an exempt response: "Agencies are not *required* to withhold information simply because a particular exemption could be legally applied . . . the law says that exemptions are supposed to be interpreted as narrowly as possible. Courts often order the release of information the agencies want to keep secret."[25]

The Center for National Security Studies also authored materials that was targeted specifically to lawyers who might be unfamiliar with the contours of FOIA; by 1980, they had already published five editions of a FOIA litigation handbook that explained relevant aspects of the Freedom of Information Act and the Privacy Act to movement lawyers who might need to understand the implications of FOIA exemptions and how to contest them. FOIA handbooks were not the exclusive domain of activist organizations. The government itself had published *A Citizen's Guide on How to Use the FOIA and the Privacy Act in Requesting Government Documents,* which was publicized by CPR alongside their other extensive list of materials.[26]

People learned about the existence of how-to guides in a number of different ways, including their promotion within many of the magazines and periodicals that also emerged out of the same moment. A question in bold in a January 1979 issue of *Organizing Notes* asked readers, "Do you have any intelligence agency files?" They urged readers who answered yes to submit those files them to the National Lawyers Guild's (NLG) Counter-Intelligence Documentation Center and *Public Eye,* an NLG-supported publication. Their goal in "collecting, indexing and analyzing documents related to counter intelligence operations by government and private groups" was broadly to make this information available to activists. In other news magazines, how-to send-away information would often appear near the end of the issue, along with subscription information. Some left-leaning books critical of the American security state included information about using FOIA in appendixes. For instance, Ami Chen Mills's book *CIA Off Campus: Building the Case Against Agency Recruitment and Research,* published as late as 1991, had a specific appendix listing several how-to FOIA guides, including those of the CNSS and the NLG.[27] These publications that fought battles over information access promoted FOIA guides as a tactic to undermine the surveillant authority of the intelligence apparatus.

Apart from print materials, people learned about FOIA from the numerous conferences and working groups focused on government spying specifically and freedom of information more broadly. A review of the conferences and political events at the time suggests the central organizing role that FOIA played in contesting government surveillance. In the 1975 "Conspiracy in America" Conference held at UCLA, the organizers, Campaign for Democratic Freedoms, brought together parties critical of the US government's political spying via law enforcement and intelligence networks. Political exile and former CIA operative/

whistleblower Philip Agee called in from London; David Graham Du Bois (writer, activist, and stepson of W. E. B. Du Bois) gave a talk titled "Conspiracy Against the Black Liberation Movement" in his capacity as a Black Panther Party spokesperson; other speakers addressed repression against labor organizing, the queer community, Chicano organizations, and international solidarity movements. The first full day of events focused on assassinations, intelligence, and the police state. Organizers began this day with the event "How to Get Your Dossier," which was billed as "A Freedom of Information Act Workshop."[28] The entire conference concluded with the panel discussion "Counter-Spies: The People's Intelligence," featuring the Assassination Information Bureau, Organizing Committee for the Fifth Estate (which would go on to found the magazine *Counterspy*), and a few other speakers.

In 1980, FOIA Inc. convened a conference specifically focused on organizing with and around FOIA. CPR's files from the event begin with details of a roundtable spearheaded by Peter Weiss, chairman of the radical and internationalist Institute for Policy Studies think tank that Orlando Letelier worked for at the time of his assassination, along with panelists set to talk about the importance of FOIA in a variety of spheres: "intelligence and foreign policy, Repression/Cointelpro, Anti-Nuclear, FTC & Consumer, Reporters and Press, and Historians."[29] According to the CPR's notes, antisurveillance and civil rights lawyer Frank Donner addressed the importance of the Media, Pennsylvania, break-in to the eventual FOIA case to gain information about COINTELPRO. Donner further argued that the "Church Committee was very subservient to the agencies' request for secrecy," echoing a sentiment pervasive throughout the conference: that FOIA must be used and defended *despite* government attempts to reform, curtail, and manage it. Marshall Perlin, attorney for the Rosenberg case, singled out the Vaughn Index as a key tool for litigators fighting to access documents. His session, which focused on attacks against FOIA, discussed obstacles to obtaining documents like deliberate release delays and the destruction of files. The destruction of files in particular, he argued, constituted an effective repeal of the act and, one that needed to be countered with know-your-FOIA-rights political education.

The annals of *Organizing Notes* chronicle repeated efforts in this period to gather people together over social issues, discuss the right to know, and teach people how to use the FOIA. Guides were made available to activists at all kind of political events and promoted in the left print culture of the time. Imagining, tinkering, learning, and practicing paper liberation was part of the moment.

As photocopied FOIA guides circulated around the country, files came to be understood not merely as ominous and authoritarian productions but as materials that could be seized and should be demanded. In this sense, *the file* was not a naturalized surveillance fixture. Rather, it was an object of struggle in at least two ways: an artifact of the struggle against spied-on dissenters but also an artifact that should be struggled *over* and repossessed. The file's shadowy production and content together could reveal the dissolute force of American power in corners all over the world. Activist entanglements in the bureaucratic machinery of document access point to the triumph of papers in the administration of life, as well as the tactical necessity of contesting the United States as a paper tiger by demanding that its most elemental unit give account of itself. For these reasons, in this period after the Church Committee findings, FOIA came to occupy a central location within the sphere of political struggle. The surveillance file was itself an idea, a process, an archive, and a weapon, but also a material object in the world and therefore one that could be expropriated.

Organizing Notes, the flagship publication of the Campaign for Political Rights, reflected this understanding of the papered nature of the surveillance state. The publication was specifically aimed at organizers working against government spying. Their very first issue, in early 1977, announced the founding of CPR, which was then known as the Campaign to Stop Government Spying (CSGS). This issue of *Organizing Notes* explains that the CSGS was created "in response to the need for a unified action around the country to stop political spying by our government agencies." They also note that "a groundswell was necessary: one so strong that meaningful action would finally be taken to stop intelligence abuses. Revelations of COINTELPRO, assassinations, secret payments, wiretapping and surveillance of law-abiding citizens, even the downfall of a president were not explosive enough to force action."[30] These early enunciations reveal that from its inception, CSGS understood not only that FOIA would be of critical use to surveilled communities but also that radical transparency was of central importance within social movements. That is to say, FOIA was at the time neither the domain solely of access professionals nor of rugged individuals intent on with highly specific queries; instead, the security state was understood as a legitimate target of collective political challenge, and as such, countersurveillant tactics were to be used for collective rather than individual ends.

CSGS noted three political goals in this first issue of *Organizing Notes*: "1) To end covert operations abroad, 2) To end political spying in the United States, 3) To end secret budgets and secret charters of the intelligence agencies."[31] The publication would go on to regularly feature articles about government spying in a myriad of sites (e.g., universities, labor organizations, communities of color), as well as FOIA stories (e.g., legislative challenges to it, important court cases that determined how FOIA could be implemented). *Organizing Notes* published articles from social justice organizations about surveillance activities in their communities, along with news updates to FOIA laws and FOIA-related lawsuits. Every issue pointed readers to a broader set of texts by including lists of other films, books, newsletters, and other media related to questions of surveillance and countersurveillance. The magazine sourced its stories from the broad coalition from which the Campaign for Political Rights emerged as well as beyond that group. *Organizing Notes* emerged out of a publication landscape abundant with stories about countersurveilling the state and revealing its covert actions. In 1975, former CIA agent Philip Agee had published *Inside the Company: CIA Diary*, a memoir exposing the brutal and unethical tactics that Agee had witnessed—and participated in—during his eleven-year tenure with the agency.[32] Agee's work detailed operations throughout South America, confirming the imperial role of the clandestine.

Other contemporaneous newsletters also focused on transparency and countersurveillance. *Access Reports*, for instance, edited and published by Evan Hendricks (who would later pen an annotated book on FOIA for CPR), focused on current news items specifically around implementations of transparency. FOIA Inc. published *FOIAlerts*. The National Lawyers Guild and Repression Information Project published *The Public Eye*, and a monthly newsletter *Recon: Keeping an Eye on the Pentagon* was available on request.[33] Even the University of Missouri published *FOI Digest*, in tandem with their Freedom of Information Center housed in their journalism school. One of the most impactful publications from the era was the journal *Counterspy*, founded by Philip Agee and other members of the Organizing Committee for the Fifth Estate. *Counterspy* was dedicated to exposing nefarious US intelligence and law enforcement activities. *Counterspy*'s work spanned from revelations of police links with the KKK to exposés of CIA abuses in Central America. The very first issue of *Counterspy* revealed a long history of white nationalist violence in San Diego and explored relationships between the Minutemen, the FBI, and the police.

Counterspy quite literally was meant to counter and oppose a specific kind of surveillant gaze, to watch the watchers, to oppose the viewing logics of US imperialism. To this end, they would publish information they received from publicly available sources (local news reports, declassified documents, etc.), but also invited whistleblowers and former members of the intelligence community to collaborate and share information.[34] Even prior to the publication of the magazine, the Fifth Estate ran a "Counter-Spy Campaign": In 1974, for instance, at Kent State University (KSU), using documents leaked from the KSU Police Department, it outed the KSU police as trying to infiltrate student groups with undercover cops and agent provocateurs.[35] In addition to printing stories about intelligence abuse, the magazine would also publish names and lists of intelligence officers: In other words, they outed spies. One such list was featured in the Winter 1975 issue, detailing names of CIA chiefs of station in dozens of countries. In late December 1975, Richard Skeffington Welch, CIA chief of station in Athens, Greece, was murdered after being outed as an American agent. Though Welch's name had first been publicly circulated in a letter published in *Athens News* on November 23 of the same year, the American government publicly blamed *Counterspy* for his death.[36] In 1978, Agee left *Counterspy* over ideological rifts with members and went on to found a new journal, *Covert Action Information Bulletin*.[37] The *Counterspy* / *Covert Action* split itself was clearly monitored by the CIA; among the many documents declassified by the CIA in 2004 were press clippings about the split.[38] But both *Counterspy* and *Covert Action* were listed as part of the broad coalition that CPR represented.

Activist organizations not only wanted to share information from formerly secret government documents, as magazines like *Counterspy* and *Organizing Notes* did, but also focused on circulating the documents themselves, as *Win* had done in 1971. The NLG Police Crimes Task Force, in concert with *Public Eye* magazine, published *Counterintelligence: A Documentary Look at America's Secret Police* in 1978. The book, over a hundred pages long, was composed almost exclusively of documents detailing the FBI's surveillance, infiltration, and harassment of activists from communities of color. The book's cover featured a caricature of J. Edgar Hoover holding bundled dynamite in one hand with a match in the other, accompanied by the subhead "The FBI's Counterintelligence Operations Against Black, Puerto Rican, Native American, and Chicano/Mexicano Movements." Their other efforts to countersurveil the state included the Counter-Intelligence Documentation Center (CDC), a group with the goal of "collecting, indexing, and analyzing documents which relate to counterintelligence operations by government and private groups."[39] *Organizing Notes* covered the CDC's efforts to serve as an information clearinghouse in an article whose title hailed the reader with a query: "Do You Have Any Intelligence Agency Files?"[40] Other organizations would follow suit, publishing magazines and books composed solely of reproduced FOIA documents, primary texts printed for public viewing.

In 1980, former interns for the Center for National Security Studies published a book simply called *Documents*, with the subtitle *A Shocking Collection of Memoranda, Letters, and Telexes from the Secret Files of the American Intelligence Community*. *Documents* is an interesting study in the information politics of the moment, as even its subtitle broadcast the media by which these paper archives were transmitted and produced: letters, telexes, and memoranda. Papers are reproduced in two ways in the book. *Documents* organizes the documents into relevant chapters, such as "The Ghostwriters and the Anonymous Letter," a chapter focusing on forged letters that the FBI would send to Black activists and their supporters to sow dissent and create distrust and doubt in the organizing world.[41] Formerly secret documents that are relevant to each chapter are retyped to transcribe what they contain, and the authors then provide written commentary to explain their significance to the reader. These retyped replications are distinguished both by their titles and by a distinct serif typeface that sets them apart from the explanatory text that appears between them. Within each chapter, retyped documents correspond to numbered photo reproductions of the original, located within an appendix. Thus every declassified text appears twice in *Documents*: once, abbreviated for narrative clarity; then, in full photographic form for indexical veracity. The dual reproductions highlight how a media history of surveillance must be equally attuned to the nefariousness of both content and form.

The inherent visual stakes in radical transparency were palpable in the literature and visual media that activists produced at the time. Consider, for instance, FOIA Inc.'s description of in-camera review during FOIA litigation: "The court also has the discretion to examine the disputed documents *in camera* [...] which means the court *sees* the documents, the government has already *seen* the documents, the requesting party does not *see* them" (emphasis mine).[42] In 1979, FOIA Inc. launched a "Save the Files," campaign, specifically trying to stop the FBI from destroying their paper archive. They wrote, "These materials constitute a significant part of U.S. people's history of the past four decades, much of which has not yet been written. It is the history of labor struggles, the Cold War and McCarthy Periods, and the day to day battles of peace and minority rights groups, environmentalists, the rising women's movement, scientists, actors, writers, and actors who defied and resisted legislative witch hunts and Executive Purges in defense of the U.S. Constitution."[43]

Saving the files from destruction meant preserving a bureaucratic archive produced in violence, but one that in its existence evidenced state repression and resistance to it. FOIA Inc.'s materials in support of this campaign mention Noam Chomsky, Paul Robeson Jr., and Harry Belafonte, among others, as supporters of efforts and litigation to stop the FBI from destroying files.[44] Information activists keenly understood the importance of mobilizing figures in the public sphere.

MULTIMEDIA MOBILIZING WITH
THE INTELLIGENCE NETWORK

Out of this feisty transparency organizing emerged the idea of a film that would simultaneously document the long reach of the surveillance state and the necessity of using FOIA to challenge it. Underscoring the centrality of the visual to ideology, the Center for Political Rights articulated the need to do a film, specifically, as an organizing tool. This decidedly visual terrain was the domain not only of CPR but of transparency politics more broadly. The idea for the film first started when the campaign was still called the Campaign to Stop Government Spying (CSGS). Numerous conversations ensued about the need for an *organizing film* specifically, and the organizers of what was then CSGS went to great lengths to solicit feedback from organizing partners about the need and shape of such a film.[45] They wanted the film to be able to demonstrate the contours of the surveillance and harassment that the US government perpetrated. What better way to show that story than in film? They were attempting to render visible the networked relations of government intelligence agencies that were pervasive in communities on the left and communities of color. Film provided the medium through which such connections between different communities and networked relations might be made visible.

The CSGS, in their proposals both to filmmakers and funders, suggested that one possible location for a shoot would be the New York Citizens' Review Commission on the FBI, which held a people's hearing to document FBI abuses, featuring testimony from Indigenous, Black, Asian American, and Puerto Rican activists.[46] Though this particular event did not feature in the film, it illustrates the desire to speak back to government intelligence with an undeterred activist's gaze. In proposing what visuals the film might feature, the organizers imagined "a diagram of agencies, shown with a pinball effect between the different agencies, can show the rapid communication between the agencies with information and dissent-suppressing programs. A map of the world can show all the countries have experienced CIA intervention. Other visuals can include the whirring of computers with telephone linkups, newspaper clippings, rows of file cabinets, pictures of police taking pictures of demonstrators, and the Church Committee hearings."[47] This diagram made it into the film, very similar to how it is described here, as a very literal visual expression of the name *The Intelligence Network*. But most interestingly, these early brainstorms demonstrate awareness both of media technologies that surveil (computational technology, the camera, the phone, the paper file), and a desire to countermap the state quite literally. The archival file with these preproduction notes contains furiously written pages that imagined how to distill the dangers of government spying into an impactful film.

In other words, the idea to produce a film was in line with CPR's broad media strategy and emerged from the paper and visual politics of the era that were brought to the fore through COINTELPRO and, to a lesser extent, Watergate. What strikes the viewer now watching the film is the amount of paper produced in this pulpy war against the state—a war in which territory is and was secretly gained through the production of files and the production of *The File*. In *The Intelligence Network*, women's rights activist and attorney Bonnie McFadden, who had herself been surveilled, notes, "What became clear from reading *my file* is if somebody parked their car in an area where a demonstration went on, they were liable to have their license plate checked and their name would then appear in the file as a participant, whether or not they knew the slightest thing about this demonstration." But *The Intelligence Network* was not necessarily singular or novel in its approach, as a key antecedent was *The Red Squad* (1972), a film produced by Joe Sucher and Steve Fischler, lifelong friends, anarchists, New Yorkers, and NYU film students. *The Red Squad* is an extraordinary film that details the efforts of the filmmakers to surveil agents of the state. We might understand the impulses of *The Intelligence Network* and *Red Squad* (along with several other films of the moment), together, as the inverse of what film scholars call "surveillance cinema": a cinema of countersurveillance, marked by confrontations with agents and other aesthetic choices.

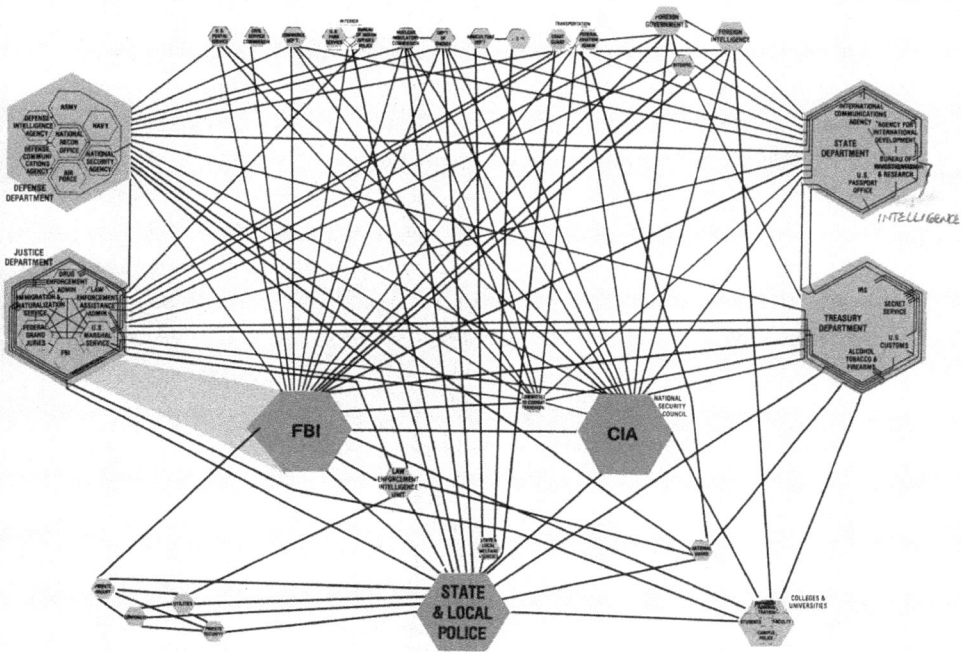

2.2 Diagram for the film *The Intelligence Network* (1979), detailing connections between law enforcement, intelligence agencies, and other actors. CPR Papers, box 11, file: "The Intelligence Network—Production."

The special debut of *The Intelligence Network* in DC that begins this chapter was just the beginning of a several-year circulation that attempted to use the film to organize in many sectors. CPR possessed two film reels that they rented out to interested parties. The film was also advertised in newsletters and in independent media catalogues, so people wrote in from all over to get information about possible film screenings. Many of the people writing in to ask about the film were from universities: professors who wanted to screen the film as part of a learning unit, or student groups wanting to program for the year. Less predictably, many people wrote in from high schools wanting to screen *The Intelligence*

Network, and from the correspondence available, it seems that these screenings were successful. CPR also screened the film at community centers and with community groups, and even put out a newsletter that explained to people precisely how to use *The Intelligence Network* to organize. In addition to self-organized screenings, the CPR sent the work to film festivals around the globe. Their film was neither comprehensive nor beautiful, but they were determined to share it widely as an organizing tool. People who were screening the film would receive a number of information packets and flyers to share with audiences. This kind of information activism—to borrow McKinney's formulation again—both semiotically and politically refused the state's gaze. CPR's press release about *The Intelligence Network* included a sixteen-page "Materials List" compiled in December 1978.[48] This list included documentary films and reading materials, both of which were emblematic of an ethos of learning, self-instruction, and empowerment that characterized that moment. CPR's pamphlet for the film, titled *Eyes Only*, indicates the centrality of the ocular both to state discourse and to contestations of that discourse.

The 1980 issue of *Organizing Notes* suggested that activists might leaflet movie theaters during screenings of *Hopscotch* (1980), a Hollywood film about a disgruntled CIA agent who attempts to leave the agency and write a tell-all memoir about agency abuses. Organizers could "use *Hopscotch* to educate and organize," the issue notes, and could even screen *The Intelligence Network* as a follow-up film.[49] Members of CPR were undeterred in their promotion of the film, which circulated prolifically as a result. A thwarted film showing illuminates the stakes in this circulation. An inmate at Leavenworth Federal Penitentiary in Kansas attempted to have the film screened at the prison for nearly a year between 1980 and 1981, but the request was denied. Reportedly, the warden said the film was "a threat to the security and orderly running of an institution . . . and of a subversive nature."[50]

In 1980 a Los Angeles–based organization, the Citizens' Commission on Police Repression (CCPR), wrote an effusive letter to the CPR about the impact of screening *The Intelligence Network* as an organizing tactic against police violence and surveillance.[51] The letter clarifies the direct impact of the film on the countersurveillant organizing work of resisting state power. CCPR had been working with many community organizations, including the Coalition Against Police Abuse and the ACLU, against the repressive surveillance network authorized by the LAPD and carried out by their Public Disorder Intelligence Division.

Together the three organizations filed a successful lawsuit in 1978 against the LAPD's program of spying on political dissidents, which ultimately prohibited the LAPD from destroying their file cards.[52] In her January 1980 letter to CPR, Linda Valentino of CCPR noted that throughout the preceding year, their coalition (comprising over two dozen Southern California organizations) screened the film on average between four and six times a month throughout greater Los Angeles: "We've had a terrific response from these programs. We've gathered many new endorsements and have brought new groups and individuals into the coalition. *After viewing the film, most people also want to know how to get their FBI or other government files. We then give out FOIA materials and instructions on how to file their requests*" (emphasis mine).[53]

She added, "The success our coalition has had in the past year, we feel, is due in no small part to our use of 'The Intelligence Network,' as an educational and outreach tool." Valentino's account illuminates how the film aided the organizing successes of and political education around antipolice violence in Southern California. But from another angle, we might glean that in the scores of undocumented community screenings throughout LA, *The Intelligence Network* inspired people to look back at the state, beyond the darkened community auditoriums and screening halls, all the way into the file cabinets that might otherwise have appeared entirely out of reach.

THE FIGHT FOR FOIA IN THE AGE OF REAGAN

The period of radical experimentation with transparency waned with both the election of Ronald Reagan and the deepening of ideological rifts among antispying and surveillance activists. President Reagan presented new challenges to the transparency movement: Organizers were forced into a defensive position as he waged a focused attack on freedom of information laws. These attacks on transparency laws were spearheaded by Orrin Hatch.[54] With Reagan's sweeping Executive Order 12356, FOIA was weakened as new classification rules took hold and information was reclassified. The attorney general noted in 1981 that he would side with federal agencies in their broad application of FOIA exemptions. And in the forty years since, FOIA has continued to be contested—more vigorously in certain moments, less so in others.

The heterogeneous coalition that had been brought together under CPR struggled under the weight of new organizing challenges and with increasingly obvious ideological differences. In particular, the place of antiracist and

The Campaign for Political Rights is a coalition of over 80 civil liberties, church, environmental, labor, educational, litigative, women's, black, latino and third world groups. Organizations affiliated with the Campaign are committed to

An End to Covert Operations Abroad

An End to Political Spying and Harassment in the United States

The Campaign is an information clearinghouse which provides speaker-scheduling services, local and campus organizing assistance, press and publicity advice and national organizational referrals. Through regular publications, press releases, phone work and meetings, the Campaign keeps local, regional and national contacts informed and up-to-date on the issue of intelligence abuse.

For further information, to schedule a speaker, establish a local group or coalition—for press, publicity or organizing assistance, contact

Campaign for Political Rights
201 Massachusetts Avenue, N.E.,#112
Washington, D.C. 20002
(202) 547-4705

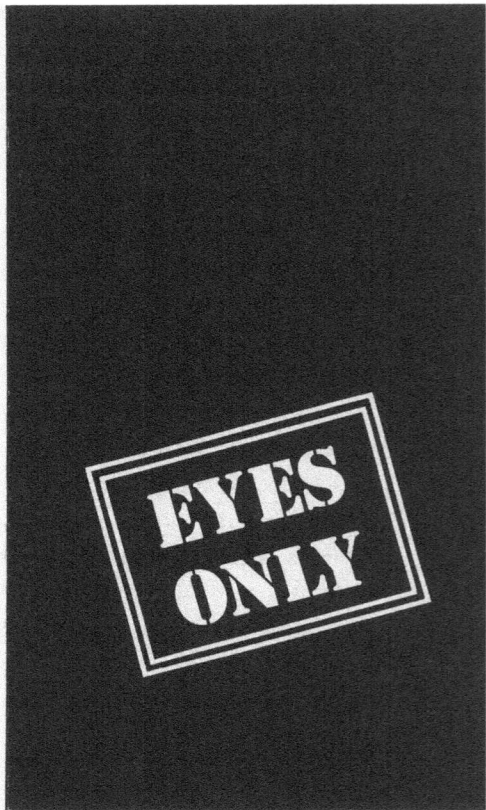

2.3 The Campaign for Political Rights "Eyes Only" brochure, produced to accompany the film *The Intelligence Network* (1979). CPR Papers, box 11, file: "The Intelligence Network—Production."

anti-imperialist organizing in their work became a source of friction. Activism around intelligence charters, legal cases around government spying, and organizing against repressive legislation had occasioned dissonant perspectives on the place of CPR within broader political struggles. After a particularly contentious board meeting in June 1981, several organizations withdrew from CPR after the coalition refused to adopt an explicit affirmative action policy in their executive committee. The Grand Jury Project denounced this as "an affront to the struggles of Black and other Third World peoples."[55] Reverend Lucius Walker, who was at the time doing faith-based antiracist organizing, pulled his organization from the CPR, noting that it was hypocritical of them to derive credibility from organizations representing "Third World People" while maintaining a predominantly white staff.[56]

In a sixteen-page missive to CPR, its member organizations, and the broader public, Ken Lawrence of the Anti-Repression Resource Team revealed the hypocrisy. He argued that CPR had betrayed its founding ideals, given that it had emerged as a coalition during the 1977 National Conference on Government Spying and that it was explicitly bound to an anti-imperialist and antiracist ethos. Lawrence expressed dismay that CPR's self-appointed doyens in critical moments appeared to center spying against white middle-class subjects rather than the victims of counterintelligence programs. In his view they focused energies "far less on the more violent repression suffered by revolutionary and minority organizations" and more so on Mort Halperin's experiences with being spied on.[57] The consequence was that Halperin, as a former government intelligence policy expert, was able to draw CPR toward the center, advancing a line of liberal-centrist reform that all but guaranteed, Lawrence argued, that "acceptable" forms of government spying would continue to be used against the left. As a committed anti-imperialist, Lawrence wrote, "In my opinion, many of Mort's failings as a civil libertarian stem from his patriotic commitment; he seems virtually incapable of acknowledging people with a different view are entitled to a full measure of civil liberties."[58] Responses to Lawrence's letter refuted the specific characterization of Halperin and CPR's actions, but in doing so they also seized on his critique of patriotism to assert a liberal politics. Esther Hearst of NCARL argued that Lawrence's contentions amounted to a "political purity" test; Rick Gutman, who organized against Chicago Red Squads, closed his letter by noting, "I ... object to your use of the term 'patriotic' as an epithet," and subsequently rearticulated antispying work as defending American ideals.[59]

These divergent ideological positions on the question of race within transparency organizing are unsurprising; coalitional work inherently incorporates divergent bodies for broad, agreed-on tactical goals. But the emergence of these fractures within an ascendant Reaganist regime indicates a changed political landscape in which the initial aspirations of—and for—transparency organizing were no longer shared or imagined by some. The field of possibilities for a broader, more radical coalition around transparency had started to narrow, as the refusal of a thoroughly antiracist approach to this work underscores. By late 1981, CPR had transformed into an information clearinghouse, and by 1984 it had all but folded.

In this interim period the group was still publishing *Organizing Notes*, and in 1982 they published a book titled *Former Secrets: Government Records Made Public Through the Freedom of Information Act*.[60] The book responded to Reagan's attack on freedom of information, presenting five hundred case studies on the use of FOIA and highlighting significant uses of the law by actors within a variety of spheres: labor organizers, disability justice activists, antinuclear and antimilitarization campaigners, racial justice advocates, and more. Notably, the book does not itself reprint the resultant pages from the FOIA requests, or the originally requested letters. Instead it is solely a compendium of requests, an index of sorts, presented together as evidence of the overwhelming impact of FOIA on the ability to utter demands in so many spheres of life. A read through *Former Secrets* gives a sense of the widespread impact of FOIA. As a historical document, it evidences the large number of people using FOIA in different social justice contexts, from organizational requests for state compliance data, to journalistic fact-finding queries, to individuals trying to understand their own relationships to the surveillance state.

But *Former Secrets* is a compendium of FOIA cases, not a repository of their results. The book was produced by Evan Hendricks, brought on to the project by the Campaign for Political Rights, who was tasked with compiling a resource list of important FOIA cases that would demonstrate the significance of the law.[61] By this account, *Former Secrets* was, in its inception, a tactical media intervention into the apparatus of secrecy that was meant to perform a countersurveillant gesture against state secrecy and surveillance. It reads as such. On each page, the reader encounters entries of different FOIA requests. Hendricks organized *Former Secrets* by the topical focus, each corresponding to one of ten chapters focused on FOIA's impacts on topics like consumer product safety, the environment, labor and civil rights, and, of course, questions of nuclear power, political surveillance, US foreign policy, and defense. Most pages within each chapter list three FOIA requests. The requests are indexed schematically, including information in five categories: Subject, Agency, Requester, Disclosed, and Result. This terse, blunt copy delivers information about not only what was requested but also by whom it was requested, giving the reader a sense of both the contours of the state's shadows and the manifold people interested in contesting the state.

No other text narratively links the requests, apart from a brief introduction to each chapter. The net result is that the reader encounters a litany both *of* and *for* countersurveillance.

In this regard, *Former Secrets* differed from publications like the 1972 issue of *Win*, the CNSS's *Documents*, or the NLG's *Counterintelligence*, as it featured no xerographic or textual reproductions of the documents themselves. But *Former Secrets* in some sense embodied the same ethos as *The Intelligence Network*; both film and index were conceived through operational need and tactical utility. Film reel and bound book were to serve specific kinds of political goals of the left transparency activists, to promote and protect FOIA as a tool to watch the watchers. The book offers a picture of just how meaningful FOIA was to people all over who were trying to get information about surveillance they knew they'd experienced yet had little ability to describe with detail. For instance, on page 161, a short entry explains that a woman (whose name remains anonymous) requested information about FBI surveillance of her only to find that the Welcome Wagon representative who greeted her family in their new neighborhood in Chicago had reported her "family background" to the FBI.[62] Her FOIA request led to a few minor newspaper stories about her findings.[63] To put it plainly, form followed function. And the book, in its simplicity, was meant to provide evidence of FOIA's relevance to everyday people. In doing so, *Former Secrets* inadvertently mapped the network of letter writers and their challenge to the clandestine reach of the American imperial project through demands for information.

Other responses to Reagan's attacks on FOIA similarly made use of print circulations to write the importance of alternate paper circulations into existence. In 1982, FOIA Inc. published *Our Right to Know! Endangered*, a newsletter detailing the Reagan administration's attacks on freedom of information. The publication was one of several strategies convened under the broad rubric of the Save the Freedom of Information Act campaign. Numerous groups weighed in on Reagan's decision in the newsletter, noting the political consequences of restrictions to freedom of information. The National Alliance Against Racist and Political Repression, the Grand Jury Project, and the National Conference of Black Lawyers were all among those who penned columns expressing the impacts that these new restrictions would have on their organizing work.

The Grand Jury Project's submission to *Our Right to Know! Endangered* was particularly pointed in its defense of FOIA against Reagan's encroachments. They condemned Attorney General William French Smith's push for changes to FOIA, noting that Smith argued that the release of information should include a clause about whether such information would be "demonstrably harmful," which could further entrench in law intelligence abuses on the basis of political opposition.[64] The FOIA's instrumental role in uncovering the COINTELPRO program illuminated the law's political significance. They argue a particularly lucid defense of the law in staunchly internationalist, antiracist, and anti-imperialist terms. I quote them at length here:

> Particularly ominous is the charge that information released under the FOIA could "fall into the hands of foreign agents." . . . We believe that both of these steps by the Reagan administrations are part of an attempt to paint many backers of just liberation struggles throughout the word as "foreign agents," and ultimately rear-guard support organizations for so-called international terrorists. This is in line with a general attempt by federal and other officials to create mass hysteria around the so-called threat of terrorism. In our view, this is nothing but an ill-founded propaganda campaign to justify government efforts to isolate, harass and repress supporters of progressive causes throughout the U.S. *Targets of these attacks have been and will likely continue to be Black and other third world activists, trade unionists, opponents of war, nuclear power, and nuclear weapons, and women's movement and gay activists* [emphasis mine]. Accordingly we will fight against any further changes in FOIA that will cover up government spying and we call upon all other freedom-loving people to oppose such changes.[65]

The other organizations who contributed to this dossier express similar sentiments, though the Grand Jury Project expressed them with the most forceful clarity. This defense of FOIA centered those bearing the brunt of the state's violence, besieged in its shadows. Further, they highlighted the connection between justifications for counterinsurgency (and intelligence abuse) and the then-emergent vocabulary of "terrorism" against the state. These connections prefigured the questions of securitization and surveillance that have come to define the contemporary moment.

CONCLUSION

I have argued here that transparency has proven itself to be an unstable, complicated terrain that varying parties have exploited for their own gain in different moments. The battle for paper and for information, often fought over murky territory, has defined social contestations since the emergence of a post–World War II security bureaucracy. But the aspirational countersurveillant use of FOIA that CPR, FOIA Inc., CNSS, and others agitated for did not come to be. Although some FOIA organizing continued through the 1980s, the end of the Cold War and the beginning of "document diplomacy" also changed the organizing landscape to some degree, as mentioned in the previous chapter. And while anyone certainly *can* make a FOIA request, successfully obtaining government documents has become the domain of lawyers, access professionals, academics, and a cadre of niche enthusiasts. The epistolary process of requesting a document remains the same, and online submissions are now allowed as well, but requests are backlogged and routinely denied. The process of successfully getting a document has become increasingly technical and arcane, requiring specific search terms, tactical creativity, and, too often, litigation. Several organizations that continue the work of making government documents public and available deserve mention, specifically MuckRock, which helps users craft and file online FOIAS, and the incredible National Security Archive (NSA), which continues to be an amazing resource for anyone looking for information about US counterinsurgency, militarism, and surveillance history. The NSA, in particular, we might understand as direct outgrowth of the activist work done by the radical left folks in DC.

What is important is not the abstraction of "transparency" within a political system, which can be used for a variety of different political meanings and leanings: For CPR, NCARL, *Counterspy*, and others, "transparency" was very deeply connected to the lives and the deaths of comrades and community members. That is to say, transparency is not a stable political tool whose meanings are innately evident by its invocation. Transparency for whom, and to what end? As I argued in the previous chapter, for transparency's early advocates, the technology of making visible was itself the politics, far more than the specifics of the documents it revealed. And in the hands of the left, transparency became an accounting of sorts, a weapon against the lies of the security state. But without a clear critique of the surveillant function of paper and imperial formation of the archive, the demand for public records has no inherent political value. Transparency, too, can arm the status quo and distribute a surveillant gaze across a broad body.[66]

While giving a talk on materials that would eventually form the basis of this book, several colleagues shared stories about how FOIA had been used by right-wing organizations intent on diminishing dissent on campus. Organized conservative blocs, they explained, would submit broad information requests to the university to gain communications about activism on campus. This deployment of FOIA as a tool against left activity in higher education wielded the right to know not as countersurveillant but, rather, as surveillant. After this visit, I encountered more stories about public records requests being used for nefarious ends to police intellectual and political work on campus. This issue has become so widespread that in 2019, the Middle East Studies Association published a "Memo on Public Records Harassment and Defense."[67] They specifically name the "abuse of public records laws" as a recent phenomenon that has a "chilling effect," particularly on research concerning contentious topics. The memo notes work on Palestine, antagonized within US academia, as one such area where academic freedom is particularly crucial. A university where I previously worked received a public records request targeting activism that was critical of the Anti-Defamation League's political positions; a student, nudged by the administration, submitted a request to access correspondence around Palestine activism circulated by faculty. In these moments, the ability of FOIA to be used by those opposing justice and freedom *mimics* the surveillant eye of the state. At public institutions, emails between faculty organizing for change can be considered part of the public record and thus demanded by hostile parties under freedom of information laws. The history I have detailed in this chapter implies not an inherent meaning of transparency but, rather, a particular moment of encounters with liberating paper that were inextricably bound up in freedom struggles of their time, even if in imperfect ways.

████████████

DO NOT TAPE OVER
—CIA, "Inventory of Videotapes"

In the Academy Award–winning documentary *Taxi to the Dark Side* (dir. Alex Gibney, 2007), Michigan senator Carl Levin shows the camera a set of documents about the abuse of detainees in the War on Terror. These documents include emails from FBI personnel based at Guantánamo Bay Naval Base (GTMO) who wrote to Department of Justice officials to express concern about prisoner abuse, yet they disclose little text. Large white boxes cover the majority of words, though a few stray sentences, titles, and notations appear here and there. Senator Levin, who in 2007 began serving as chair of the Committee on Armed Services, bemoans onscreen the erosion of government transparency he encountered while investigating torture claims in this capacity. With piercing eyes, the senator points to the documents in hand and says, "But the emails are what is called *redacted*, which means there are big holes in these emails. Now, some of these emails are *totally* redacted so we don't know what they say at all. . . . You can't see anything on these documents. One after another where there is *nothing*."

Redaction is an art of censorship, the application of a white or black box to conceal information when a document is compelled into the public through law.

3.1   Senator Carl Levin, in *Taxi to the Dark Side* (dir. Alex Gibney, 2007), emphasizes the redaction of torture documents.

In the same vein as Moss and Moynihan, his Cold War predecessors in the capitol, Senator Levin's sentiments reflect widespread concerns over the lack of accountability regarding abuse in US military prisons that emerged during the War on Terror. In 2002, as the Bush administration began to capture prisoners and detain them within an archipelago of military facilities worldwide, legal scholars debated the ethical limits of the brutalities unfolding within these sites and the extent to which the US government had secretly sanctioned torture through what came to be known as Enhanced Interrogation Techniques (EIT). These debates centered around a set of documents—legal memos, to be precise— that carefully deliberated the conditions under which a prisoner could be tortured. The "Torture Memos," as these documents came to be known, penned an ideology of "intelligence gathering" through distress. When the first of these documents were made public in 2004, large sections were redacted. In their very being, the censored files told a story about war and the administration of violence. As critics encountered the opaque boxes, they wondered what was contained within them. The marks of censorship appeared not to cloak but to reveal.

We now know that these legal memos were created not in the abstract but in response to the US detention of people whom they deemed "high-value" prisoners in 2002 and for whom internationally recognized and legally binding standards of imprisonment were intentionally defiled. The Torture Memos indexed not a thought experiment in legal permissibility but, rather, an official, legal relation to the humanity of those detained persons who existed in the public sphere only in relation to the blacked-out spaces circulating in redacted memos. But as Cathy Scott and Adrian Levy reveal in *The Forever Prisoner*, one detainee in particular was at the center of these memos: a Palestinian born in exile, Abu Zubaydah, whom, they argue, the CIA willfully miscast as part of al-Qaeda and involved with the 9/11 attacks. Legal scholars have long argued that torture does *not* produce actionable intelligence broadly but also that in Guantánamo and other detention facilities specifically failed to produce any meaningful information; evidence for the latter argument was documented meticulously in the 2014 Senate Select Committee on Intelligence Report on Torture. But Abu Zubaydah's case was that of guilt by association: After imprisoning him for decades, the US government now admits it has nothing to charge him with but refuses to release him from his confinement in GTMO.[1] For years his situation has been defined by the regulations on information associated with American military detention.

Increased secrecy measures under the Bush-Cheney administration and the subsequent nondisclosure of data allowed torture and detention programs to function with systematic efficiency. Only five days after 9/11, Dick Cheney hinted at the brutal architecture of American intelligence that would unfold in the aftermath: "We also have to work sort of the dark side, if you will. We're going to spend time in the shadows of the intelligence world. A lot of what needs to be done here will have to be done quietly, without any discussions, using sources and methods that are available to our intelligence agencies if we're going to be successful."[2]

The term *dark side* euphemistically referred to covert military and intelligence actions that would remake entire lifeworlds. Under the auspices of the US-led Global War on Terror, men from all over the world, mostly poor and Muslim, were captured by US forces, secretly transported to black-site prisons, and subject to indefinite detention without legal recourse. This program of Rendition, Detention, and Interrogation (RDI), brutal in its execution, operated with the impunity afforded by clandestine lawfare. The RDI program lived in an interconnected network of military prisons, black sites, and rendition routes that were hidden from view on official maps and thereby evaded public scrutiny.

Artist and geographer Trevor Paglen has referred to this militarized configuration as a "dark geography."[3] While GTMO is the best-known such site (since it is an official US facility), under the pretext of the Clinton-era policy of "extraordinary rendition," detainees were tortured in dungeons in far reaches of the globe. Slowly the experiences of these men have come to light, mostly through the memoirs of former detainees. But the years of imposed silence on and redaction of detainees created another inescapable prison—an endless and racializing loop whereby detainees stood outside the law on paper yet whose advocates' only recourse was to demand the release of papers. Indeed, detainees in GTMO were not allowed to file a writ of habeas corpus until 2004, after two years of detention without charge; even this paper that modestly declares that a person exists before the court was initially denied.

As with the Cold War–era covert operations and infiltration practices detailed in previous chapters, documentation was ironically central to secrecy. Classification facilitated the RDI program, as files both created legal pretext for state violence and documented the theater of operations. Lawfare through paper was not unique to this moment, and neither was the militarization of bureaucracy, of course. Rather, we should think of these things cumulatively: The infrastructure of the War on Terror hinged on a bureaucratic intelligence apparatus honed during the nuclear era. Securitized file production and classification were accumulations of Cold War practices and logics, and the aesthetics of censorship bear the literal imprints of previous transparency battles. Document redaction as a form emerged from disputes over bureaucratic authority, state violence, and imperialism. Arguments over disclosure, exemption, and classification from civil rights advocates like Ralph Nader or the more radical lawyers of the National Lawyers Guild, for instance, shaped the meaning of the law in the decade after FOIA's 1966 passage. These bureaucratic treatments of the document render it a palimpsest; accrued histories of warfare spring forth from its redacted pages.

But certain important pivots had happened in the intervening years between the end of the Cold War and the beginning of the War on Terror. Though document access and the contestations over paper had been central to organizing against Cold War intelligence abuse, the existence of the internet and the access to electronic paper transformed the public meaning of the redacted document in the War on Terror. The social movement–based information networks, publications, and organizations I discuss in chapter 2 had meticulously sought to convey the data gleaned from government files and, when possible, visually reproduce the most provocative ones for public consumption. In the context of the post-9/11 world, files were imminently easier to share yet in many ways much harder to access. The War on Terror emerged coeval with the rise of digital culture, and as a consequence, redaction took shape as a legible form in the public sphere and, later, as a signifier in its own right. Electronic file-sharing meant that digitally reproduced papers spread rapidly and widely on the internet as visual texts, not simply as content or information. The public *visually* experienced the wars fought after 9/11 through redacted paper detritus circulating online and in other media.

The role of information activism in the contestation around American imperialism since 9/11 has differed from earlier times in another significant way. Challenges to the RDI program and requests to gain access to information largely took place in legal form, within courts, and through an insistence on due process. Unlike for the FOIA activists of previous generations, the demands to disclose secret files were not caught up in a broader revolutionary movement politics or an anti-imperialist worldview. The organizations that emerged in the 1970s began to disappear by the end of the 1980s, their structures eroded by the very same efforts of surveillance and policing they had sought to expose. Responses to this transnational carceral crisis emerged most prominently not from grassroots community efforts but, rather, from liberal rights organizations like the American Civil Liberties Union (ACLU), the Center for Constitutional Rights (CCR), and Human Rights Watch (HRW), who called on the state to provide greater transparency. These organizations, particularly the ACLU and their affiliates, led the charge to advocate for declassification of RDI with the dual purpose of building legal cases against unfair detention and publicly exposing torture practices endemic to militarized punishment. Though community and grassroots organizations organized protests against the War on Terror, the fight over documents entered the public sphere through lawyerly entanglements and public art and media projects. This shift toward the courts reflect that FOIA itself was no longer the people's countersurveillance.

With a historical view, it might appear that the blacked-out or censored document would be the antithesis of what both liberal politicians who championed freedom of information and the subversives who demanded radical transparency had fought for. Yet this chapter challenges Senator Levin's sentiments: Redacted documents are not *nothing*. A redaction does not foreclose interpretation of the paper it lies on. On the contrary, censored spaces function as images rather than simply as absent text, and they require a more profound hermeneutics. "You can't *see* anything on these documents!" he exclaims on one hand, yet on the other he presents them precisely for the viewer to *see*. A contradiction emerges: The documentary camera is meant to witness the spectacle of nonsight. In other words, rather than *nothing*, redaction suggests a dialectical relationship between seeing and not seeing, between the empirical and the unknown. Unintentionally, from the redaction of state documents, a visual politics emerged that exceeds transparency's failures. So, too, my focus on redaction below may reveal some of the political and epistemological limits to those efforts toward transparency that I detailed in the previous chapters.

Redacted spaces by their very nature expose the hems, patches, and tears in the textile from which American papered bureaucracy is sewn. Redaction renders the processual transparent. FOIA documents are scored with all kinds of notations, marks from bureaucratic circulation: a crossed-out "Top Secret" stamp, a declassification date, the alphanumeric codes on the corners of blacked-out boxes. These notations—both methodologically systematized and therefore decipherable and seemingly random—index multiple layers of authorship, the progression through time, and administrative circulation. In his magisterial work *Culture and Imperialism*, Edward Said suggested *contrapuntal reading* as a method of textual analysis: "A contrapuntal reading must take account of both processes, that of imperialism and that of resistance to it, which can be done by extending our reading of the texts to include what was once *forcibly excluded*" (emphasis mine).[4] Though Said's theory emerged from narrative text, from this method I extrapolate redaction as the very visualization of forcible exclusion. In other words, redaction paradoxically evinces a contrapuntal aesthetic.

This chapter, then, is dedicated to a reading of censored documents through which I suggest a broader idea of redaction and contrapuntal aesthetics. An analysis of a few primary texts from the RDI program that hinge on the detention of Abu Zubaydah reveals the uncanny readings that redaction provokes, even in situations where sight is subject to extreme regulation. I compare two differently redacted versions of a memo written by Assistant Attorney General Jay Bybee on August 1, 2002, authorizing the use of several torture techniques; we now know that these memos were drafted in relation to the capture and torture of Abu Zubaydah in 2002. Caught in Pakistan, he was rendered to Thailand, where he spent months being relentlessly subjected to physical, psychological, sexual, and sensorial abuse. But for at least six years during the Bush administration, little was known about these circumstances. The differently censored versions of the Bybee memo demonstrate how reading these documents *with* redaction (not in spite of it) proved a critical method for analyzing the multitude of declassified documents, particularly in the period of information blackout. Although incongruent with the intention to conceal, these redacted spaces visually signified the ungraspable dimensions of detainee torture. While Abu Zubaydah was being tortured in Thailand, the CIA recorded ninety tapes of these interrogations, and two more of Abdul Rahim al-Nashri being tortured. In 2005 they destroyed these tapes, and they have refused to release descriptions of what was on them. I examine the only official record of these materials in the public sphere: a redacted inventory of these ninety-two now-destroyed videos. Through this document, I show how information refracts through multiple dimensions of visual power, including the censoring power of redaction, the muscle of destruction, and the biopower of transparency. Reading these documents contrapuntally underscores the brutal binds between information practices, state violence, and the unintended possibilities of refuting the security archive's racializing logic.

BIOPOLITICS BETWEEN SUNSHINE AND SHADOW

Shortly after his inauguration as the first new president after 9/11, Barack Obama summoned Supreme Court Justice Louis Brandeis's oft-repeated dictum "Sunlight is said to be the best of disinfectants" when he asked executive departments and agencies for a renewed commitment to FOIA and a return to "accountability through transparency."[5] In the seven-and-a-half years between Dick Cheney marshaling the shadows and Obama calling in sunshine, some millions of documents accumulated in the dark. To be sure, not all of these proliferated invisibly. Some leaked; others were debated in FOIA lawsuits for years. But as Obama came to power, transparency—as both metaphor and mechanism—offered a way of imagining and talking about statecraft. As I detailed in previous chapters, government transparency emerged as a site of ideological struggle during the Cold War, mobilized by differing political factions for different political ends; when the Soviet Union fell, these debates continued with new valences and actors.

Between the Cold War and Bush's War on Terror, President Bill Clinton and Attorney General Janet Reno at least officially endorsed greater transparency measures, urging government organizations to share information expediently, and encouraged the growing ability to electronically file-share. Federal information policy scholars observed that after 9/11, FOIA's strength significantly diminished.[6] During the George W. Bush presidency, new information classification categories eroded the authority of FOIA, and declassification practices became somewhat erratic. Exemptions to FOIA were encouraged and applied beyond their original mandate. Information access professionals were trained to evade disclosure, and memos were issued reinforcing this shift.[7] The Justice Department helped create new categories, including, for instance, "sensitive but unclassified," "for official use only," and "sensitive security information."[8] This era also marked another shift in information classification policy, one that moved practice away from centralized decision-making. Instead, a more polycentric regulatory schema allowed varying agencies to more independently make their own disclosure policy determinations. Such postmodern arrangements made it difficult for civil rights lawyers to take legal action under FOIA to get the government to release information about detention to the public: In the absence of centralized decision-making schema, withholding exemptions often lacked clarity. As Lotte Feinberg suggests, the use of these categories "presents a number of problems, beginning with the fundamental 'tension' of competing goals: that of 'securing the nation' from attack while simultaneously 'keeping the public informed.'"[9]

Ironically, the creation of digital archives and the broad implementation of e-governance emerged out of an era of the covert, a clandestine common sense. Feinberg notes this tension between access to government documentation and "securing the nation" materializes as crisis in government agencies around defining what documentation should remain classified, what can be declassified, and what other documents may be considered "sensitive" but not "classified." The differential classifications proved quite haphazard; documents once public became sensitive without explanation.[10] The attempts to web-scrub this information newly classified as sensitive were vexed, as search engine caches and digital archives might have stored documents and posts beyond the bounds of government servers.[11] The rise of electronic file-sharing—particularly in unsanctioned document dumps facilitated by government whistleblowers—imperiled the exclusive safeguarding of the "state secret," a notion that emerges out of the mid-twentieth century's ballooning defense industry and the rise of nuclear weaponry. Though government documents had repeatedly and regularly been made public in the predigital era, it was primarily their *content* that was shared, not the document as primary source material. Riffing off of Walter Benjamin, we might alternately imagine our analysis of redacted aesthetics as analyzing *the art of the document in the era of electronic reproduction.*[12]

In 2003, the ACLU filed a lawsuit against the government asking them to disclose documentation of detention and interrogation under FOIA; in 2004, the first Torture Memo was leaked; and in the subsequent period, documents came to public light intermittently and often heavily redacted. In 2009, under the new Obama administration, the Justice Department released memos related to torture, interrogation, and detention that were written during the Bush presidency. As these documents now clearly show, a series of secret memos issued by varying government agencies between 2002 and 2005 set into motion substantive shifts in official guidelines on the treatment of detainees that violated both international agreements and conventional interpretations of American law. As legal scholar David Cole remarks in the introduction to his compendium of the torture documents, they demonstrate the precise legal maneuvering through which torture was rationalized.[13] Several of these memos directly corresponded to the torture of Abu Zubaydah. Clark and Levy meticulously document, in the summer of 2002, the Bush administration's internal process of legally authorizing the violent interrogations of Abu Zubaydah in response to the demand of his interrogators, psychologists Bruce Jessen and James Mitchell, who developed new techniques based on the Survival, Evasion, Resistance, and Escape (SERE) program, along with Abu Zubaydah's unique profile. In their drafting of the August 1 memos, senior officials in the Bush administration consulted Jessen and Mitchell's notes, observations, and documentation of their interrogations of Abu Zubaydah, even drawing from personal diaries and childhood memories.[14] By manipulating the definition of what was considered legally permissible, the documents reveal how brutal practices like waterboarding, sleep deprivation, physical binding, caloric restriction, and other psychological tactics were routinized as part of the CIA's "enhanced interrogation procedures" on the literal body of Abu Zubaydah and through his unique subject position.[15] While the unredacted memos now expose plainly the legal rationalizations concocted to justify torture, the struggle to reveal their content demonstrated how the US government approaches the question of access. These demands for government transparency and greater accountability were met with an uneven response:[16] Documentation from the detention program has been released over the years, often in fragments, only after legal pressure.

Foucault's work on governmentality illuminates the logics of government administration and the forms of political subjectivity that transparency advocates operated within. In his lectures at the Collège de France during the late 1970s, Foucault began to consider how the idea of "the population" emerged alongside modern conceptions of statehood and an art of governance. This newly imagined category—the population—existed to be managed. Visualizations of this population through institutionalized technologies of sight, including statistics, figures, and bureaucratic documentation, became the basis for government rationality. Governmental apparatuses are primarily concerned with how populations should be made to live, what Foucault called "biopower": the regulation and calculated optimization of life within modern societies. Paper management was and is crucial to the management of human life.

Governmentality, however, is not simply the way the state sees its subjects but also how citizens self-govern. As Nikolas Rose and Peter Miller note about the emergence of biopower, "Liberal doctrines of freedom went hand in hand with projects to make liberalism operable by producing the 'subjective' conditions under which its contractual notions of the mutual relations between citizen and society could work."[17] Liberalism's paradox, therefore, is that while governing through an idiom of freedom and seeming to promote subjective choice, individual liberties are regulated by biopolitical constraints on what constitute appropriate citizen behavior.[18] In other words, biopolitical technologies of citizenship circumscribe this taut relationship between individual liberties and the rule of law. FOIA requests sit between two different governmental mechanisms, what Dean calls "the technology of agency," or the empowerment of citizens to "take control" of self and community, and "the technology of performance," or the regulation of institutions to create citizens' trust through notions of "accountability, transparency, and democratic control."[19] When active citizens empower themselves to demand transparency, it can be a demand for better governing through the restoration of trust: a technology of performance. Therefore, FOIA claims work through the citizen's biopolitical subjectivity, reinscribing redress for injustice within a fundamentally governmental mechanism.

Transparency, then, is an optic mechanism to make visible institutional documentation for the optimal functioning of liberal government. This governmental notion that seeing better means governing better is reflected in both the state's capacity to visualize the population through instrumentalized categories of knowledge (e.g., statistics) and the citizens' ability to access these documents themselves. The move toward open governments (particularly in the digital era, where many states have adopted e-government statutes) reflects this idealized relationship.[20] However, making some things visible is always a way of making others things invisible, imperceptible, or hidden from view. The visual aspects of these discourses of accountability infuse the language of access: We often hear various actors bringing information *to light*, keeping citizens *in the dark*, allowing the public *to see*, and of course making government *transparent*. This language of the visual is hardly incidental; in this idiom, to make accountable is to render the visible, a visuality that is articulated through the governmental document.

As a visual metaphor, *the transparent* is that which allows light to pass through and enables an object to be unmitigatedly seen. Perception is a variegated terrain, however, and that particular transparent gaze is but one way of knowing.[21] Transparency, or rather the vision associated with it, is paradoxically always situated and only partial.[22] Seemingly transparent images have a vexed relationship to the subject they portray;[23] the photographs of abuse from the Abu Ghraib detention center, for instance, were often summoned as proof of America's failings rather than to viscerally account for what detainees experienced.[24] In other words, what appears to be transparent is already refracted through a racialized prism, a gendered prison, a prism that contains within it patterned stories of difference. Transparency is ideological. Moreover, many contemporary torture techniques deliberately escape this kind of transparency: Modern democratic states prefer torture methods that are imperceptible to the eye—a shift from earlier periods, when techniques applied to prisoners would leave scars on the body.[25] Debates over waterboarding, for example, and whether it constituted torture, flourished in the absence of a visual record.[26] In these kinds of instances it is untenable to make actions truly transparent through an optic field of perception.

The fragments of information within these documents affirm that detainees are not biopolitical subjects under American law: Their lives are not optimized through regulation and management, nor are they given the liberty to self-govern through the idiom of freedom. Instead they are incarcerated and brutalized, subjected to a violent bodily regulation: what Achille Mbembe calls "necropower."[27] Mbembe suggests that biopolitics is not an adequate theorization of modern power, arguing that we must account for the ways that geographic isolations, war machines, and technologies of death have decimated populations and created subjects through life-negation.[28] Detainees in GTMO and other US military prisons and black sites were detained indefinitely without charge, stripped of their rights, rendered to other countries, and incarcerated without political or legal recourse. Their state-sanctioned geographic isolation stems from the notion that the citizen population needs to be inoculated against them.[29] As Mbembe argues, biopolitics, necropolitics, and discipline are different mechanisms of power that together define relations in modern nation-states. Within this discourse, the negation of detainee life occurs in order to optimize life for the "population" of the United States. If biopolitics are visually mundane, necropolitics may be both visually mundane and spectacular: visually excluded or strikingly on display.

Though the demand for transparency—through FOIA requests, for instance —may arguably make biopolitical subjects, the memos themselves highlight a fundamentally necropolitical form of governmentality. Authorizing documents —memos, detainee files, and other official communications—create forms of governmental knowledge in order to routinize detention and brutal interrogation methods under the rubric of inoculating the population from terrorist violence.[30] The detainees' renditions into files, figures, and statistics create a rational order in military prisons; their bodies are thereby made visible to the state through bureaucratic categorization. Unlike biopolitical archives that include, for example, readily accessible data about demography, insurance, and fertility rates, these necropolitical archives remain inaccessible to the public, available only to selectively authorized state officials until declassification. I explain these interwoven relationships between normative biopolitics and carceral necropolitics to highlight the disjunctures between the governance of citizen populations and detainee "enemy combatants." When government documents instrumentalize necropolitical violence in particular, redaction takes on a nefarious quality for the viewer.

Within this archive of carceral violence, detainees exist as a necropolitical subject, submerged within the bureaucratic prose of the military record. This was particularly true for Abu Zubaydah, whose torture and the legal architectures built around it came to stand in for *all* detainees. Torture cannot be made transparent through mere reversal of the security archive's logic. Abu Zubaydah was wrongly identified as a top al-Qaeda official. Accounts suggest he had been involved in a minor way in coordinating logistics with them from Pakistan, forging passports and arranging flights, though he was not part of their organization or involved in 9/11. But he was deeply critical of Western imperialism, as himself a stateless person. His father had been a refugee from Jericho during the Nakba in 1948, fleeing to Gaza only to flee again in 1956 after the Israelis massacred hundreds of Palestinians in Khan Younis that November.[31] The archive demands readings against the grain, and the detainee demands context: They are not a person within these documents. Rather, for the abuser, they are a subject composed in bureaucratic, legal prose on whom the maximum admissible amount of torture should be wrought. And in the American liberal imagination, the detainee was only the body on which American ideals are eroded. Detainees did not write themselves into this state archive, with few exceptions: detainee testimony within Combatant Status Review Tribunals, correspondence, and other personal papers. Their status, then, is not unlike the figure of the subaltern, whose archival traces have been theorized extensively by postcolonial scholars. For these scholars, the subaltern are a colonized and subjugated class who were made visible to the West through government bureaucracy (the census, colonial documentation, etc.), or animated in the imagination through the landscape of literature and art.[32]

These colonial archives are innately archives of epistemic violence as they manifested in both regulatory and physical brutality; governmental records existed to facilitate domination and manage the possibilities of insurgency. As a field, postcolonial studies can still offer reading strategies that can point to the traces of the detained. Within colonial archives, scholars have shown how a discursive analysis of colonial language as well as structured absences within documents can reveal subaltern histories. These methods utilize colonial documentation in deliberate opposition to its intended purpose. In a literary context, Said called this a "contrapuntal reading," that is, a dynamic reading against the grain that summons all that exists outside the frame. In his theorization of a contrapuntal mode of reading, a musical metaphor, Said also points to a visual mode of analysis: "In reading a text, one must open it out to both what went into it and what its author excluded. Each cultural work is a *vision* of moment and we must juxtapose that *vision* with the various re*visions* it later provoked."[33] While Said was not writing about the visual per se, his argument mobilized the metaphoric power of sight. Contrapuntal analysis, seen in this light, foregrounds the material conditions under which something is made visible: the ideology of a particular mode of being seen, the practice of making visible, and the forcible exclusions that are redacted from sight. In other words, this Saidian mode lends itself seamlessly to a visual study of militarism as a tessellated assemblage of state documents, redactions, notations, photographs, databases, aerial views, views from below, and combat footage. Paper, in particular, is the grist of administrative violence, the aesthetics of which invite an understanding of both the imperial narrative and resistance to it. We might reread redacted paper in this way—its layered authorship, its possession and circulation, and its location within a militarized frame.

Alongside Said, the scholars of the Subaltern Studies Group narrated the travails of the detained, dejected, and disinherited through colonial archives, or what Ranajit Guha called "the prose of counter-insurgency" in a 1983 essay by the same name. While subaltern studies largely focused its attention on the colonial past, their methods are useful for reading the prose of the imperial present. Documents from the torture archive would constitute what Guha would call "primary discourse," with "production and circulation both necessarily contingent on reasons of the state."[34] In his well-known essay Guha examines the language of primary discourse, showing how coded expressions demonstrate the instrumental complicity of administrative knowledge in producing the conditions of subalternity. In this sense, the bureaucratic archive does not simply provide verifiable information: It is an object of inquiry and a site of deep, textured discovery. These documents can be turned around on the colonial gaze—providing just as much (if not more) information about the colonizer as the colonized. Whereas Guha argues for a rereading of the very colonial language used to describe insurrectionary acts, I argue that the act of redacting this bureaucratic prose in fact denaturalizes the perceived neutrality of the document that subaltern scholars have worked to undo.[35] Although it may seem that redacted documents would disallow the kind of close examinations of texts that Guha undertakes, paradoxically redaction can provoke contrapuntal readings with respect to documentation of the necropolitical. In other words, a redaction renders a visually mundane document spectacular. In the next section, I explore some of these cases through close readings of redacted documents, showing how reading with redaction interrupts the seamlessness of a text, compelling the reader to ponder unspeakable, unrecordable traumas of detention that escape governmental record.

READING WITH REDACTION

In 2005, *The Onion* published an article titled "CIA Realizes It's Been Using Black Highlighters All These Years," satirizing the wanton censorship of government documents made public. The parody appeared just one year after the first Torture Memo leaked, and it hailed readers with a wry lede: "A report released Tuesday by the CIA's Office of the Inspector General revealed that the CIA has mistakenly obscured hundreds of thousands of pages of critical intelligence information with black highlighters." The piece captured the ethos of the moment, as people were increasingly frustrated with the kind of redacted and furtive political life that defined the War on Terror. An absurdist parody of the War on Terror's nontransparency, rendered transparent.

Two documents — dated August 1, 2002 — exemplify the legal correspondence that came to be known as the Torture Memos. These Office of Legal Council missives, drafted by Assistant Attorney General Jay Bybee, appeared to respond to CIA queries about whether treatments of prisoners (specifically Abu Zubaydah and fellow detainee Khalid Sheikh Muhammad) would be considered torture under both the Convention Against Torture and, more importantly, the US Criminal and Penal Code.[36] Instead, the memos intentionally provided legal cover for wildly disavowing internationally held standards of prisoner treatment. The first of these memos, leaked in 2004, was for Alberto Gonzales and broadly discussed legal implications of using varying torture techniques, and, significantly, did so by rewriting definitions of suffering, harm, and pain. The second memo, drafted to John Rizzo, discusses Abu Zubaydah's treatment while at a black site in Thailand. I discuss here two differently redacted versions of this latter memo to show how redacted views shape our readings.

Prior to President Obama's massive document disclosure in April 2009, a heavily redacted version — nearly unreadable — had been made available to the ACLU under a FOIA request asking for data on detainee abuse. (As part of the Obama administration's efforts to create more government accountability, the 2009 release was only lightly redacted. It does, however, conceal some description of Zubaydah's interrogations.) On July 24, 2008, the ACLU received the substantially redacted version in response to a FOIA request.[37] The document was released after the ACLU took the Central Intelligence Agency to court under FOIA, but it was so heavily redacted that the ACLU staff themselves seemed confused by what they were seeing. On the ACLU's *Blog of Rights*, Suzanne Ito noted this uncertainty, writing, "According to news reports, this memo lists the specific interrogation methods for use by CIA personnel against prisoners in secret detention centers overseas. But we can't be sure, because a typical page from this document looks like this." Directly below her entry, Ito posted a page containing four black rectangles that clearly cover different paragraphs. If the text was unintelligible, what warranted its feature on the *Blog of Rights*? The memo's significance rests on more than words. In the full PDF, some text remains uncovered, but the focus on this page illustrates Ito's argument. According to the ACLU's website description of the PDF file, the document shows how "[the] Justice Department authorized alternative interrogation methods." However, to the casual reader—if not to seasoned ACLU lawyers—such authorization might not be readily apparent.

Whether flipping through the entire document or scrolling through the PDF version on a computer, the viewer finds page after page of neatly arranged opaque boxes.[38] The document eludes rational comprehension, as legal justifications for torture are concealed under an array of darkened boxes. Since the majority of the document appears this way, the viewer cannot extract much empirical information from the text itself. And as an attempt at governmental accountability and biopolitical citizen empowerment, it fails. Instead, what emerges seems fragmented and inscrutable. Within the memo, the bits of available text provide a dispassionate assessment of what can constitute torture, with nearly all references to specific acts, studies, or procedures coated liberally with black ink to conceal them. Despite the scarcity of visible words, we can consider several dimensions of the redacted document. First, the mere existence of this file in its redacted form confirms a discussion and discourse, unlike a Glomar "neither confirm nor deny" response. Additionally, there are quantifiable ways to measure the contents of the document—the length (eighteen pages), the size of paragraphs, and so on—as well as qualitative notations such as crossed-out "Top Secret" headers at the top of every page, for instance. Further, while readers certainly employ deductive reasoning to work around textual absences, meaning is also created through the visual spectacle of nondisclosure. This meaning emerges from the experience of reading a redacted document, where blacked-out spaces evoke more than just the desire to uncover the invisible. By closely examining this memo, we see how redaction actually creates multilayered and unintended meanings that exceed governmental instrumentality of the document. The document, then, functions more as an image than as a text.

The last page of the August 1 memo exemplifies how such unintended meanings are created. As with the preceding pages, this last page is heavily redacted. Besides Jay Bybee's signature, we see only a cryptic sentence fragment in print: "Your review of the literature uncovered no empirical data on the use of these procedures, with the exception [REDACTED]."[39] The quote is striking. It provides an awkward closure to the seventeen pages of text that precede it, and it is peculiar that such a short and seemingly inconsequential fragment that would be submerged between data and conclusion was deliberately left uncovered. However, here it reads as a clue and a fragment of the deductive process. The eye might linger on the "empirical data," or ponder the exceptional case that remains redacted. Further, it may even underscore for the reader the work of the empirical within necropolitical rationality—that the redacted spaces that precede it are calculated and rational arguments drawing on literature and scientific reasoning. And indeed, we now know that the psychologists Jessen and Mitchell drew directly from their social science training to craft and implement techniques of torture on Abu Zubaydah. In the absence of a larger account, the fragment offered an uncanny yet ultimately apt glimpse into the racist nexus of lawfare and social science. Yet when compared with the same final page in the currently available version, the contingency of this reading becomes clear. The literature review returns to the mundane, and the empirical data returns to being a method. These words simply signpost, disappear between description. Thus, although its intended purpose is to conceal the facts of interrogation, the visual spectacle of redaction ironically makes contrapuntal readings immediately available to the reader.

In April 2009, the August 1 memo was rereleased in lightly redacted form, under the auspices of President Obama's promises of transparency in American war. The document extensively discussed the legal basis for utilizing a variety of violent techniques that would and could be applied during the interrogation of Abu Zubaydah: stress positions, confinement boxes, facial slaps, sleep deprivation, and waterboarding.[40] In the moment the memo was drafted, Abu Zubaydah was recovering from injuries sustained during his capture, from which he had nearly died due to sepsis. Though until that point he had been cooperating with FBI agents conducting interrogations, the CIA-commissioned team of Jessen and Mitchell wanted a free hand to extract *more* by employing a brutal maximalist treatment against him. The legal status for these "enhanced interrogation" tactics, created in the context of Abu Zubaydah, had long-ranging and far-reaching impacts for those rendered through American detention sites—here addressed in the context of Abu Zubaydah, they more broadly catalogue the musings of lawyers ready to supply legal justification to the CIA. Yet to a reader unaccustomed to the norms of legal writing, the experience of reading the un-redacted memo is bizarre. On the one hand, the memo documents a calculated,

Your review of the literature uncovered no empirical data on the use of these procedures, with the exception

Jay S. Bybee
Assistant Attorney General

3.2 Memorandum from Jay S. Bybee, Assistant Attorney General, to John Rizzo, general counsel for the CIA. The memo was issued August 1, 2002, and released in 2008.

that such consequences would result here. Because you have conducted the due diligence to determine that these procedures, either alone or in combination, do not produce prolonged mental harm, we believe that you do not meet the specific intent requirement necessary to violate Section 2340A.

You have also informed us that you have reviewed the relevant literature on the subject, and consulted with outside psychologists. Your review of the literature uncovered no empirical data on the use of these procedures, with the exception of sleep deprivation for which no long-term health consequences resulted. The outside psychologists with whom you consulted indicated were unaware of any cases where long-term problems have occurred as a result of these techniques.

As described above, it appears you have conducted an extensive inquiry to ascertain what impact, if any, these procedures individually and as a course of conduct would have on Zubaydah. You have consulted with interrogation experts, including those with substantial SERE school experience, consulted with outside psychologists, completed a psychological assessment and reviewed the relevant literature on this topic. Based on this inquiry, you believe that the use of the procedures, including the waterboard, and as a course of conduct would not result in prolonged mental harm. Reliance on this information about Zubaydah and about the effect of the use of these techniques more generally demonstrates the presence of a good faith belief that no prolonged mental harm will result from using these methods in the interrogation of Zubaydah. Moreover, we think that this represents not only an honest belief but also a reasonable belief based on the information that you have supplied to us. Thus, we believe that the specific intent to inflict prolonged mental is not present, and consequently, there is no specific intent to inflict severe mental pain or suffering. Accordingly, we conclude that on the facts in this case the use of these methods separately or a course of conduct would not violate Section 2340A.

Based on the foregoing, and based on the facts that you have provided, we conclude that the interrogation procedures that you propose would not violate Section 2340A. We wish to emphasize that this is our best reading of the law; however, you should be aware that there are no cases construing this statute; just as there have been no prosecutions brought under it.

Please let us know if we can be of further assistance.

Jay S. Bybee
Assistant Attorney General

3.3 Memorandum from Jay S. Bybee, Assistant Attorney General to John Rizzo, general counsel for the CIA. The memo was issued August 1, 2002, and released in 2009.

necropolitical legal reasoning that at some moments is utterly chilling to read. But on the other, the discussion primarily occurs in such an arcane bureaucratic language of law that parsing meaning, let alone intention and implication, is challenging. Put differently, the legalese is its own obfuscation, and the seemingly transparency of the document reveals a lexicon that is anything but. This is a different kind of nonsight.

In one particularly chilling section, we find an extended argument about the legal basis for placing insects into a confinement box *with* a prisoner. The discussion extends to disturbing rationalizations of minutiae about what, legally, the torturer could be allowed to let the prisoner believe about the dangers of that insect's sting. In the middle of this descriptive paragraph lie two redacted lines. The preceding and subsequent sentences are produced here:

> If, however, you were to place the insect in the box without informing him you were doing so, then, in order not to commit a predicate act, you should not affirmatively lead him to believe that any insect is present which has a sting that can produce severe pain or suffering or even cause his death. [RE-DACTED] so long as you take the approaches we have described, the insect's placement in the box would not constitute a threat of severe physical pain or suffering to a reasonable person in his position.[41]

The redacted lines provoke the reader's imagination. What cannot be uttered? What exceeds the horror of the previous lines, a debate on the legality of lying about insect venom? Directly following the redacted portion, the sentence fragment begins with "so," leading the reader backed to the rectangular blackened space preceding it. Within the unredacted document, the "so" reads as rather inconsequential, an innocuous word only signaling how the reasoning through which the author concludes that certain practices of torture are in fact legal and permissible. A comparative reading thus tells us that what remains concealed are government information and rationalizations about its necropolitical practices —which, to be sure, should be made publicly known—but their revelation does not in fact produce "transparency" with respect to the experience of the detainee. Transparency if understood to be produced through this kind of revelation, is an instrument of the state and a technology of agency for the liberal subject who demands access to these knowledges. The psychological horrors of torture, already obfuscated in the bureaucratic language of the memo, in some ways may appear more prominent when the document is interrupted by the unfathomable blacked-out stripes that bracket these peculiar fragments. As such, the concealed information, while important in a legal context, is extrinsic to the contrapuntal reading that the redacted document enables.

Even within this more "transparent" document, these redacted spaces disrupt narrative, as they create points of rupture that disallow seamless reading. They change how you read and the words you dwell on, infuse a mundane word with suggestions of the necropolitical. In another instance, a blacked-out portion of a paragraph describing how mental health experts produced a psychological profile for Zubaydah, in accordance with the practice of creating psychological assessments for detainees, is followed by the seemingly innocuous phrase "as we indicated above," beginning the next paragraph. Perhaps the "above" refers to points made before the redacted portion, visible to the viewer. Perhaps the reasoning is hardly controversial. However, without knowing what lies beneath the blacked-out segments, the simple phrase beckons us back into the ungraspable and reminds us of what we do not know. Our reading of these documents is always a visual act, shaped both literally and metaphorically by the things that are beyond our view.

Redacted documents, and the experience of reading them, are of course made most meaningful by the context in which they circulate. Turning back to Benjamin, in the age of electronic reproduction, documents—and their redaction—present as a visual art. The reproduction of paper online happened prolifically in antitorture blogs and torture archives during the War on Terror. As a visual image circulating within this online sphere, redaction became an aesthetic signifier. In 2008, responding to the release of eighteen heavily redacted documents, Rachel Myers addressed this particular form of appearance for the ACLU *Blog of Rights*. She notes, "While the documents do, in fact, reveal the word 'water boarding' or some variation, they leave pretty much everything else to the imagination. The pages that haven't been completely withheld . . . have the *clandestine blacked-out look that's become a sort of trademark of this administration*" (emphasis mine).[42] Her "favorite" of these documents, she continues, only contains the phrases "These enhanced techniques include" and far later on the page, "Water Board." Myers does not attribute the document to any specific file released the day before and does not bear any other markers to suggest where it's from. Within her post, the page becomes a floating signifier for the Bush administration, a *look* that represents an immanently familiar and meaningful kind of visual experience.

That trademark *look* of the War on Terror made its way onto websites, into art galleries, and onto book covers. Even the website design for the ACLU's Accountability for Torture website, an online resource dedicated to issues of detention in the War on Terror, drew from this aesthetic. On the banner at the top of the page, the phrase "Accountability for Torture" emerged from between black lines. To one side the phrases "enhanced techniques" and "the water board technique," written in a faded typewriter font, peeked out from between the redacted lines. "Accountability" ruptures the redacted spaces that, taken alongside a row of stars descending on the left, constitute a nefarious version of the American flag. The entire image evokes a faded, perhaps even faxed document: a site of governmental knowledges about the detained body, torture techniques, and authorization. The ACLU's Torture FOIA and *Blog of Rights* designers and contributors are not singular in their mobilization of the visual and conceptual currency of redaction. The National Security Archive, a clearinghouse of declassified government documents relating to US intelligence and security, boasts a WordPress blog that is rather appropriately named *Unredacted*.

Within this contested field of public accessibility, there exist uninterrogated assumptions about the way digitization affects viewership of these documents. The "public" becomes naturalized within discourses about democracy, based on the idea that the citizenry can access digitized documentation uploaded to websites by computer users. Within e-government discourses, the emphasis on making information available online rests on the assumption that the "citizen" and the "user" are equivalent, digital divide notwithstanding.[43] Although people have disparate levels of access to computing technology, the push to achieve more equitable online access dovetails with the idealization of the digital public sphere as a democratic practice. Following this logic, in order for e-government to realize its potential, US citizens need to be able to somewhat equivalently use online resources; the utopia of such transparent practices hinges on the idea that "the public" (or "the citizen") and "the user" should ultimately be coterminous.[44] This slippage between "the public" and "the user" highlights the significance of the digitization of FOIA documents; beyond simply being an incidental medium of transmission, online accessibility is itself an ideological statement. Michael Warner and Jodi Dean have troubled Habermas's enduring idea of "the public" as an antitheocratic and democratic space, exposing how the public's constitutive other is "the secret."[45] It is not innately the sharing of information that creates a public, but that which is perceived or classified as a secret which creates an idea of the public. The unrevealed document is but the public's secret-sharer, a constitutive private archive that chronicles the quotidian and instrumentalized forms of violence for the eyes of few, the lure of its release informing how the public comes to be understood.

Website aesthetics and online practices show the importance of redaction and the interrelation between the visible and what Akira Mizuta Lippit calls the "avisual" in the digital realm. On the internet, which is idealized as an accessible and accountable public, redacted aesthetics and the circulation of redacted documents point to the failures of transparency and the impossibility of complete sight. This becomes especially important in a time when the illusion of endless searchability retrenches documentary evidence as the only way of acknowledging injustice and visual proof becomes a most important site of redress, think for example of the copwatcher's video, on the one hand, and the cop's body-camera, on the other. The redacted document offers no illusory and dangerous sense of cogency or completeness.

VIDEOTAPES ARE NOT EVIDENCE

In early November 2005, Jose Rodriguez, director of the CIA's National Clandestine Service, ordered the destruction of dozens of videotapes, thinking, perhaps, that certain things were best left unseen. Contrary to the advice of friends and colleagues at the White House and the Office of the Director of National Intelligence, he gave the green light to the rest of his clan at the CIA to expunge a particular set of indexical images recorded in the detention program the CIA had been running since 2002.[46] The ninety-two tapes in question depicted interrogations of two detainees in secret prisons in Thailand and northern Europe, Abu Zubaydah and Abdul Rahim al-Nashri. Of the collection, ninety depicted the torture of Abu Zubaydah and two of al-Nashri. After privately purging them, the CIA denied their existence in public and in court. It took two years and the threat of a *New York Times* scoop for the CIA to admit the videos had once indeed existed. Despite this acknowledgment, in the midst of heavy litigation from civil rights organizations like the ACLU, the CIA's approach to document release related to these tapes continued to be miserly at best. They refused to release either transcripts of these videos or descriptions of what they contained.

In 2009, during the long-standing federal case *ACLU et al. v. Department of Defense et al.* (No. 04 Civ. 4151), presided over by Judge Alvin Hellerstein, the CIA admitted that it had destroyed precisely ninety-two videotape recordings of interrogations, which originated from CIA black sites. Yet even then the CIA insisted that videotapes were made with the specific intention of reviewing interrogations to ensure that protocol was being followed and no unauthorized techniques were being used. In 2003 an agency-issued memo granted CIA Inspector General John Helgerson—an agency-appointed watchdog—access to the videos, noting they would be destroyed shortly after. By the time Helgerson arrived in Thailand to review the interrogation videos in late 2003, fifteen of the ninety-two tapes that a CIA lawyer had reviewed earlier in the year had been destroyed. According to Larry Siems, these were "blank or broken and twenty-one hours of interrogations described in the logs and cables were missing from the video record, including two waterboarding sessions."[47]

Helgerson's research resulted in a classified report he issued in 2004 called "Counterterrorism Detention and Interrogation Activities (September 2001–October 2003)," which was released in lightly redacted form in 2009. This publication, along with increasing pressure being placed on the US intelligence world by members of the US press who in the meantime were publishing and reporting on the controversial images taken by US soldiers of Abu Ghraib prisoners as well as the existence of the Torture Memos, led the CIA in November 2005 to destroy the remaining black-site interrogation tapes within a climate that was becoming more publicly hostile to the idea that the American government had tortured.[48] At the same time, in November 2005, during the Zacarias Moussaoui trail, the CIA swore in federal court that no videotapes of interrogations existed. Two years later, however, Michael Hayden admitted in a December 2007 email to CIA employees that these interrogations had indeed been taped during the early years of the interrogation program. He wrote, "The Tapes were meant chiefly as an additional, internal check on the program in its early stages. At one point it was thought the tapes could serve as a backstop to guarantee that other methods of documenting the interrogations—and the crucial information they produced—were accurate and complete. The Agency soon determined that its documentary reporting was full and exacting, removing any need for tapes."[49]

But of course the obvious question remained unaddressed: If the interrogations followed procedure, why destroy the tapes? The refusal to release these transcripts only further confounds the question, since neither text exists in the public sphere. Clearly, the risk of culpability lay in both the indexical and visceral qualities of video, the ability of the interrogation video to evoke a strong response from the viewer. Moreover, a transcription itself only records specific aspects of the interrogation, while with visual images, a "punctum" can betray the photograph's intended meaning, and, similarly, document redaction can lend itself to a contrapuntal reading that subverts concealment.[50] However, the transcription as a text can obscure the bodily experiences of torture by translating the encounter between interrogator and detainee as dialogue. Indeed, though torture may incorporate verbal threats, torture is hardly limited to the spoken word; the experience of torture is primarily within the body and senses. Though a video of an interrogation would mimic the eye of the torturer and neither fully capture nor translate pain, images are often unwieldy and behave in ways that defy the logic of their production. During the ACLU's case against the Department of Defense and the CIA, the CIA successfully argued against even releasing descriptions of the videotapes in question. Although a description of the video would itself be a translation of a translation, Hellerstein's ruling barred the potential to pinpoint the embodied acts of enhanced interrogation.

The ACLU argued, among other things, that the CIA had committed a crime by destroying these tapes while FOIA requests for them were still pending. While Hellerstein ultimately did not find the CIA guilty of any wrongdoing, the case did produce a number of documents and memos that shed light on the tapes and their destruction.[51] One document titled "Inventory of Videotapes" is a nine-page PDF file that lists all of the missing tapes in question. The heavily redacted document contains an itemized list that is ninety-two lines long with nearly all the dates and times blacked out. While some descriptions remain visible, we can see that tape 92, for instance, bears the label "#3" and its accompanying description reads, "Use and rewind #3"; directly underneath is the word *Final*.[52]

The very first of these tapes is for Abu Zubaydah, the unnamed "Detainee 1." The description of the tape, rather ironically, is covered over with a black redaction line and followed by the instruction "Do not tape over." This redacted reading unintentionally of course, points itself to the CIA's transgression of its own policies. "Do not tape over" sits next to taped-over text that presumably describes a (destroyed) video that has been, effectively, taped over. The image exemplifies Lippit's description of avisuality: "All signs lead to a view but at its destination nothing is seen."[53] The text hails the reader as visual spectator, yet the redacted space merely points to the trace of its originary visual object.

This document illuminates the entwinement of these visualities: It is through demands for *transparency* (via FOIA) that we know about the *destruction* of these videotapes; we only know them in their *redacted* form, through a *bureaucratic*

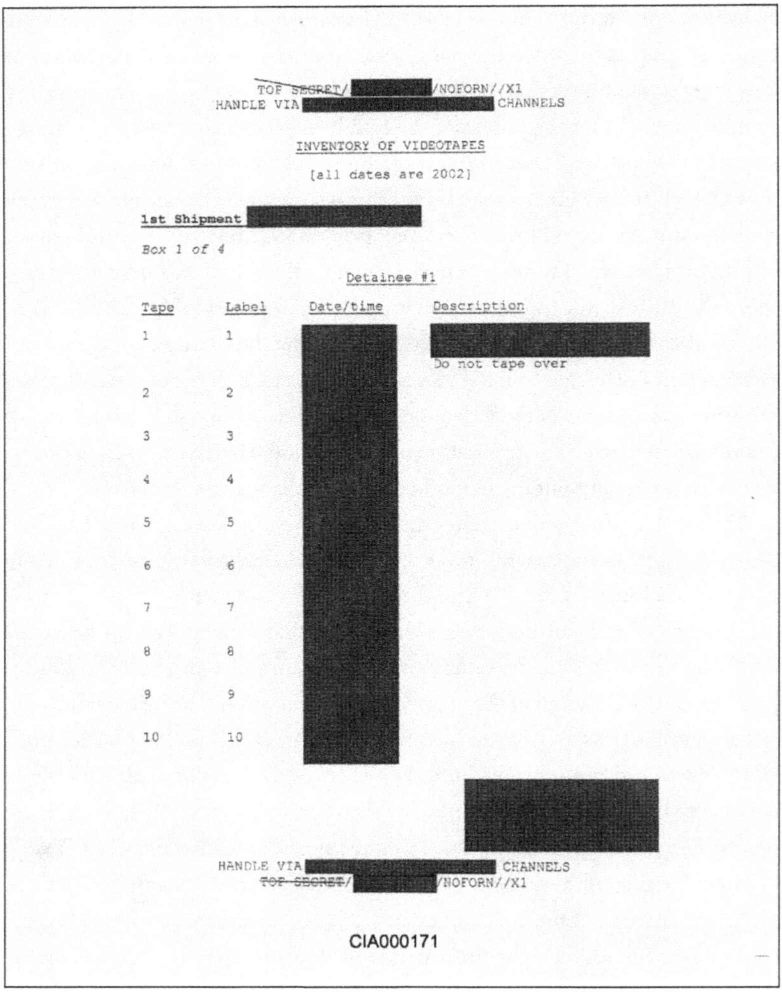

INVENTORY OF VIDEOTAPES

[all dates are 2002]

1st Shipment ▮▮▮▮▮▮▮▮

Box 1 of 4

Detainee #1

Tape	Label	Date/time	Description
1	1	▮	▮▮▮▮▮▮▮
			Do not tape over
2	2	▮	
3	3	▮	
4	4	▮	
5	5	▮	
6	6	▮	
7	7	▮	
8	8	▮	
9	9	▮	
10	10	▮	

CIA000171

3.4 First page of the redacted inventory of the ninety-two torture and interrogation videos that the CIA destroyed in 2004. Declassified in 2009.

representation of detention. Although FOIA requests, redacted documents, and legal memos reflect a desire to attain "evidence" within the juridical sphere, it is through the production of this legal discourse that a visual quality of detention becomes fathomable. The tapes of detention would appear to be the closest (most proximate) visual evidence of detention because of their visual and aural indexical qualities. That is, if these videotapes still existed, civil rights advocates would undoubtedly mobilize them as substantiating proof of the brutality of Enhanced Interrogation Techniques (torture). Further, they might also prove that the interrogations went off-script, meaning that interrogators and handlers used officially unsanctioned interrogation methods—beyond Enhanced Interrogation Techniques, even—and violated international conventions against torture.

Thus, the potential existence of these texts, for good reason, was seen as key in the carrying out of justice within the juridical realm by both the CIA (who sent strict instructions to have them destroyed) and the activists who sought access to them. Marita Sturken illuminates the limits of visible evidence in her discussion of the video footage used in the Rodney King trials, in which four officers from the Los Angeles Police Department were charged with assault with a deadly weapon and use of excessive force. On March 2, 1991, Rodney King was pulled over by the police for speeding and beaten mercilessly by four police officers for resisting arrest. The incident was captured on video by George Holliday, a bystander who was at home and used his personal camcorder to film the event. The footage circulated in the news and created a public uproar against police brutality and the police department's racist practices. Holliday's seemingly incontrovertible video footage was key in the prosecution's case. However, the defense team showed the video in short, staccato segments that created the impression that King posed a threat to the mob of armed officers. The jury failed to find the officers guilty of any wrongdoing.[54] Sturken argues, "What had been so popularly seen as incontrovertible evidence of excessive police force when the videotape was first released became, in the course of the first trial, an ambiguous document that was used instead to prove the police were vulnerable to and threatened by King." She continues that the "ambiguity" surrounding the Rodney King video "undermined assumptions about the nature of the documentary image. If this image was not evidence, then did visual evidence exist?"[55] Similarly, the public availability of the Abu Ghraib image archive did not lead to a restructuring of the legal justice framework; instead it resulted in a more targeted prosecution of the low-level soldiers involved in the scandal. Images of Iraqi torture victims were quickly renarrated as twisted expressions by American soldiers, a Stanford Prison Experiment–like scenario in which they recklessly wielded power in an environment that was new, scary, and foreign to them. Thus, even though access to the ninety-two interrogation videos would certainly have brought a form of juridical attention to the state's use of Enhanced Interrogation Techniques, by no means would they have guaranteed justice.

Redacted documents thus do not translate as the unrecorded event or as recorded evidence. Instead, the redacted legal document and memo indicate that there was once an image, but it is now destroyed. What then constitutes a visual reading of the destroyed image? Scholars like Lucas Hilderbrand and Laura Marks argue for a reading practice of the aesthetics of the decaying and degenerating image that focuses on the spectator's experience of seeing them.[56] Yet what do we make of the image that has already been destroyed? How do we read the image that no longer exists? It would seem that in the instance of the destroyed videotapes, one would need to consider several aspects of their destruction. Writing (or thinking) about the destroyed image is a somewhat speculative endeavor. I do not write *about* the destruction of these tapes; rather, I write *around* their destruction. I write from within the space of their erasure by describing the media and technological landscape in which they were produced as well as the issues regarding the wider practices of storing and transferring media files in use at a particular moment. Writing from this erasure is not, however, about piecing together the originary image. It requires one to dwell in the trace, to consider both the production of the tape as well as its destruction.

The phrase "destroyed videotapes" conspicuously stands out from the media context in which they emerged. Interrogations were likely captured on digital cameras: At that time, high-quality videocassette-based digital recording devices were widely available on the consumer market. Although it is possible that the interrogators used analog video cameras, it is also possible that the destroyed "videotapes" of interrogations were actually high-definition digital recordings. But we do not know. The destruction of "videotapes" brings to mind images of broken and shattered mini-DVDs or even VHS plastic cartridges, the shiny magnetic ribbon once contained within their shell strewn about. In the age of digital reproducibility, the destruction of media often refers to more than just the materiality of a singular object. The digital reproduction of image files has changed the character of both preservation and circulation of the recorded image, and the destruction of a recording does not simply translate as the material destruction of the "tape," but the erasure or deletion of a digital file. To be sure, digital files themselves take a material form insofar as they exist on a hard drive or server but take on a very different materiality from that of a cassette tape. Even though digital reproducibility is not a guarantee of permanence, and file-sharing is not innate to this technology, the idea of the "destroyed video-tape" may not adequately captured the media on which these images were created or what happened to them. Again, we do not know.

As a redacted inventory, the spectator sees several different lists—numbered and catalogued—and understands those to represent videotapes. However, the contrapuntal aesthetics of redaction gesture toward the unknowability of the practices these tapes may capture. Returning back to Lippit's discussion of the different orders of invisibility, we see both the destroyed image and the covered-up image. The redacted document engages a kind of invisibility that is about the covering up of the image—we know that the document exists within the government archive yet is hidden from view. The destroyed videotapes are invisible, however, because they no longer exist; they are beyond the purview of sight.

The videotapes should not be considered evidence in their totality. If the tapes existed (or if they were made publicly available), they would doubtlessly provide insight into the brutality of interrogation measures. Of course, their intended purpose from the outset was precisely to function as evidence—interrogators recorded interrogations so they could review them to verify clues or assess what further information could be extracted from the detained body. Thus, some of the limitations of what these video recordings could show are bound by their intended purpose outlined by the CIA and the impossibility of representing the totality of detention as a condition or experience. One could imagine that "softening-up" measures for interrogation, for instance, would have no use-value within an economy of interrogation and thus may not have been taped. Or, one could imagine the desire to see the interrogation tapes obscuring the usefulness or relevance of watching the more mundane but perhaps far more telling twenty-four-hour surveillance videos of the detainee's cells. In other words, what kinds of recorded moving images are allowed to work as evidence, both within the juridical and the experiential context of spectatorship?

The destroyed videotapes of interrogations were not the only kind of moving images recorded at detention facilities. For instance, when Khalid Sheikh Mohammad was initially captured and brought to a black-site detention facility in Europe (Mohammad later guessed that it might have been Poland), he was "kept naked for nearly a month, wrists shackled to the ceiling and ankles to the floor, in a wooden-walled room equipped with closed-circuit cameras where he was monitored 24 hours a day by a doctor, psychologist and interrogator."[57] In Guantánamo, cell blocks are also subject to video surveillance, in concert with the guard's patrolling gaze.[58] These video cameras were the subject of scrutiny during an investigation into the deaths of detainees Mani al-Utaybi, Yasser al-Zahrani, and Ali Abdullah Ahmed, who in 2006 were found hanged to death in their cells in GTMO. Although their cell blocks were videotaped, the human rights report "Death in Camp Delta" suggests these videos were never properly reviewed during the Navy Criminal Investigative Service (NCIS) inquisition.[59] The report cites NCIS's failure to review the surveillance footage from the cell block and facility (as well as the "pass-on books" and other surveillance texts). Moreover, it notes that the "combat camera"—which is supposed to be turned on when there is an incident in a cell and the Immediate Response Force is called to investigate the cell as well as any bodies that need to be transported for medical care—was directed to be turned off.[60] A footnote cites the following testimony from a released FOIA document: "Someone called for a combat camera. I am combat camera qualified so I volunteered to videotape the event. I ran the video camera for approximately two (2) minutes until I was instructed by [REDACTED] to halt taping."[61] In the summoning of the "combat camera," the videotape is intended to ensure that within the juridical context, the image could protect against allegations of wrongdoing. Inversely, the order to turn off the tape during the Immediate Response Force's investigation can intimate acts of misconduct that transpired within the detention center.

Thus, the destroyed interrogation tapes stand as just one example among the variety of ways that cameras were used at detention centers and black sites. The sustained focus on these tapes as opposed to others within legal discourse reinscribes the idea that torture and injustice must be "visible" and "spectacular" for it to register as such. A twenty-four-hour circuit video of a cell block that does not depict the beating of a detainee could not be called on as evidence of violence, eliding the violence of incarceration itself. In this regard, the destroyed tapes may have captured some Enhanced Interrogation Techniques or other excesses, but they do not capture the brutality of detention in its entirety. As discussed in the introduction, the most popular image of Guantánamo underscores this point: The picture of detainees kneeling in sensory deprivation gear rarely registers as torture, though it may register in some way as mistreatment. People expect torture to be spectacular and visible, but modern torture techniques deliberately avoid this sort of exterior detection.[62] Furthermore, the kind of torture depicted in these images where detainees are placed in a stress position while wearing sensory deprivation gear are designed to place a durational and cumulative strain on the body. However, no multihour tape of these practices exists (as far as we know), nor is it clear what images that do not necessarily possess visceral or haptic qualities would evidence to the spectator.

The destroyed tapes, however, signal the impossibility of seeing torture. Unlike the redacted image, which always works against and through the possibility of seeing what lies underneath, there is no transparent image that can be revealed in these tapes' absence. There is no shrouding of the truth, the veil of which itself must be subject to critical analysis. There is no recovery of the source document, whose indexical properties in the end could only have captured certain aspects of torture's brutality to the detriment of seeing the brutality of detention itself. Instead, all that exists is the trace of torture left behind by these destroyed tapes. What makes the destroyed interrogation tapes function as evidence is the imagination of the spectacular, visceral violences that may have been enacted on a detainee's body and the mundane, avisual condition of imprisonment that make it so dastardly and insidious. In this way, the videotapes are evidence, yet the videotapes are not evidence. As erased texts, they cannot function as evidence within the juridical realm. However, their destruction evidences the fear of legal repercussion. The desire to see these destroyed documents represents both the claim to juridical justice and the investment in the indexical as positivist proof of wrongdoing. But beyond juridical positivism, the desire to see these images points to the sense that there exists a true haptic image that conjures the experience of torture.

CONCLUSION

The ACLU's case against the CIA to release information about the destruction of these videotapes compelled Leon Panetta to produce a Vaughn Declaration, which, as I discuss in chapter 1, is a reasoned accounting of FOIA exemptions and is compelled through litigation. In the declaration, Panetta writes, "I have determined that no meaningfully segregable information can be released from the operational documents at issue. In some instances, relatively innocuous words or sentences, some of which may even have been released in other contexts, are so inextricably intertwined with the classified information that their release would produce only meaningless, incomplete, fragmented, unintelligible words or sentences."[63] Panetta's disclosure and its medium of appearance encapsulate the arguments of this chapter. In arguing for the wholesale censor of the torture documents, he inadvertently points to the new, emergent meanings produced from redacted readings. Even as he argues that the release wouldn't produce meaningful information, he suggests the possibility of imbuing "relatively innocuous words or sentences" with new meanings in this fragmented form. Panetta's Vaughn Declaration, as an auxiliary document adds to an endlessly proliferating archive of security papers that produce a detention as a media event, scaffolded by the law, which itself is but a collection of documents and statements. The discursive production of rendition/detention networks is enmeshed in this tangle of censored and spectacular appearances. Papers do not merely document; they create the law, shape the racialized and imprisoned subject, and produce discourse and common sense about war. In this sense, there is no "meaningfully segregable information," because the papers, the tapes, the auxiliary documentation, in *all* their forms (released, redacted, destroyed) are documents that illuminate the visual landscape that makes detention possible.

In the post-9/11 world, new infrastructures of permanent war resulted in the law, and transparency laws in particular, being an important site for antiwar work. Despite the repeated attempts to diminish the potency of FOIA by successive regimes, before and certainly after 9/11—through amendments to the law, normalization of national security emergency, and the improper use of FOIA exemptions—the redacted document has emerged as its own cultural form. Even with the ebb of the radical social movements dedicated to transparency, new forms of aesthetic intervention and reading practices have taken hold. FOIA as a law has become technically precise and in practice requires savvy lawyers to navigate government obfuscations. Yet in the same moment, released documents have come into public view: as black-and-white patterns, negative space and text, both familiar and unexpected, floating signifiers in an increasingly networked image world.

A POSTSCRIPT (2024)

I began writing this chapter during a period in which lawyers, writers, and activists were still scrambling to declassify and obtain information about the torture program, whereby the ability to apprehend GTMO from the standpoint of its victims was entirely circumscribed within a redacted aesthetic, determined in totality by classified archive. Over a decade later, documents continue to come to light that illuminate the experience of detainees and the character of the program. In 2023, Abu Zubaydah, his lawyer Mark Denbeaux, and clinical psychiatrist Jess Ghannam copublished a report detailing the conditions of his detention.[64] A collection of Zubaydah's personal artwork depicting his experience of being tortured accompanied the work, and the index included each image with a first-person description of what was being shown. These forty illustrations, which I will not reproduce here, are harrowing. Zubaydah draws himself in varying states of torture or duress; his naked body forced into stress positions, subjected to sexual torture, water torture, and sensorial torture. Nearly all the pictures are drawn in black pen, accented most commonly with blue and red pen and, occasionally, what seem to be markers or highlighter: art instruments of the imprisoned. Many images directly illustrate the conditions of torture that were legally sanctioned in the Torture Memos. In several, Zubaydah drew himself naked confined inside a box, illustrated with stark linear hatches that emphasize personal terror of the imprisonment. To show abuse—slaps, slams, and baton hits—he draws on a comic lexicon, using effect lines to animate the viscerality of the blows. Giant insects surround him in another image, surreal yet anatomically correct, pen marks emphasizing their sting.

The drawings are horrifying both for their realism and in their creative, expressive language; his accompanying description of them give voices to a terror that for decades has otherwise only dwelled in the opacity of redaction. Along with other testimony that emerges from prisoners, these documents will surely form a powerful part of the torture archive. As the authors note, "Not only are these drawings a powerful testament to what the CIA and FBI did in the wake of 9/11, they are the only evidence now [as the] CIA destroyed the only video evidence of detainee torture."[65] To this point, despite the surreal elements in the drawings that represent the visceral and sensorial horror of torture, illustrated faces of the FBI and CIA interrogators were redacted from the drawings, deemed too realistic by the government.[66] Instead, standing over Abu Zubaydah's naked portraits, figures drawn with meticulous details such as wrinkle marks and pockets on their clothes, have the all-too-familiar black boxes covering their faces. I end here with this final thought: The fact of redaction, even in the release of this important material, draws us back to the very visual conditions that materially structure confinement.

In my work since 2016 that draws on the FBI file amassed on my father when he was a Black Panther, I realized how pink and glitter could be used like a kryptonite, or weapon, against J. Edgar Hoover and this whole surveillance system. Pink seemed even more defiant than scribbling on documents or ripping them up.
—SADIE BARNETTE, "Across Space and Time"

On January 20, 2017, the day of Donald Trump's first presidential inauguration, I found myself wandering through the Oakland Museum of California. The day was marked by protests and a sense of despair, and I found myself in the company of dozens of others who, like me, had come for the exhibition on view, *All Power to the People: The Black Panther Party at 50*. The exhibition showcased both historically significant material from the Black Panther Party as well as art inspired by their work. In what euphemistically has been called "the *new* Oakland," longtime residents have fought to counter the remaking of the city by the influx of tech money, real estate developers, and an expanded policing apparatus. *All Power to the People* was, like similar efforts, an insistence on the political and social histories that the city and region holds. Entering the exhibit hall, we encountered a sculptural replica of the wicker chair that Huey Newton posed with for his famous portrait taken in 1968. The exhibition also featured a large wall installation of the Black Panther Party's ten-point program, a library of their publications, historic photographs, and other paraphernalia related to the organization.

Wrapping around toward the end of the exhibition, I walked into a corner covered from ceiling to wall with redacted FBI documents, deliberately stained with spray paint, glitter, and gemstones, all pink and black. A vintage security camera appeared to be watching me from above. Peering at the documents that were arranged on the wall, between the blacked-out lines and glitter, bits of a story emerged. A framed family photograph was fastened to the wall, next to an ironically and subversively enlarged image of a letter signature: "Very Truly Yours, J. Edgar Hoover." Fragmented parts of Rodney Barnette's surveillance file, lovingly arranged by his daughter, artist Sadie Barnette, as an intimate and subjective encounter with the security state. Barnette began working with these documents in her art after she and her father used FOIA to obtain his file, as ways to grapple with the intrusion of the FBI into her family history as well as the broader impact of surveillance on Black communities in America. Together Barnett's family pored through the documents delivered on a CD. In her exhibition at UC Davis titled *Dear 1968, . . .* , she installed the redacted works along with personal photographs from her family archive. Barnette created a piece specifically for the show that reads in italic and serif fonts, "Dear 1968, Love, 1984," a juxtaposition of memories of that moment with the conditions which made her future self (born in 1984) possible.[1] On first look, the piece seems to be a monochrome print, a graphic design utilizing font and color-blocking in black-and-white to visually reference the contrasts of redaction. But on closer look, the piece is actually a graphite drawing, the letters drawn by hand, and the shading a meticulous cross-hatching rendered with pencil. As an introduction to the show and thematic centerpiece, the work subverts the apparent objective facticity of print with the subjective, the human, and the handmade. Throughout her ongoing *FBI Project* (2016–), she deploys color inversions, shine, and symbols of femme life to assert a new relation to the redacted material, reproducing them in a variety of installation spaces, and through a variety of media. In a powdered graphite piece from 2020, she reproduces a terse surveillance memo about a copy of the Black Panther Party newsletter, inverted in black and bursting with outlines of Hello Kitty.

Barnette's work with her father's FBI file sits within a growing body of visual and installation art grappling with the aesthetic dimensions of the US security archive, past and present. Coinciding with both the beginnings of the War on Terror and the inauguration of the digital age, numerous art projects have proliferated that attend to the increased circulations of redacted documents within

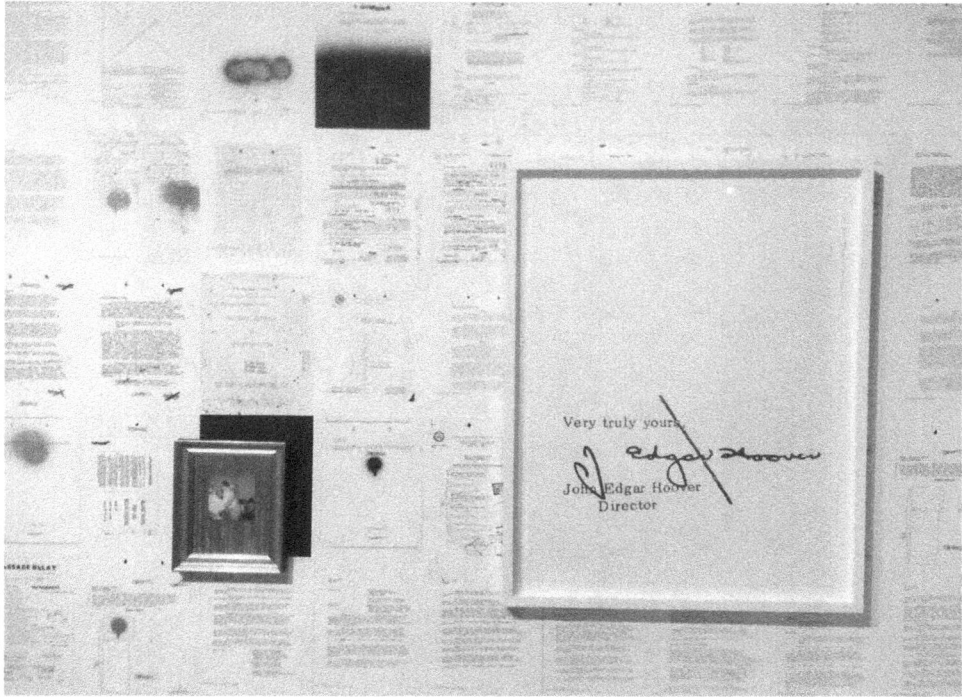

4.1 The author's encounter, on the day of President Donald Trump's inauguration in 2017, with Sadie Barnette's FBI drawings, installed for the *Black Panther Party at 50* exhibition at the Oakland Museum of California. Photo courtesy of Esmat Elhalaby.

the public sphere. As I argue in chapter 3, the experience of looking at redaction inherently conjures the contrapuntal; the viewer must reckon with the existence of attendant, hidden, accompaniment to the official story. Redaction can point to, or make available, the limitations of the official archive, created to uphold, proliferate, justify, or sustain imperial bureaucracy. For this reason alone, they lend themselves intuitively to artistic applications. My turn to art in this final chapter emerges from what I see as an inherent, and maybe even inescapable, entanglement between the security archive and creative processes. That is to say, the bloat of the security archive has produced reams of declassified files; how could they not be incorporated as found objects in art? Artists make work using

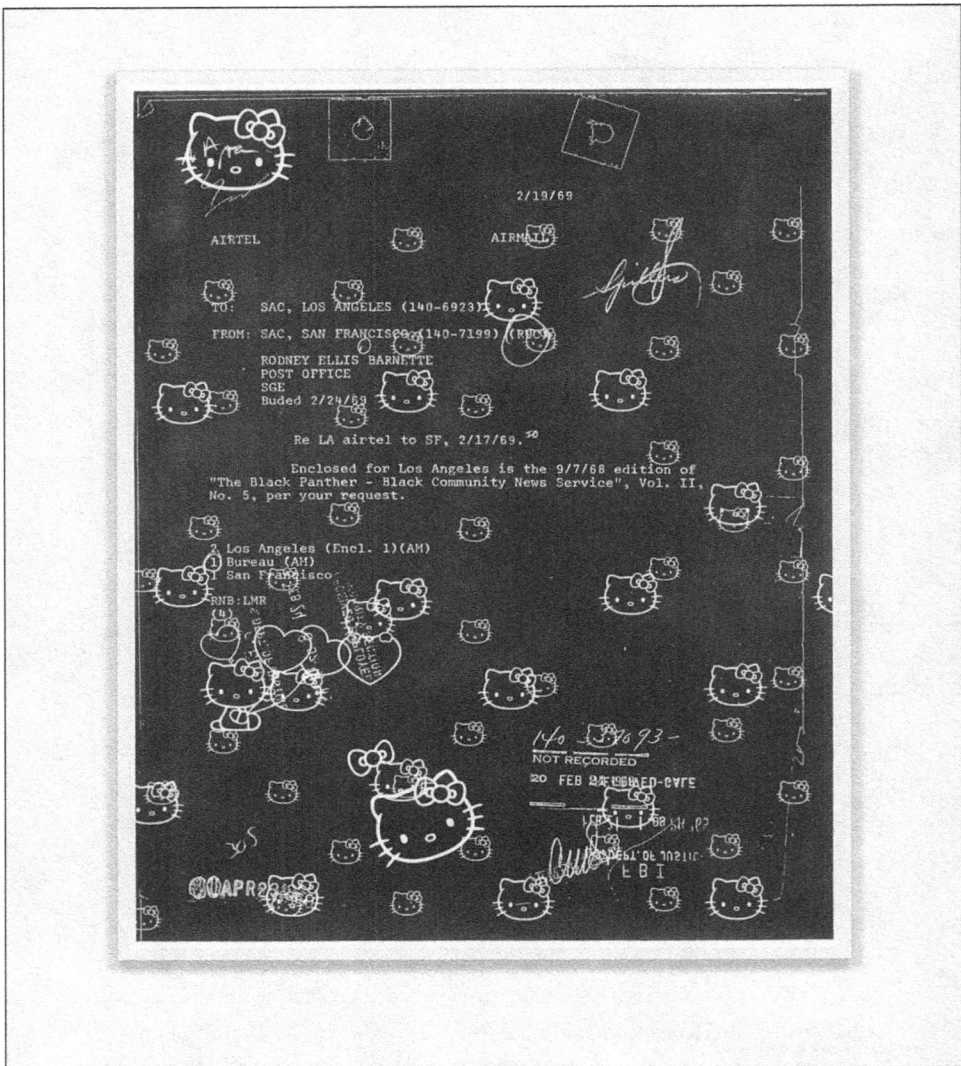

4.2 Sadie Barnette, *FBI Drawings: Black Community News*, 2020, powdered graphite on paper, 114.3 × 91.4 cm.

the material around them; but of course, endlessly proliferating, visually striking, and emotionally resonant papers *readymade*, as it were, for visual consumption, would find new life in the hands of artists. Following the cultural history
of freedom of information and the militarized histories that make it meaningful
leads us invariably to art, to people constructing meaning out of the papers that
have shaped and destroyed so many lives[2] and in these creative manipulations,
we find a wrestling with the secrecy/transparency dialectic, but with a possibility that refuses the terms of the dialectic as binary.

Art can interrupt a facile view that transparency is always already a just cause,
but also dually invite us to think about that which exists through and beyond
the possibilities of opacity. Through art we might be invited to think about the
politics of looking, our desires from the documents, and, most importantly, the
meaning of these documents for the human condition under imperialism. In
the interaction between the classified/declassified, other meanings, reckonings,
conversations can spring to life, though this too is not guaranteed. Artists can
use the visual relationships between text and paper, black print and white material, obscured codes and the multiple authors on a redacted page (writers of text,
redactors of words, stampers of classification), and the technically distinct kinds
of redactions (the hand-drawn blackouts, computer-generated white-fill boxes,
the completely blacked-out lines or paragraphs that might render on special-
ized software). These are all elements that can be played with for visual artists,
alongside other techniques. Performance, literary, and multimedia audiences
also work with the idea of aural erasure in their work.

The sheer number of artists working with this material is striking, as are
the varied artistic outputs. While close readings of redacted art can be independently intriguing, my purpose here is not to engage in a close reading; inadvertently, such work can get lost in the singularity of the artist's intervention or
the dramatic aesthetic appearance of the work, at the expense of thinking struc-
turally about the proliferation of security bureaucracy and the politics of transparency. There is a limit to how much can be said about redacted art individually
without engaging a history of paperwork. Instead, I offer a partial inventory of
redacted art to underscore the widespread cultural traction of the form and to
highlight how artists are drawn to—and repurpose—redaction for radically different purposes. Can this panoramic view of artistic interventions help us think
about the broader possibilities of viewing, engaging with, and repurposing archives of violence? The papers of power? Though varied in approach, style, and

medium, crudely, there are two ways artists utilize these found objects: first, to criticize the failures of US liberalism and democratic aspirations; and second, and more powerfully in my view, to grapple with intimate and community histories and legacies of violence.

REDACTION AS A FLOATING SIGNIFIER

Redacted documents, particularly those that are completely blacked out, bear an uncanny similarity to the works produced during the abstract expressionist art movement that took hold in a Cold War America.[3] The visual resonance with Mark Rothko's work in particular is striking, specifically his paintings from the mid-1940s, many of which were painted on vertically oriented canvases. Large boxes of one color—"color fields," as they came to be known—were modulated in tone and arranged straight on top of each other and against colored backgrounds. The visual effect is nearly identical to the arrangements of redacted spaces on a completely censored page, though of course these paintings predated FOIA and the circulation of redacted documents in a meaningful way. Art historian Anna Chave notes, "Rothko's pictures are often said to be comprised as sheets of color, a term suggesting flat and uniform surfaces, but closer study reveals modulation of color and a varied surface. More apt is the (also commonly used) term *veils*, evoking a quality of transparency as a sense of things only partially apprehended through an intervening screen."[4] What can be said of this connection?

In his work on the origins of abstract expressionism, Serge Guilbaut reconnects the emergence of the form to the early politics of the Cold War. Guilbaut reveals how that the abstract expressionists like Rothko, Jackson Pollack, and others took expressly apolitical stances as the US government weaponized their work in the service of building postwar American cultural hegemony.[5] Continued controversy around the role of the CIA itself in promoting the abstract expressionists remains. Frances Stoner Saunders and others working on the "cultural Cold War" have revealed how the US government promoted abstract expressionism and other styles of art and writing as foil to the political scripts of Soviet and communist art worldwide. This cultural flex of soft power was meant to emphasize the freedom and individuality of the artist and their effort to push the edges of the avant-garde.[6] Some have attributed the artist Ad Reinhardt's exclusion from the US-government-funded export of American modern art to his explicit left politics and allyship with socialism and communism.[7] Reinhardt's post–World War II contributions to abstract expressionism, particularly his late "Black Paintings" (1955–67), all-black canvases that explored the contour of color and monochromatism, bore a striking resemblance to the work of Rothko, with whom he was at times in contention.[8] Yet even apart from the government promotion of abstract expressionists in the trenches of the cultural Cold War, art historians link to their disavowal of figurative art with the magnitude of atomic warfare and the inexpressibility of nuclear devastation. As Guilbaut succinctly notes, "In order to speak to horror without accepting it, some artists experimented with an abstract idiom."[9] To wit, what we now understand as a redacted aesthetic is tethered inescapably to a postwar militarized cultural and political landscape, the emotional horror of a nuclearized planet, and splitting of the world in three.[10]

Far more than the mere doppelgänger of modern art, the redacted document springs forth from similar tensions around the politics of imperial visuality, secrecy, and transparency that defined the latter and its viewing publics. Redaction art conjures Cold War America, and the art of redaction summons a longer history of militarized prohibitions around information access. Visual artist Arnold Mesches's series of paintings *The FBI Files*, completed between 2000 and 2003 and based on his own FBI file, clarifies these connective threads.[11] In 1999, Mesches, who had in his youth been associated with the Communist Party and whose work continued to make social commentary throughout his career, had received the nearly eight-hundred-page file, based on surveillance from 1945 to 1972 inaugurated during the Second Red Scare.[12] Notably, the work began before the events up September 11, 2001, but continued through the beginnings of the War on Terror, and in the years after former intelligence analyst Edward Snowden revealed that the National Security Agency had been spying on Americans, Mesches wrote in to *Cultural Politics* to connect the new disclosures with his work on his own Cold War surveillance.[13] The works, drawing from the detritus of Cold War filing cabinets, found meaning publicly in the unfolding War on Terror. Further, even as he received the documents at the turn of the millennium, it was the work of the abstract expressionist movement— one that Mesches had himself lived through—they conjured. Mesches wrote that the redacted papers reminded him of Franz Kline, whose large black-and-white paintings were distinctive in their composition. Kline's broad, black brushstrokes had movement in them; they were not boxy or modular like those of Rothko but, rather, burst forth against large white canvases with angular, off-kilter movements of the painter himself. "The sheer aesthetic beauty of the pages themselves," Mesches remarked, "the bold, black, slashing, eradicating strokes—looked like Franz Kline's color sketches, with the typewriter's words peeking through."[14] Mesches's reference to Kline's work in particular indexes a moment in the history of redaction in which the censorship marks were themselves likely done by hand. Unlike the declassified documents released at the height of the War on Terror and beyond, which typically have been rendered in software, what Mesches was seeing and responding to was the movement of the censor's hand on paper.

The counterhistories of FOIA that made possible these artistic interventions are inextricable from the stories they now tell. This book has brought forth the visual dialectics that have characterized postwar discussions of American transparency. These discussions—though not reducible to machinery—are inextricable from the technologies that facilitate them and the visual ideologies that mediate them. The dialectic between secrecy and transparency during the Cold War that I catalogue in chapters 1 and 2 is possible only through the technology of xerographic paper reproduction and responds to the advent of nuclear technology. Edward Shils, John Moss, and Daniel Patrick Moynihan were collectively concerned with forms of American liberalism that might be imperiled by the restrictions on sight that had emerged through paper classification. They argued not against visual regulation but for a rational, enlightened form of circulation that balanced America's growing imperial endeavors with its purportedly liberal foundations.

While interrelated, the different landscapes they map reveal distinct but sometimes overlapping political terrain. Many creative approaches to redacted documents highlighted the relationships between document and government process: a "paper trail" approach. These works use the document deliberately and purposefully to stage an investigation or encounter for the viewer that provide evidence of some kind. For instance, artist Edmund Clark and researcher Crofton Black's Magnum Foundation art book *Negative Publicity: Artefacts of Extraordinary Rendition* juxtaposes redacted torture documents with varying kinds of ephemera, photographs, and descriptions of the torture program.[15] Clark and Black's project resonates with that of artist and scholar Trevor Paglen. Paglen's voluminous body of work focuses on the production of detention's geography through paper, the uneven circulations of such papers, and the artistic challenge of attempting to see that which is concealed or obscured by the scopic regime. For instance Paglen's *Signs Unseen* (2018–19) exhibition at the Smithsonian included both photographic material attempting to index the limit of military secrecy (bases blacked out on a map, but photographed from afar, military satellites imaged in orbit), but also works that used declassified documents and materials as part of his craft.[16] Redacted papers, in these works, are part of a story of sleuthing and sifting through fragments of documentary evidence.

Ian Allen Paul's fictive website *Guantánamo Bay Museum of Art and History*, first posted online in 2012, imagines an alternative history and future in which the naval base and prison have been decommissioned in 2010 and repurposed as a site of memory. Paul invited artists to create work from within the diegetic space of the museum, many of which drew from documentary material from Guantánamo. One work in Paul's fictive museum is Jon Kuzmich's *Interrogation of al Qaeda Operative*, a three-minute-long video exploration of previously classified materials from Canadian child detainee Omar Khadr's redacted file. Steve Mumford's watercolor series from Guantánamo Bay (2013) presents another approach to the issue of censorship and visual restriction in GTMO. These works, painted at the base itself, stayed within the convention of landscape watercolors and portrayed the interaction between nature and the militarized built environment on the base. While creating the pieces on site, though Mumford was allowed to see certain areas, he was not allowed to paint them; his watercolors are thus punctuated with spots left entirely blank on which he writes "classified." The negative space conjures a spectacle of redaction.[17] Unlike other works with redacted materials, Mumford's situates classification into the literal landscape that is restructured from public view.

Another approach to working with classification and visual regulations on sight was taken up by L. M. Bogad, author of *Cointelshow: A Patriot Act*, a play performed and ultimately published by Oakland's PM Press. The one-person, one-act performance features a fictional FBI bureaucrat, "Chris White," giving a "friendly" lecture on COINTELPRO at a community event. White interacts with the audience, narrating a crooked history counterintelligence made palatable, alongside a slideshow of redacted documents. Halfway into the show, White's character begins to receive mysterious letters from his rebelling left brain, and he reads them out loud to the audience. A covert Cold War between the two halves of his mind ensues. "The left brain is unreliable," the right brain writes, "it will betray us and think secret thoughts. The audience will hear all your classified information. . . . You must silence the left brain by any means necessary." Bogad's piece was written in response to his encounter in the 1990s with redacted FOIA documents detailing COINTELPRO, which prompted him to contemplate the disturbing histories of domestic counterinsurgency and the implications of this history for the present. In the introduction to the play, Bogad writes that despite encountering absurd and bizarre counterintelligence stories while initially reading the documents, "I didn't decide to write the play until I discovered a document that was *completely* censored, *completely* blacked out, *eradi-redacted*, before being released in the name of 'freedom of information.'" He has performed this show as a living, evolving piece since then, as it took on a new character in the wake of the 9/11 attacks and the subsequent implementation of draconian legislation like the Patriot Act. The pamphlet form of the play, published first in 2011 and then again in 2017, contains reflections on the continuities between domestic practices of spying, disinformation, and infiltration during the 1960s and 1970s and the post-9/11 moment through the Trump era. Bogad's retelling of his encounter with the redacted document speaks to the broad intrigue of redacted documents as raw material for art: "What was under those redaction marks? What if we could get a tour of that underworld, of that haunted space, seemingly empty but in fact filled with the ghosts of repression, the shades of resistance?"[18]

Some cultural workers play with aurality and performance of redaction in staged readings of declassified texts. PEN America and the ACLU collaborated on a performance project called "Reckoning with Torture" that debuted at Cooper Union in 2009; half a dozen actors, writers, and lawyers read declassified Torture Memos to a ticketed public audience at the theater. During the readings, Jenny Holzer's *Redaction Paintings* provided background visuals on a display loop, underscoring the relationship between the redacted looks and experience of hearing the word *redacted* read out loud. An ongoing project of public performance grew out of the event, and a script assembled from different government documents was made available online via ReckoningwithTorture.com to parties interested in staging their own readings. Director Doug Liman from the *Bourne Supremacy* series signed on to direct an interactive documentary of the project, driven by personal uploads of recordings and ones taken at ACLU-sponsored events. Ultimately, despite some media fanfare and a multicity tour, the project did not take off, and as of publication of this book the "Reckoning with Torture" website and Twitter handle were online but had been inactive since 2014. However, this style of performative and sober readings of redacted texts has been taken up in other contexts, notably in response to a heavily redacted version of the "Investigation into Russian Interference in the 2016 Presidential Election," authored by Robert Mueller, being made public. The "Mueller Report," as it came to be known, prompted a new crop of artists to take interest in redaction as a subject of painting and drawing, as well as new staged readings of redacted texts with public figures.[19]

My brief accounting here notes both the broad utilization of censored material in art and the profoundly different meanings of these works to artists and their communities. As I have suggested, these artists and their viewing publics differ greatly in their investments in what such documents might mean for understandings of state violence. As a floating signifier, redaction can conjure the contrapuntal, but in the artists' hands can determine whether this powerful raw material will transform into politically significant work or that which is aesthetically pleasing but intellectually empty. To explore the latter example, I turn to the best-known artist working with these materials: the conceptual artist Jenny Holzer. Holzer, a white American artist who began silk-screening reproductions of redacted documents onto linen canvases, inaugurating what she termed "Redaction Paintings," in 2005 in the midst of public outcry about the censoring of RDI program documents.[20] Holzer, as an already established artist, was among the first to work with these materials during the War on Terror. As such, her art has been widely written about and exhibited. Holzer called attention to the spectacle of nonsight, often partnering with different civil liberty and information access organizations to bring attention to the issue of secrecy and diminished civil rights. Early in her career, she had admired Rothko, Reinhardt, and the abstract expressionist movement, but after being unable to emulate their work well (by her own admission), she moved on to other kinds of artistic experiments.[21] In some ways, her *Redaction Paintings* might be understood as a turn back to these early interests, but imbued with social commentary that the best-known abstract expressionists fastidiously avoided. Holzer's oeuvre remains the most recognizable and lauded within the world of redaction art. For instance, Joshua Craze argued that "Holzer turns words into images so we can read them, as if for the first time."[22] She partnered with the ACLU and the National Security Archive, and her art has been circulated in conjunction with many civil liberties events.

Yet for all the ways in which Holzer has been summoned in critical spaces, it is unclear that her art does more than riff on the contrapuntal aesthetics already present in the documents themselves. Drawing from Pamela M. Lee, for artists like Holzer, "visualizing redaction amounts to monumentalizing such censorial gestures, escalating and exposing them to the clear light of day as representation."[23] Unlike other artists working with redacted materials, Holzer's materials bear no trace of what these documents mean for the subjects they represent or the lives they destroyed. Her engagement with redacted documents presents a one-dimensional view of foreign policy, a simple reversal that in Craze's laudatory words "take a position inverse to that of the US government, which asserts that these documents are nothing but content."[24] I understand the sentiment and the desire to read a deeper analysis into these visually striking works that hung at the Whitney, the Guggenheim, and the Tate. But the materials become self-referential, dwelling in the spectacle of redaction and the affective responses they provoke rather than the material, social, lived histories of people and places they describe. Despite their abstraction and interpretive possibility (which, arguably, can be attributed more to the documents themselves than her engagement with them), the tragedy that emerges in Holzer's work is inescapably that of censorship and accountability, a lamenting of the absence of sight. The paintings primarily replicate the ambiguity in the documents themselves, and as such inadvertently lend themselves to the simple sense that redaction *is* the violence and that a presumably reasonable American viewer should desire the document to be restored.

Holzer's body of work with redaction over the last two decades is now voluminous; she has exhibited around the world and her work has adorned the walls of the most elite art institutions. Several of Holzer's best-known paintings portray redacted handprints; the images reproduce with indexical fidelity a blacked-out silhouette of a hand, each drawing from military documents investigations into detainee abuse that were released only through FOIA cases brought by the ACLU. One such piece is her well-known 2007 work *DODDOACID*, currently held at the National Gallery of Art, gifted to them by the artist along with another handprint painting.[25] The painting is impressively large (58 by 44 inches) and the disembodied, larger-than-life handprint can be read through noncontiguous shapes: imperfect ovals gesture toward fingers, imperfect circles suggest fingertips, a painter's palette shape implies a palm. The disjointed forms hang in negative space, partially framed by redacted document titles and punctuated with a few FOIA exemption codes that would have been added when the original file was being redacted for release. The visual elements, the black-and-white, the painting's size, and the political context summon the kind of contrapuntal aesthetic I have discussed previously. Of course, the spectral, haunting nature of the handprint was present in the original document, which only adds to the uncanny, discordant experience of that indexical bind on canvas. This would have been especially true in the moment of its debut, when people were still gathering information about the kinds of horrors that happened to the people detained by America's post-9/11 wars. And redaction served as an apt visual metaphor for the disappeared, murdered, and maimed. Paradoxically, this is why DODDOACID is such a vexed work. Who has been redacted? Whose handprint haunts us? Contrary to what may appear at first glance, the handprint in question belongs not to a victim of US imperialism but, rather, to one of its foot soldiers. Like many of Holzer's handprint paintings, this image was taken from the files investigating American soldiers who were accused of abuse; this one was drawn from a document about the subject's arrest. The redacted hand does not, in fact, belong to the redacted person. In other words, the viewer beholds an alleged *abuser's* literal imprint, not that of the abused. What is being conjured by the aesthetics and the dire, life-shattering context of American war is so at odds with the existential purpose of the document and the person we encounter in this form. This visual slippage raises important questions about the ways redaction can visually signal, and the politics that animate the work.

In a sense, Holzer's work emerges from a similar kind of crisis of transparency articulated by earlier advocates like Congressman John Moss and the journalists of the right-to-know movement, discussed earlier in this text, who were unable to reckon with the inherent violence of imperial modernity. The *fact* of redaction is itself a crisis for liberalism, not for the bodies of the tortured nor for their homelands, but rather for the illusion of democracy as transparent and accountable that Western hegemony hinges on. Holzer's support of the Israeli art world underscores this myopia and the disconnect between liberal notions of transparency and radical claims against the violence of the settler colonial state. In 2017, she was the guest of honor at the annual "Women in Art" luncheon hosted by the British Friends of the Art Museums of Israel, during which time she donated art worth $50,000 dollars to support Israeli art programs.[26] The arts in Israel have been well documented as part of a state-sanctioned *hasbara* (public relations) campaign; activists and scholars of the cultural boycott have noted weaponization of the arts in the service of normalization of the occupation, erasure of the Nakba (past and present), and justification of ongoing

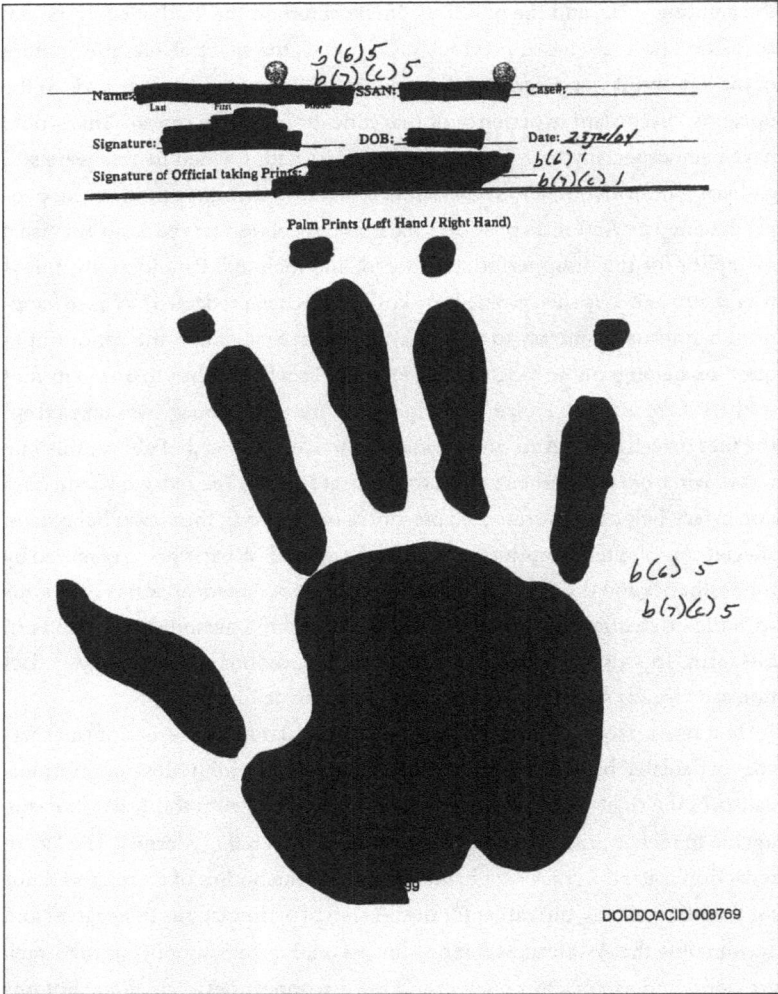

4.3   Jenny Holzer, *DODDOACID*, 2007, oil on linen, 147.32 × 111.76 cm, from the *Redaction Paintings* series.

settler colonialism.[27] Underscoring this point, Holzer contributed DODDOACID to an exhibit curated by Israeli artist Raphie Etgar at the Museum on the Seam. Etgar and the museum occupy the Barmaki house, built by the Palestinian architect Andoni Barmaki, who was expelled with his family during the Nakba, and whose attempts at reclaiming their house have been rebuffed.[28] The museum is a classic example of Israeli "artwashing," the normalization of occupation through the cultivation of an art community. The Museum on the Seam claims to be a site of peace and multiple perspectives yet is one physically premised on the violence of ethnic cleaning, not unlike the Israeli Museum of Tolerance itself, built in Jerusalem on the grounds of the historic Mamilla Cemetery—"a profoundly ironic gesture," in the words of Saree Makdisi.[29] The Etgar exhibition in which Holzer showed her redacted silkscreen was called *The Right to Protest*.[30] In other words, the redacted soldier's handprint, itself an obfuscation, contributed to the liberal obfuscations invoked by calls to "dialogue," which refuse to address the illegal theft of Palestinian land. The function of such protest art within an occupied space is clear. Holzer's characteristic style of obfuscating the absence of critique with provocative aesthetics is well suited to this endeavor.[31] Incidentally, the painting in question is now held by the National Gallery of Art in the United States, gifted by the artist along with several other *Redaction Paintings*. Holzer's transit in the art world only underscores how her *Redaction Paintings*, despite their superficial provocation, are relatively tepid and statementless.

Viewing her work in this broader landscape, it is hard to shake the feeling that her engagement with declassified documents reflects a long-held desire to emulate the work of abstract expressionists more than one to lay bare the violent contradictions of empire (which she admits to in interviews).[32] The work reads especially hollow in comparison with the tender and sensous treatments of redacted materials by artists grappling with the weight of US state violence and the thwarting of anticolonial, antiracist, and anticapitalist dreams.

REDACTION ART AS COMMUNITY RECKONING

Apart from Sadie Barnette's work, the approaches I have detailed thus far, pioneered mostly by white artists, remain enthralled with the dialectic between sight and nonsight at the exclusion of a consideration of the racialized subjects who are at the center of these document's productions and whose racialization hinges on these forms of concealment and disclosure. But many other artists, have vitiated the bureaucratic authority of redacted papers by appending them with representations of the racialized subjects they produce. In the spring of 2019, artist Titus Kaphar and writer/attorney Reginald Dwayne Betts presented *Redaction*, an exhibition of thirty collaboratively authored prints at MoMA PS1 that addressed the personal and subjective within a racist American criminal justice system that imprisons people unable to pay cash bonds. Kaphar and Betts's exhibition included coauthored pieces. As Kaphar drew portraits of these incarcerated individuals, Betts wrote poetry by redacting legal documents related to incarceration, subverting their white authority. Kaphar then screenprinted these onto his drawings, creating haunting documentary portraits on which the archival violence of law is literally suspended.[33] The collaboration between the two artists offered a way to address the subjective and real impact of such documents on the people whose lives they rendered. Together their personal and subjective treatments of the documents called forth the traces and subjects created by and through documents and made clear the stakes of mass incarceration. Both Kaphar and Betts draw inspiration from tradition of Black radical critique rooted in their communities, emerging from activist endeavors alongside "whispered stories of family members and friends." From 2012 to 2013, Rajkamal Kahlon, as artist-in-residence with the ACLU, created *Did You Kiss the Dead Body: Visualizing Absence in the Archive of War*, a project consisting of original visual art, interviews, and text addressing the RDI program and race after 9/11. On autopsy reports, Kahlon drew European anatomical renderings (bodies, faces) and marbled the papers in a Turkish and Iranian style with pale red ink.[34] The dual effect imbued the redacted document with a sense of life it extinguished and the death it detailed, as a contest to the racializing force of paper within imperial statecraft.[35] These fleshy amendments called into question the bureaucratic rendering of violence onto the bodies of Arabs, Africans, and South Asians.[36] Kahlon's project and that of Kaphar and Betts visually conjoin security bureaucracy with the subjects of racialized violence, which makes the victims not just abstract entities but actual persons. As Betts succinctly put it, "We're redacting to reveal."

The look of redaction thus speaks to many artists' desire to address the racial and imperial histories that appear hidden to some but are manifestly visible to others. As a symbolic gesture of document diplomacy, in 2013 the CIA declassified a small number of papers relating to their instrumental role in the coup d'état against Iranian Prime Minister Mohammed Mossadegh that had taken place sixty years earlier, in 1953. The documents affirmed pieces of what was already, in Shiva Balaghi's words, an "open secret" that had been detailed in memoirs of American operatives (accounts that Balaghi described as "rambling recollections of spies") yet remained elusive in official and public accounting.[37] Shortly after the 2013 release, Iranian diasporic artist Bahar Behbahani encountered these documents and began contemplating the intimate participation of Donald Wilber, one of the American operatives named in the release. Wilber's public life was as a scholar of Middle East architecture and appreciator of Persian gardens. Behbahani had encountered his scholarly writings as a student in Iran, as he remains a major figure in the field. The revelation that he participated in the complete subversion of Iranian democracy and played a key role in the coup was an unnerving shock. She delved into both the declassified files and Wilber's life, creating large abstract paintings with laborious applications of modulated color to consider the interplay between memory and historical record. She then applied blocks of black paint that conjured the redacted spaces of Wilber's report to the CIA: "The feeling that I had, what he [Wilber] or Americans or British, did to the culture, they redacted the most beautiful part. So I can redact my own paintings, I worked 12 hours, 24 hours on just one inch of the painting, and it's hard to redact yourself. And I wanted to really feel that."[38]

Her project culminated in the *Garden Coup* series. Behbahani's works are haunting and visually referencing abstract art traditions in the same breath as poetic, architectural, and fine arts traditions of Iran, and bursting forth from clandestine memories of the American coup. These large and visually striking mixed-media pieces present another visual approach to reconciling ideas and images of state violence. Behbahani produced these pieces both in opposition to the shadow life of Wilber's scholarship as well as in conversation with Balaghi's writings on the incomplete declassification of the Iran coup files. Within this oeuvre, the Persian garden becomes both physical and allegorical site for Iranian political history as it references the strange interplay between Wilber's public life as an appreciator of garden landscapes and his covert life within the CIA. As Balaghi writes, "Bahar's occupation with the history of Persian gardens is not so much to do with documentation but with the evocation of something intangible, an attempt to capture something deeply personal, something chimeric."[39] At two solo exhibitions of the paintings in 2016, Behbahani installed a table in which viewers could read parts of the documents through a sheet of glass that covered the length of the tabletop. The exhibitions invited viewers to interact with and call into question the documents as evidence of this open secret. At the Moscow Biennale, Behbahani's paintings were accompanied by seven tables of graduated height atop which the documents emerge from Russian soil, partially covered and drawn on by the artist. These installations underscore the materiality of documents as artifacts, forensically bound to both the shadow state and the landscapes (political and national) that they secretly shaped.

Several other exhibitions remain notable for their display of redacted documents, redacted art, and materials that riff on the dialectic between secrecy and publicity. Like Behbahani's table, others have focused on the interactions between document and viewer/participant, rather than the aesthetic manipulation of the redacted page. Chilean artist Voluspa Jarpa's work is particularly notable in this regard. Since 2010 she has been producing artworks based on the heavily redacted documents the US government released in 1998 that detailed their clandestine interference in Latin American affairs. In her 2016 exhibition, *En nuestra pequeña región de por acá*, scrolls of American government documents dangled down as streamers from the towering ceilings of the Museum of Latin American Art in Buenos Aires. These hundreds of papers, censored with clean, modernist redaction marks, were culled from the declassified archives of Operation Condor and installed by her to highlight the documentary terms of America's brutal intervention in Latin America. Jarpa's work might be understood as a counterpoint to the kind of document diplomacy I discuss previously as a way of public reckoning with US imperial documents. In a similar vein, multimedia artists Mariam Ghani and Chitra Ganesh have had an ongoing collaboration since 2004: *Index of the Disappeared*, a Brooklyn-based archival project investigating and reckoning with the US security state's disappearing of South Asian and Arab persons in the aftermath of 9/11. The project utilizes publicly released government documents, some of which have been creatively manipulated by Ghani and Ganesh. The artists see the censored information as "not flaws in the archive but, rather, the key to its organization," playing with the contrapuntal aesthetic of the redacted pages, and foreground the experience of immigrant and radicalized communities in their artistic vision.[40] Much of the scholarship on Ghani and Ganesh's collaboration has focused on the way they engage multiple media: manipulating redacted documents, creating an alternate questionnaire framing the encounter with the security state, staging archival encounters with redacted documents, creating watercolor portraits, and more.[41] Rather than the release of papers being a point of catharsis or closure, for artists like Jarpa and

4.4 Bahar Behbahani, *Consolidating the Plan*, 2015–16, mixed media on canvas, 183 × 137 cm, from the *Garden Coup* series. Photo courtesy of Bahar Behbahani.

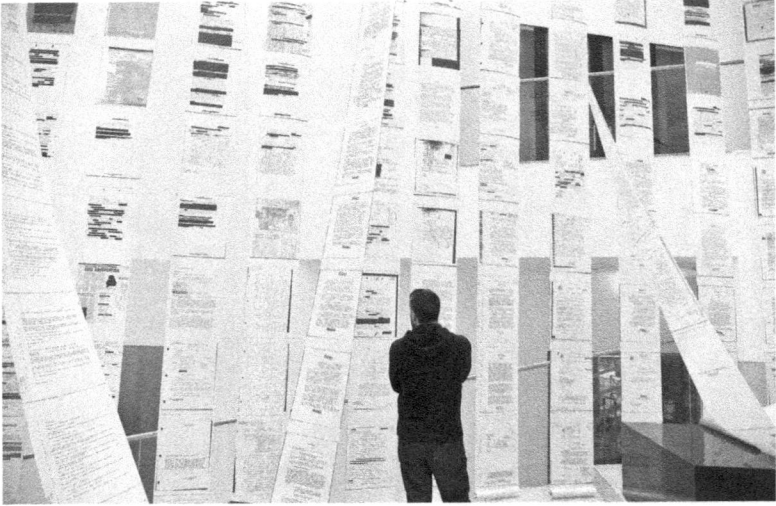

4.5   Voluspa Jarpa, installation view from *En nuestra pequeña región de por acá*, exhibited at the Museo de Arte Latinoamericano de Buenos Aires, Argentina (2016). Photo courtesy of Voluspa Jarpa.

Ghani and Ganesh, working with redacted materials makes clear the links between and the racialized politics of memory and the papers of imperialism.

Other artists responded to redacted aesthetics across media. Poets experimented with the strange paradoxical lyricism that can emerge from the censored document. Erasure poetry is certainly not singular to the War on Terror context; artists have long experimented with erasure as a kind of found practice, and the form has resonated across and in relation to the spectacular, uncanny presence of redacted material in the public sphere. For instance, several pieces in Solmaz Sharif's volume of poetry *Look* (2016), a compilation of experimental work utilizing and reframing fragments of military prose to meditate on the personal and sensorial dimensions of war, explicitly emerge from government documents. Travis Macdonald published the first volume of *O mission repo* (2008), which was drawn from the 9/11 Commission Report, using and riffing on redaction to craft the work. Though erasure poetry certainly has a longer history, the presence of militarized redacted documents in the post-9/11 public sphere intensified the meaning and circulation. Redaction poetry—or erasure poetry—became far more prevalent and recognizable than it had been in the past, in part because the form allows for a kind of recognition of the violence of the government documents and an interaction of—or intervention of—the poet. In this same period, M. NourbeSe Philip's published *Zong!*, a collection of erasure poetry drawing from the legal record of the 1781 horrific mass-murder-by-drowning of 142 Africans at sea, perpetrated so the ship's owners could collect insurance money. As Jenny Sharpe argues, *Zong!* powerfully meditates on the silences and erasures within official documentation through its own erasure: "Phillip's experimental poems do not tell a story so much as convey the ghostly presence of lives within a document that treats those lives as immaterial. They summon transported Africans caught between life and death, filled with humanity and also drowning in its negation."[42] In other words, *Zong!*, through poetic experimentation, calls forth the originary and racial violence of the document itself.

Redaction art can behave in multiple ways in multiple spaces, speaking to distinct ideological tensions in each. There is no essential meaning to the juxtaposition between text and the censor's mark. The paratext, context, and site specificity of the artwork shape its interpretation by viewing publics. Even as redaction bears a contrapuntal aesthetic, how artists interpret and make meaning from this visual dialectic can vary widely. Some artists play with the redaction and its visual aesthetics without mention of politics or the visual logic of censorship.[43] For them, redaction becomes a form to play with, a way of riffing on the interplay between different kinds of texts and intertextually. The look of redaction, for some, points to a dialectic between secrecy and publicity that orders a liberal governance; creative manipulations like Holzer's exploit this tension. Her work staunchly centers American liberal governance rather than the victims of America. Another example of this orientation might be found in the aforementioned reactions to the redacted Mueller Report. The fixation on Trumpism suggested the politics of corruption were exceptional, latently undergirding a myth of American democracy. These narrative orientations might best be characterized as an American contortionism that transposes victimhood from the brutalized onto the state itself: The victims of America are not the wounded, maimed, or dead in this frame; rather, America is its own victim. In this anamorphic mirror of liberal white supremacy, an incomprehensible emphasis emerges as reflection: Redaction aesthetics are deployed for patriotic ends.

But, more interestingly, for other artists, working with redaction becomes a way of reckoning with the documentation that destroyed an anti-imperialist movement, disappeared loved ones, or subjected their communities to violence. For these artists, the spectacle of redacted documents does not spark a myopic crisis of American values, but instead makes visualizable the grist of imperial and racial violence that has ravaged so many communities. It is these latter works that I find arresting and revelatory in their refusal of the racializing logic of statecraft. Jarpa and Barnette begin from the facticity of American counterinsurgency, and consider the relationships oddly mapped and tragically negated through these documents. For instance, in Bett's and Behbahani's respective explorations of redacting-to-reveal and redacting-to-reenact-state-violence, we see the gesture toward the social and subaltern histories that are shaped by paper archives but remain nonetheless negated through them. These explorations do not diverge; rather, they similarly map a landscape in which Americans can simultaneously conceal and reveal, neither confirm nor deny, both create and destroy.

Intimate treatments of paper reveal how contours of life are both shaped through and described within the files of a security bureaucracy. They gesture toward living with disappearances and through disappearance. They conjure the shadowy tragedies of the carceral geography; the affect of living with and through coups and dictatorships; the brutal totalities of the police state; the artless masculinity of a machine gun; the shadowy presence of the agent provocateur; the senseless murder of a rising revolutionary; the creep of ethnonationalism; the forever absence of beloveds; the sensual experience of what Naomi Klein calls "the shock doctrine." In contrast to liberal Americanist redaction art, in these productions the dueling juxtapositions of black-and-white—the censored and uncensored—evokes an intimate reckoning with mass violence and government suppression, not a crisis of American consciousness. In other words, the difference might be distilled into that between art that regards the pain of others (to summon the conceptual work of Susan Sontag), and art that emerges from the wound itself; on one hand a meditation on the paradoxical impasses of *representation* in translating violence to privileged populations living at a distance, and on the other, the urgency of mobilizing any and all remnant objects, aesthetics, and symbols to sketch the violence of the state.

As I detail in previous chapters, the desire for transparency is vexed, slippery, and politically contingent on its relation to power. On the one hand, liberal notions of transparency are a ruse, promising an endlessly deferred notion of citizenship predicated on the continuation of the imperial. On the other, wrestling with the declassified archive—and struggling for declassification—can be an intervention in the racial state, a form of countersurveillance as radical transparency activism. Art and community-based practices of looking back provide yet another model for what it means to think about radical entanglements with archives of surveillance and violence. Algerian American journalist and filmmaker Assia Boundaoui's work grapples with what it means to bring formerly secret documents into the public sphere, exemplifying what I've argued throughout the book: Declassification is most meaningful when reconciled within a movement or community frame. Across both her documentary film *The Feeling of Being Watched* (2019) and an in-progress *Inverse Surveillance Project*, Boundaoui worked to excavate volumes of files that the FBI produced while they surveilled her community in suburban Chicago. *The Feeling of Being Watched* chronicles a yearslong FBI surveillance operation of her tight-knit, predominantly Arab and Muslim neighborhood in Bridgewood, Illinois. The film might be characterized as both autoethnography and an ethnography of the state; Boundaoui's first-person account highlights intimate and personal repercussions of FBI's racialized spycraft, while the film's critique of surveillance as both bureaucratic and muscular points to more structural questions. The piece documents the convoluted process of trying to obtain the records using the Freedom of Information Act and to account for the experience of living under the shadowy presence of the state.

In 2016, Boundaoui used FOIA to request files from Operation Vulgar Betrayal —an FBI witch hunt inaugurated in the 1990s that attempted to connect finance of "terrorism" with her community and their participation in charity and fundraising work.[44] The film begins with her recounting significant moments in her childhood framed by encounters with the surveillance state, including chilling but mundane recollections of intelligence-gathering in her community and the arrest of her downstairs neighbor Mohammad Salah, a Palestinian American. She narrates how in the early 1990s, while on a humanitarian visit to Palestine,

Salah was arrested, tortured by the Shin Bet, and forced to sign a false confession in Hebrew, a language he could not read, testifying to being a financier and Hamas leader. He was imprisoned for five years; on his return to the United States and to his community in Bridgeview, the FBI used the false confession to initiate Operation Vulgar Betrayal. In the United States, Salah was acquitted of all charges based on this investigation, but his case was the pretext for the surveillance of Boundaoui's community, and the reason for a constant presence of the FBI in their community. Furthermore, the film offers a lawyers' view that the case's implications were wide-ranging and created a broader pretext to criminalize the Palestinian resistance movement in the United States.[45]

In *The Feeling of Being Watched*, at every turn a subjective encounter with paper, documentation, and surveillance frames the story Boundaoui tells. Instead of simply narrating the surveillance of her community, we are drawn into the process of unraveling years of memories and trauma alongside the quest to declassify and unredact the whole Operation Vulgar Betrayal file. These scenes draw us into the intimacy of the story. She clicks through the FBI digital vault of released documents, she scans the microfilm of old papers covering the FBI investigating her community, the printer spits out the declassified documents, she scrolls the online FOIA request portal hunched over her laptop, she rips open the envelope containing her FOIA denial, her hands handle voluminous stacks of paper, she places documents thoughtfully on the wall. In her telling, the surveillance archive and the struggle for it becomes personal; there is no recounting of her own history or of her community's without the strange, uncanny eye of the state watching them.

Her focus on storytelling and personal encounters with this surveillance state only underscore the subjective, intimate meaning of this FOIA cache and the broader case she files. As she and her family go through the first batch of documents together, close-up shots of shock on their faces and hands on the papers invite us into the *feeling* of being watched. "It's been weird to find things that directly relate to our lives in these very bureaucratic and administrative documents," Boundaoui says. They are looking at documents that detail the FBI's pursuit of Salah and her parents' encounter with the FBI who were watching him. Her sister, a moment later, says, "You see that? That's so creepy!," pointing to a page redacted with a white text box: "It's just like 'blank' has been surveiled."

In some ways, *The Feeling of Being Watched* is a contemporary and fully realized version of what the filmmakers of *The Intelligence Network* were hoping to

4.6 In a scene from her film *The Feeling of Being Watched* (2018), Assia Boundaoui affixes FOIA documents to her wall documenting surveillance of the Arab American community during Operation Vulgar Betrayal.

accomplish. Like that film, Boundaoui's is clearly crafted in an organizing context, meant to galvanize her community around the violence of the surveillance state. After the scene above, Boundaoui gathers her family's signatures for a follow-up FOIA request. At another point, she goes door-to-door with the aim of collecting enough signatures to unredact names in the surveillance file. *The Feeling of Being Watched* thus animates the practice of FOIA and the active process of demanding a certain kind of transparency from the state. In the aftermath of this film, and with the bounty of documents obtained through FOIA, Boundaoui conceived of a community cocreation project reckoning with the now-public documents. This, the *Inverse Surveillance Project*, was a way for Boundaoui of collectively describing the practices that might look back at the state and making sense of the heavy redactions throughout the archive. In her writings and interviews on the piece, she emphasizes the importance of a collaborative process as a way to create space to collectively reckon, heal, and renarrate.

In the summer of 2022, she and other community members installed a sculptural labyrinth inside a community center in Chicago, which they collaged inside and out with documents from Operation Vulgar Betrayal. Fabric that they'd embroidered collectively in a Palestinian *tatreez* style was hung at the end of this process, in order to shape and reshape the encounter with the surveillance archive. By installing this work in the community, holding art and embroidery workshops in the weeks leading up to it, and being explicit about the destructive weight of the state's eye, the *Inverse Surveillance Project* offered one way of transforming the community's relation to the papers. In an interview on the installation, Boundaoui notes that it picked up where the film left off, as a way to grapple with the question of what it means to "watch back" and "imagine a new narrative in that redacted space."[46] Further, the site specificity of the work and the cocreation process offered a way of experimenting with the redacted spaces and reimagining the question of the archive's rightful owners.

CONCLUSION

Redaction emerges from a Cold War structure of feeling but has taken hold as a legible signifier with the coemergence of the War on Terror and the digital public sphere. There are many kinds of redacted documents, not all of them similarly spectacular. What I submit here is a view of redacted art—and redacted aesthetics —as not simply reflective of tensions, ideologies, or sentiment. Redaction's contrapuntal aesthetic goes beyond the merely representational or semiotic; as a sign it is utterly contingent on the conditions of production that make it legible. In other words, even if the sign (redaction) is delinked from the signified (that which is censored, or, alternatively, state violence), the sign itself is coherent only within a particular media landscape. To draw from Walter Benjamin, the art of manipulating this aesthetic only emerges from a technological adoption of multiple kinds of reproduction, including, first, the xerographic reproduction of the bureaucratic paper that bears on it the labor of those who redacted, and second, the digital censorships and circulations and processes that mark the present. These are works of art in the age of secret reproductions.

The redacted document in its mere existence reflects a number of material and social relations that are relatively new and themselves emerge out of an endlessly proliferating security bureaucracy. This particular artistic approach makes use of the raw materials that have emerged in the postwar era as the fundamental form of the state. Redaction art must be understood in relation to traditions like abstract expressionism, which haunts its visage, and also found object art or readymade art, as modern art movements that drew from and repurposed real-world objects. When these papers are reimagined as art, it is not simply the technique of the censor that constitutes that artistic practice, but the object itself that demands consideration as a specific thing in the world. In that sense, redaction art offers not just a symbolic or a semiotic intervention but one that reflects a papered form of militarism. In other words, redaction art is *inescapable* because it emerges from a readily available archive that is always expanding and creating new surveilled, policed, incarcerated, dominated subjects. Redaction is an aesthetic and a floating signifier, but only because it became so as a technique applied to circulating and securitized objects—papers, whether digital or material. The distinction may appear slight, but I'm drawing attention to the difference between locating the aesthetic narrowly within the representational aims of political art, or more capaciously as built from the raw materials of a militarized surveillant bureaucracy. The aesthetics of redaction spring forth from a logic of circulation and classification coeval with the nuclear era that proliferated within a post-9/11 digitally mediated sphere. In other words, redaction coheres in the public eye only because FOIA, a Cold War technology, compels formerly classified documents into public view in this way.

What I have attempted to do here is to situate these aesthetic practices in a longer history of American imperialism and the emergence of America as global hegemon. The works I've detailed above in varying ways emerge from—and call attention to—the grist of state violence. I have argued that redaction bears a contrapuntal aesthetic, one that betrays the utility ascribed to censorship by the national security state. The art moves us because it responds to a longer genealogy of transparency that we inherit as cultural lookers. In redaction the nationalist specters of Moynihan, Moss, and Shils appear, as do the American exceptionalist ideas that frame what they saw in the blacked-out boxes. But I have also shown how the ghosts of America's victims appear in redacted spaces, endlessly haunting the pages. In redaction we see the impossible, destructive visuality of atomic light and the slow violence that environs nuclear proliferation—communities ravaged by the creeping ruination of their social and material worlds.[47] Through paper censorship we sense the dreams of radical transparency and the feverish memories of unruly break-ins to the FBI. These ideas already animate this art of censorship, its materials, its rhetorics. Experimenting with redaction and the surveillance can itself be a reckoning, an acknowledgment, a way of reimagining. As Sadie Barnette remarks, "In my work since 2016 that draws on the FBI file amassed on my father when he was a Black Panther, I realized how pink and glitter could be used like a kryptonite, or weapon, against J. Edgar Hoover and this whole surveillance system." Her use of elements associated with femme and queer life are deliberate acts of rebellion. She continues, "Pink seemed even more defiant than scribbling on documents or ripping them up."[48] In the hands of Barnette, Jarpa, Behbahani, and scores of other artists working with formerly classified material, a possibility emerges through and beyond transparency.

In the end, documents exceed the instrumentality of their author but tell a story of paper infrastructure and racialized statecraft. The various notations on the declassified documents tell stories of their circulation, the structuring logics of government sights, and, paradoxically, of subaltern survival. We see redacted aesthetics in many places, whether to represent the actions of the security state itself or to vaguely reference the shadowy or the politically authoritarian, as a simple scroll through Netflix might confirm. Not only have redacted aesthetics become more recognizable since the advent of digital technology that allows people to *see* the reproduced redacted document on a screen; I contend that redacted aesthetics might also be understood in the context of state practices of seeing and surveilling that define the contemporary world. Redaction is most interesting not on the walls of great art institutions but, rather in works tethered to places made and unmade in the long history of American imperial endeavor. I've dwelled in the life of redaction because multiple histories and ideas congeal around it. Some have used redacted documents to tell a story of the decline of an American democracy that they believed existed. Others have visually demanded that we must consider documents from the standpoint of their victims, to borrow the oft-cited formulation of Edward Said.[49] What it comes to is this, more or less: Our *modern art* of war emerges because the modern *art of war* hinges on paper. And by reckoning with the haunting of censored frames, the arcana of black boxes, we might also remember that a demilitarized horizon could be just out of view.

I found myself writing and remembering, beyond the boundaries of what I was supposed to be filling in. But it was by doing this, and not trying to confine myself to the government's prescribed blacked-out spaces, that I felt myself recovering the feeling of the original pages.—MOHAMEDOU OULD SLAHI, *Guantánamo Diary: Restored Edition*

Mohamadou Ould Slahi's remarkable writings about his detention without charge in US custody inspired *A Thousand Paper Cuts* in its early stages as a project. I first encountered Slahi's authorial voice in April 2013, when *Slate* published "The Never Before Seen Memoir of a Guantánamo Detainee," a three-part installment of portions of a testimony that Slahi, still imprisoned in GTMO, had written between 2004 and 2005, shortly after being taken into US custody. The works published in *Slate* had been edited for clarity by the writer Larry Siems. Replications of Slahi's handwritten originals, composed as letters to his lawyers, accompanied the *Slate* series as PDFs, with words, phrases, and paragraphs censored in a strange pattern. Readers of the online magazine experienced Slahi's memories through his writing, punctuated cruelly by a heavy-handed redactor's mark. Though some former detainees had published accounts of Guantánamo, none had done so *from* Guantánamo. By that point his prison writings were eight years old, but they were also in the present tense: He was still detained without charge, still erased from the map, interred. I followed Slahi's story closely.

12 ▮

interrogation before the day of around end
of August, "Birth day Party" as ▮ called
it. ▮ brought an apparently Marine who
wore a ▮
▮ I told you, I'm gonna bring some
people to help me interrogate you," said ▮
sitting inches away in front of me. ▮ offered
me a metal chair. The guest sat almost sticking
on my knee. ▮ started to ask me some
question I don't remember "Yes or No?",
shouted the guest loudly beyond belief in a
show to scare me, and maybe to impress ▮
who knows. I found his method very childish
and silly. I looked at him, smiled, and said, "Neither!"
The guest drew the chair from beneath me violently.
I fell on the chains, Oh, it hurt. "Stand up,
Mother fucker" shouted both, almost, synchronous.
Then, a session of torture, and humiliation started.
They started to ask me the questions after they made
me stand up, but it was too late by I told them
million times "whenever you start to torture me, it is
not gonna say a single word". And that was
always accurate, for the rest of the day, they made
exclusively the talk. ▮ turned the conditioning
Air Condition all the way down to bring me to freezing.
This method had been practiced in the camp at least
since Aug 02. I have seen people who were exposed

E.1   Excerpt of Slahi's handwritten memoir, as published by *Slate* on April 30, 2013.

Slahi, a Mauritanian engineer, had been kidnapped from Mauritania in 2001 under the auspices of the US-led War on Terror, on a flimsy accusation of involvement with a plot to blow up the Los Angeles International Airport a few years earlier, prior to 9/11. He was detained in Mauritania and subsequently extraordinarily rendered to Jordan, then to Afghanistan, and finally to GTMO, where he spent fourteen years. While in captivity, he taught himself English and became prolific in his new language.[1] He wrote two novels, penned a self-help book, and drew up a handwritten petition for a writ of habeas corpus, which, while drafted in 2005, wasn't granted until 2010. The habeas petition inaugurated the possibility of a deeper account of his imprisonment, as did the meeting with his lawyers.[2] Once Slahi was given access to lawyers, his chronicle poured out as a series of letters addressed to them; in later writings, he notes that these were intended to be assembled in book form, though it is not clear exactly when this idea took shape.[3] For five years, the letters sat in a secured government storage facility outside Washington, DC, viewable only by his legal team during highly structured visits. Though his lawyers spent years trying to release the documents, it was only by waiving attorney-client privilege—and then waiting more years for further clearance—that the lawyers were able to declassify Slahi's work in 2010.[4] Slahi recorded the details of this letter-writing process:

> In order to avoid suspicion, I divided my writing into sections that looked like long letters to my attorney, keeping the writing small and keeping track of the page numbers, starting each new installment with the next page in the sequence, so the manuscript could be assembled into a book that I dreamed would somehow escape the prison where all of these "privileged" materials lived. Of course I was not smarter than the American censors. The government soon figured out what was happening, and refused to declassify these "letters" the way they declassified poems and letters other detainees wrote.[5]

We should pay particular attention to the form of this account as *letters*, even as they were later collected and published as a widely read but heavily redacted memoir (more on this shortly). Our appraisal of Slahi's story might gain from what Sharon Luk has called "the life of paper," accounting for the way the writing and exchange of letters reveal a tender, sensuous, and ontological dimension of racial capitalism. In thinking about the "epistemological interruptions emanating from imprisoned populations, the pressures they exert at the thresholds of human being, and the aesthetic significance of letters to mediate social move-ment," as Luk does, a social history animating the memoir comes into view.[6] Disappeared within a tropical gulag, a muggy labyrinth of CCTV cameras, con-certina wire, and other molded metals, the letter was a particular medium. Given his conditions in Guantánamo, and the select options to represent himself, le-gally and discursively, Slahi's literary accomplishment is astounding. With just paper and pencil, Slahi wrote himself into the world.

By 2015, after a long battle with the courts, an edited version of the redacted letters would be published as a memoir under the title *Guantánamo Diary* by Little, Brown, even as Slahi was still a prisoner in GTMO, though cleared for re-lease. *Guantánamo Diary* met critical acclaim in book form. Yet the *Guantánamo Diary* memoir was not a simple photographic reproduction of Slahi's handwrit-ten letters. It was not a diary either, or an exact transcription of Slahi's letters into type. Larry Siems, a writer from the PEN USA association who had just finished writing *The Torture Report*, a book-length appraisal of Bush's RDI program and its trail of documents, was procured to edit and help publish the piece. In the introduction to the original memoir he writes, "It has been edited twice: first by the United States government, which added more than 2,500 black-bar redac-tions censoring Mohamedou's text, and then by me." Later he continues, "I have edited the manuscript on two levels. Line by line, this has mostly meant regular-izing verb tenses, word order, and a few awkward locutions, and occasionally, for clarity's sake, consolidating or reordering text. I have also incorporated the ap-pended flashbacks within the main narrative and streamlined the manuscript as a whole, a process that brought a work that was in the neighborhood of 122,000 words to just under 100,000 in this version."[7]

Of particular note is Siem's addition of copious footnotes throughout book, many of them paratextual notes to the redactions, drawing from existing docu-mentation in order to speculate on what lay beneath the censor's mark. Notes were culled from official government documents like the transcripts from Ad-ministrative Review Board hearings, the Schmidt-Furlow Report, and other materials procured through FOIA requests or other litigation. Some of these footnotes give context for Slahi's movements and his detention, but more nota-bly they reflect Siems's attempts to grapple with the redactions in the text. These notes, he writes, represent "speculations that arose in connection with the re-dactions, based on the context in which the redactions appear, information that appears elsewhere in the manuscript, and what is now a wealth of publicly available sources about Mohamedou Ould Slahi's ordeal and about the incidents and events he chronicles here." He goes on to clarify that he is not trying to "uncover classified material" or "reconstruct redacted text" but instead intends to "present information that most plausibly corresponds to the redactions when that information is a matter of public record or evident from a careful reading of the manuscript."[8] The notes foreground the necessity of politically informed interpretive speculation in the reading of the text, as they do the legal infrastructures that literally made the book.

The memoir brought attention to his case, ultimately expediting Slahi's passage back to Mauritania the following year. In 2019, a "restored" version of the memoir was published: After being freed, Mohamadou met and worked collaboratively with Siems to "fill in" the gaps left by the redactor's pen. Slahi writes in his introduction to the restored version, "Often it felt like we were trying to restore a very ancient building." Later he continues, "I found myself writing and remembering, beyond the boundaries of what I was supposed to be filling in. But it was by doing this, and not trying to confine myself to the government's prescribed blacked-out spaces, that I felt myself recovering the feeling of the original pages."[9] *Recovering the feeling of the original pages.* By 2021, the memoir was turned into the action/drama film *The Mauritanian* (starring Jodie Foster), and the book was republished and rebranded under the same name. In the short period after it was declassified, Slahi's work was published as a series of articles, printed as a memoir under three different titles, translated into multiple languages, and turned into a film.

With so many layers of textual, political, and aesthetic meaning, what do we make of *Guantánamo Diary* in its multiple iterations? A number of excellent academic texts have elaborated the textual meanings of redaction and the literary contours of Slahi's work, and the existence of the memoir more broadly. For instance, both Zeinab Mcheimech and Yogita Goyal place the work within a frame of American slave narratives; Eleni Coundouriotis argues for reading it through the lens of postcolonial literary criticism and anti-imperial writing; Elizabeth Swansen and Alexandra Moore suggest that Mikhail Bakhtin's chronotopes allows for a uniquely relevant temporal and spatial analysis; and Erin Trapp argues that the redactions present an "aesthetics of alterity ."[10] And as Rebecca Adelman poignantly notes, the ruse of transparency in cultural productions that emerge from Guantánamo like Slahi's create a fiction of intimacy that is both historically burdened and one-sided.[11] The memoir is a rich and important text that will surely continue to be written about for years to come. I offer something slightly distinct, circling around memoir and through its transit.

My concluding thoughts are simple: Following the paper trail in Slahi's story reveals how the infrastructures of surveillance and militarism make redacted aesthetics relevant in the first place. We can trace these at every juncture: the letters written by hand; the attempts to evade the government's censor; the viewing regulations within the government's holding facility near Washington, DC; the years of litigation to free them. After public release, the letters went through multiple editorial iterations in the hands of others, as two different books (redacted and restored), and found new life rewritten written in a screenplay, and brought to the big screen. In other words, Slahi's story makes sense only through the literal transit, circulation, and reproduction of the pages on which his memoir was written. These pages must be understood through the structural antagonism between oppressed and oppressor. As such, they reveal the workings of paper and power, the way that paper is a material battleground within racial capitalism. Perhaps what Slahi means when he suggests he was *recovering the feeling of the original pages* is more than the repair of a broken narrative; perhaps he is more precisely describing a reencounter with the paper archive, an intimate challenge to the bureaucratic mechanisms that produced his detention.[12] In confronting these redacted portions, Slahi encountered the biopolitical order that produced the conditions of his detention while reencountering his own form of life-writing, penned in response to—and under—duress. The restored version marked where the original redactions had existed, as faded gray shadows frame Slahi's newly repaired prose.

One of the most-commented redacted passages in Slahi's memoir is a several-page account of a series of polygraph tests administered on him. In the original memoir, the account is wholly redacted, and the reader is left to imagine the encounter over several pages of completely blacked-out text.[13] In the restored memoir, Slahi fills in these spaces, revealing that the results of the test were negative; the most dramatically censored piece of the manuscript was the one the government believed might display his innocence. Of course, the polygraph itself is another technology of writing the body, a nonconsensual form of reading and writing Slahi into the bureaucratic archive. Like the rest of his memoir, Slahi's repaired account of this redacted memory is incredibly beautiful. This is a remarkable feat, considering he learned English only as a prisoner. His mobilization of English presents another layer of visual refusal; he did not write his memoir in Arabic or in German, languages of work and learning for him. Rather, he learns the language of his captors and speaks through it, mobilizing colloquial expressions and reanimating this language with beautiful and haunting vignettes of prison life. (As a correlated note, Slahi also started learning Spanish in Guantánamo, so he could understand former Venezuelan President Hugo Chavez's speeches on TV: "He [Chavez] kept saying *la burguesía, la burguesía*," Slahi reflected after his release, "I know what *la bourgeoisie* means, but *la burguesía* I didn't understand. I decided to learn Spanish just to understand what he was saying.")[14]

In some ways, *Guantánamo Diary* represents a complementary but different kind of text and process than what I've examined here. Slahi's lawyers spent years in litigation to free the memoir, yet unlike other texts in this book, the document is not a bureaucratic state-authored account. The declassification of Slahi's writings meant freeing them from government imprisonment, which ultimately shaped the possibilities for Slahi's life outside the cage. In this instance, the redactions concern the voice of a person writing under conditions already characterized by regulations on sight, movement, and time. *Guantánamo Diary* presents us with a view of redaction and paper transparency that is stitched back to the fundamental terms of confinement and unfreedom. To wit, Slahi writes in a piece for the book *Prison Writing and the Literary World*, "As for the restored text, I cannot claim that I always accurately reproduced what the censors tried to obliterate, but I did my best—and honestly, I cannot say for sure that I did not in fact reproduce everything the way it was in the original. The only way to know is for the US government to follow the law and give me back what they confiscated illegally."[15]

In this book I have refused a facile binary between the politics of opacity and transparency and have eschewed the idea that one is a place of possibility and the other an antagonist of freedom. Slahi's words quoted at the beginning of this chapter illuminate the inherent interplay between seen and unseen; the very form of his writing (epistolary) was a necessary attempt to evade the censor. That is, Slahi hoped the letter form might obscure the true intent of his writing to the surveillor's eye, with the idea that a memoir would make it out of confinement and into a wider view. Of course, there are compelling reasons to be suspicious of what Mark Fenster calls "the transparency fix," as there are important reasons to demand that files be disclosed and unredacted.[16] Likewise, strategic invisibilities, ways of dwelling in the unseen or the uncategorized, can of course refuse punitive gazes.[17] As I discussed at the outset of this book, opacity can represent an ungovernability, an anarchic approach to a biopolitical order that diminishes life through categorization. But it is most helpful to think about the dialectic between transparency and opacity as fitting within what Stuart Hall so elegantly called "the double movement of containment and resistance" in his canonical essay "Notes on Deconstructing 'the Popular.'"[18] Though Hall was writing about the contradictions and possibilities within popular culture, at core his analysis of media productions grappled with their circulation, the meanings they acquired as they traversed the public sphere in both overdetermined and unexpected ways. In the end, what mattered to Hall was a text's relation to social movements of the dispossessed, the kindling of popular consciousness, and the interests of capital and the state, not the inherent radical possibility of popular culture, as many mistakenly extrapolate. So too is the case with formerly secret documents. There is no determined justice in the reveal. Can we imagine a transparency without guarantees?[19]

It is these very ambivalences that resonate in Slahi's work, even in different iterations as a public text: a redacted handwritten scanned photocopy, an edited and finessed memoir from a major publisher, and a blockbuster film. How does each repetition—with difference—embody and refract such movements of containment and resistance? What do the paratextual, editorial, and reproductive processes baked into each version reveal about the multifarious logics of visuality and avisuality?[20] In *Guantánamo Diary*'s remarkable transit lies this story, one that resonates more broadly across a transparency landscape shaped by imperial and military infrastructure. Put differently, *Guantánamo Diary* reveals just how profoundly the medium is, indeed, the message.

In the present moment, it has become more challenging to think dialectically about secrecy and transparency due, in part, to the ascendance of a cyberlibertarian position: the naive presumption that data drops and tactical leaks will transform the world order, or that greater visibility begets justice.[21] The rugged individualist sensibility that a lone actor (often white) who can singularly reveal wrongdoing stands in distinction from the movement-led relationships to information access that I've discussed in this book. And of course, in addition to the many document caches whose stories have occupied the public sphere (the Wikileaks papers, the Panama Papers, the Senate Select Committee on Intelligence Report on torture, the Benghazi emails, etc.), *data* presents a related but distinct horizon.[22] The relentless and increasing amounts of data in any form, document or otherwise, produced off our lives, desires, movements, and bodies, will not be reconciled by mere reversal. And as we enter a new era marked by deep fakes and ultrarealistic images and texts produced by artificial intelligence, we are forced to question what realism we demand from texts. Transparency is neither an inherently singular concept nor an inherently singular bulwark against the violence of a war-making, policing, and surveilling imperial state. If anything, what I have called for here is a position that emerges first and foremost from the belief that the question of ownership of papers, images, and data must be reconciled within a radical frame, and read against the grain alongside memories, stories, oral histories, and other absences and hauntings that are even more slippery. We already have so many guides pointing us in this direction. For instance, with Michel-Rolph Trouillot, we renarrate histories and reexamine the silences produced by evidentiary claims; with Avery Gordon, we summon the restless specters around us; with Robin Kelley, we dream surrealist and utopian dreams.[23]

In our encounters with the shadow archive, perhaps we are always *recovering the feeling of the original pages*, even as we grapple with the ghosts of imperial pasts and the ghouls of the imperial present; even as our daily activities have been wholly subsumed within the relentless data-producing, content-driven machinery of algorithmic life, and "paper" is just as often digital artifact as it is pulp; even amid the ongoing percussions of war, war by other means, and police warfare; even in the midst of multiple unfolding ecological catastrophes which have been long anticipated in the annals of science reporting and government produced data on water, air, land, and climate. Our ongoing, multiple crises compel a reckoning with the paradoxes of evidence: to think with and beyond "truth" in a post-truth era. In other words, as we refuse the authority of imperial states and their imperial knowledges, we might feel our way through the shadow archive, finding the materials we need to organize. Or we might even break into the proverbial office, shattering the window and stealing documents, with shards of glass stuck between papers. We might seize the data that is rightfully ours, destroy the data that cannot be salvaged for a radical, humanist vision. It is in reckoning with these contradictions that we will create a different story. Toward a new history we write with our words and our bodies!

ACKNOWLEDGMENTS

It feels odd to write acknowledgments in a time of such misery.

The accelerating pace of planetary destruction and live-streamed racialized cruelty are unbearable and staggering. This book began while I was trying to process the horrors of American wars and their secret prisons made by paper. It is off to press, now, in an era in which the heinous details of the Gaza genocide are live-streamed on devices across the world, for all to behold. From the quietude of my home in Toronto, this attempt at writing against militarization, far too long in the making, feels like a feeble offering in such times. I don't know where this labor of writing will go, but it wouldn't exist without support, friendship, and guidance of many people. And, dear reader, if it means something to you, I'm grateful to you too. Acknowledgments are necessarily incomplete and imperfect; my sincere apologies to anyone I have failed to mention by name here.

I am grateful to my friends and fellow travelers from USC, where I spent many days as a graduate student: Inna Arzumanova, Patty Ahn, Sophia Azeb, Umayyah Cable, Jolie Chea, John Cheney-Lippold, Jih-Fei Cheng, Araceli Esparza, Analena Hope Hassberg, Veena Hariharan, Nisha Kunte, Priscilla Leiva, Nic Ramos, Mark Padoongpatt, Laura Portwood Stacer, Evren Savci, Orlando Serrano, Sriya Shrestha, Tasneem Siddiqui, Margarita Smith, David Stein, and Gretel Vera Rosas. Akhila Ananth was the best writing partner a girl could ask for. Crystal Mun-hye Baik has been a fellow traveler along many routes, and many more await us. I benefited from the feminist mentorship of Sarah Banet-Weiser, alongside Macarena Gómez-Barris, Priya Jaikumar, and Kara Keeling. I also learned so much from Ruth Wilson Gilmore, Jack Halberstam, Lanita Jacobs, Josh Kun, Curtis Marez, Fred Moten, Viet Thanh Nguyen, and Nayan Shah.

Teshome Gabriel, Sondra Hale, Vinay Lal, Bob Nakamura, and Don Nakanishi made lasting impressions on me at UCLA that have carried me through decades.

This project transformed from my time working at the American University of Beirut, the campus that taught me how to be a professor and so much more about how to think. I was grateful to share space with many wonderful people there: Anaheed Al-Hardan, May Farah, Alice Kezhaya, Hatim El-Hibri, Tala Makhoul, Salwa Mansour, Steve Salaita, Nadya Sbaiti, Nazanin Shahrokni, Hana Sleiman, Samhita Sunya, and Adam Waterman, among them. Tamara Abdul Hadi, Jackson Allers, and Nisreen Kaj made Beirut home. Regular and lively lectures at the Center for American Studies and Research taught me about intellectual community and the spirit of engaged debate. I understood more about the dialectics of transparency while thinking with colleagues in Lebanon than is possible to account for in this book.

My colleagues at UC Davis made it a special place during my time there. Thank you, Javier Arbona-Homar, Charlotte Biltekoff, Ryan Lee Cartwright, Ofelia Cuevas, Jemma DeCristo, Rana Jaleel, Caren Kaplan, Erica Kohl-Arenas, Laurie Lambert, Justin Leroy, Susette Min, Eric Smoodin, Julie Sze, Grace Wang, and Suzy Zepeda. I will be forever indebted to Caren who has taught me so much about friendship, scholarship, and rebellious thinking through the years. And thank you, as well, to so many of the graduate students who enriched our Hart Hall conversations, especially those who were regular participants in the Critical Militarization, Policing, and Security Studies cluster, including Gaby Kirk, Zunaira Komal, Andrea Miller, and Robert (Bobby) Moeller. I was lucky enough to hire Bobby as a research assistant at an early stage in this work and benefited from his attentive eye and research skill.

I completed this book at University of Toronto, arriving while the COVID-19 pandemic protocols were still in effect. I'm grateful that despite the distancing, early outdoor meals, and awkward "mask or no mask?" moments, I met a cadre of ethical and kind scholars. A special thank-you to my colleagues in the Institute of Communication, Culture, Information and Technology, especially Jeffrey Boase, Marie-Pier Boucher, Julie Chen, Nicole Cohen, Beth Coleman, Alessandro Delfanti, Negin Dahya, Brett Caraway, Sarah Cherki El Idrissi, Dan Guandagnolo, Kate Maddalena, Jeremy Packer, Samar Sabie, Sarah Sharma, Steve Szigeti, and Lilia Topouzova. At UofT I am lucky enough to be surrounded by a brilliant and ethical community of scholars, including: Hulya Arik, Comfort Azubuko-Udah, Carolina Sa Carvalho, Deborah Cowen, Chandni Desai,

Robert Diaz, Nisrin Elamin, Rachel Goffe, Uahikea Maile, Robyn Maynard, Max Mishler, Maíra Mendes, Nada Moumtaz, Alejandro Paz, Bhavani Raman, Lauren Richter, Natalie Rothman, SA Smythe, Yvonne Sherwood, Omar Sirri, Shauna Sweeny, Alissa Trotz, and Adrien Zakar.

I have also benefited from conversations so many others, fellow travelers, mentors, and friendly colleagues across continents, including Dena Al-Adeeb, Samar Al-Bulushi, Rebecca Adelman, Sasha Ali, Neda Atanasoski, Natasha Bissonauth, Lisa Bhungalia, Abbie Boggs, Antoinette Burton, Katherine Chandler, Hardeep Dhillon, Mitra Ebadolahi, Bene Ferrão, Keith Feldman Sarah Emma Friedland, Rhonda Frederick, Maryam Griffin, Suleiman Hodali, Christine Hong, Ren-yo Huang, Aamer Ibrahim, Regine Jean-Charles, Manu Karuka, Liam Kennedy, Laleh Khalili, Alex Lubin, Sean Malloy, Manijeh Moradian, Amaka Okechukwu, Terry Park, Oiyan Poon, Elliot Powell, Jasbir Puar, Lauren Richter, Roï Saade, Ragini Shah, Khanum Sheikh, Sue Shon, Balbir Singh, Davorn Sisaveth, Hana Sleiman, Dean Spade, Wendy Sung, Jennifer Terry, Kehaulani Vaughn and last but not least Ather Zia. David Lloyd, Sarita See, and Neelam Sharma are the best traveling supper club. Thank you to Sadie Barnette, Bahar Behbahani, Voluspa Jarpa, and all the artists whose work demands us to rethink the power of archives in the terms of the dispossessed. And I am especially grateful to all the inspiring activists and revolutionaries who have refused to accept paper in the terms of the state. I hope this book does justice to you.

Practically, this book would not have been possible without the fellowship support of the UC Humanities Research Institute, the UC Davis Humanities Center, and the Charles Warren Center for Studies in American History at Harvard University. Thank you to Genavieve Clutario, Lorgia García-Peña, and Ju Yon Kim, as conveners of our Warren Center fellowship, who navigated an unbelievably tumultuous year that coincided with the start of the pandemic. Monnikue McCall took extra care of us as fellows. Early on in this project, I was lucky to speak with Nate Jones, Michael Morisy, and Evan Hendricks, each of whom gave me insights about the workings of FOIA in the world. A special shout-out goes to the archivists at the Wisconsin Historical Society, who are brilliant intellectuals and deeply generous people. I am particularly grateful to the archivists at the Howard Gotlieb Archival Research Center at Boston University, who made sure I received digital copies of the research files I was supposed to pick up in person on the day of the COVID-19 shutdown in March 2020.

Thank you to Courtney Berger, my editor at Duke University Press. From our first meeting, Courtney understood this project and the kind of work I hoped it would do. I'm grateful to her for shepherding this book from those early stages, and to the anonymous readers who read my work with such insight, sharpness, and generosity. Laura Jaramillo and the entire team at Duke deserve special mention for their diligence and care with this work. I appreciate their patience as this book moved along at its own pace. A very early experiment with this material drew from my graduate work and was published as "Beyond the Public Eye: On FOIA Documents and the Visual Politics of Redaction," *Cultural Studies Critical Methodologies* 14, no. 1 (2014); some of that article appears in chapter 3.

I am fortunate to have a beautiful family and supportive community. My parents were my earliest teachers and have remained my loudest cheerleaders. From my mom I learned an expansive way of seeing and being, along with an appreciation for art. She is the one who taught me the word *aesthetic*. This book is dedicated to her. Thank you, mom. Rishi and Luna flew in to save the day many times. So did Erica, Pato, and Nilo. (Sriya, Samhita, Tamara, and Nadya too.) R and L show me the beauty of chaos and the chaos of beauty. Esmat, you read every word of this book with a sharp and loving eye. Thank you for carrying me across cities and continents. It is you, my infinite shoreline.

NOTES

INTRODUCTION

Epigraph: Mao Tse-tung, "U.S. Imperialism Is a Paper Tiger," 67.

1   Department of Homeland Security, "The Race Paper," Center for Constitutional Rights (CCR), https://ccrjustice.org/sites/default/files/DHS%20Race%20Paper%20-%20COC%20v%20DHS%20FOIA.pdf. A PDF of the DHS correspondence is available on the CCR website, along with more contextual information about the "Race Paper" FOIA: "DHS 'Race Paper,'" Center for Constitutional Rights, May 22, 2019, https://ccrjustice.org/dhs-race-paper.

2   The corresponding CCR/CoC case was dismissed in court in 2018. See the order of dismissal at CCR, https://ccrjustice.org/sites/default/files/attach/2019/02/Dkt%2071%20-%20Signed%20Stipulation%20and%20Order%20of%20Partial%20Dismissal%20COC%20FOIA.pdf.

3   Letter from Color of Change and Center for Constitutional Rights FOIA to DHS and FBI, July 5, 2016, https://ccrjustice.org/sites/default/files/attach/2019/04/COC_FOIA.pdf.

4   The Center for Constitutional Rights and the Color of Change first sent this FOIA request in 2016.

5   Spencer, "Black Identity Extremists."

6   Color of Change and Center for Constitutional Rights, "DHS 'Race Paper' Briefing Guide," March 2018, https://ccrjustice.org/sites/default/files/attach/2018/03/COC%20FOIA%20-%20Race%20Paper%20Briefing%20Guide%20031918.pdf.

7   Kaplan, *Aerial Aftermaths*; Feldman, "On the Actuarial Gaze"; Adelman, "One Apostate Run Over, Hundreds Repented"; Smith and McDonald, "Mundane to the Memorial"; Gates, "Policing as Digital Platform"; Browne, "Digital Epidermalization"; Sturken, *Tangled Memories*, 19–42, 122–44.

8   Sontag, *On Photography*, 153–82.

9   Nixon, *Slow Violence*, 16. Nixon also discusses the "representational bias against slow violence," which provides another visual paradox of the indexical impulse.

10   Mirzoeff, *Right to Look*, 1–4; 25–29.

11   US Department of Justice, Office of Information Policy, "United States Department of Justice Guide to the Freedom of Information Act," n.d., https://www.justice.gov/oip/doj-guide-freedom-information-act-0.

12   "Statement of Nate Jones, Director of the Freedom of Information Act Project of the National Security Archive, George Washington University Before the United States House of Representatives Committee on Oversight and Government Reform on 'Ensuring Transparency Through the Freedom of Information Act,'" June 2, 2015, https://docs.house.gov/meetings/GO/GO00/20150602/103592/HHRG-114-GO00-Wstate-JonesN-20150602.pdf.

13   Schwellenbach and Moulton, "'Most Abused' Freedom of Information Act Exemption Still Needs to Be Reined In."

14   Reddy, *Freedom with Violence*, 39.

15   Rault, "Window Walls and Other Tricks of Transparency." Rault connects the settler colonial promises of accountability-through-transparency with the colonial and modern architectures of transparency that ravage the airspace for wild birds.

16   Letter to Professor Robinson from Angus MacLean Thuermer, November 14, 1974, released by CIA on July 7, 2005, https://www.cia.gov/readingroom/document/cia-rdp80b01495r000300070011-3.

17   Cook and Markowitz, "History in Shreds"; Wittner, "Blanche Weisen Cook and World Peace," 92–93.

18   MacKenzie, *Secrets*; Theoharis, *From the Secret Files*; Theoharis, "FBI Surveillance During the Cold War Years"; Theoharis, "The FBI and FOIA"; Theoharis, "Researching the Intelligence Agencies." MacKenzie's work was posthumously published, and thus there isn't a continued body of work looking at the evolving politics of FOIA. Theoharis was prolific in his writing; in addition to what I have cited there are many more dealing with intelligence abuse. Notably, he was not only writing about the FBI and FOIA, but as an early user of the transparency law, he was party to the debates around its implementation and served on the Church Committee. Also, some of his early texts point to the materiality of organization practices in the service of power. For instance, in "FBI Surveillance During the Cold War Years," he details the minutiae of how J. Edgar Hoover avoided disclosure through personal and peculiar managerial treatments of paper; counterrevolution by file.

19   Diamond, *Compromised Campus*.

20   Price, "On Using Archives and Freedom of Information Act for Anthropological Research"; Price, *Cold War Anthropology*; Price, *Threatening Anthropology*; Price, *Weaponizing Anthropology*.

21   Churchill and Vander Wall, *The COINTELPRO Papers*; Churchill and Vander Wall, *Agents of Repression* made a profound impact on the writing of this history.

22   Maxwell, *James Baldwin*; Ratner and Smith, *Che Guevara and the* FBI; Friedly and
      Gallen, *Martin Luther King Jr.*; Carson, *Malcolm X.*

23   I also want to emphasize the centrality of the redacted document to the left his-
      tories and histories of communities of color. These are critical to the method of
      writing our stories. Of course, oral history is one of the foundational methods
      of ethnic studies, but my contention is that reading the redacted document, too,
      must be understood as paramount to the ethnic studies project.

24   Vang, *History on the Run*, 84–90.

25   Kim, *Interrogation Rooms of the Korean War*, 18–19.

26   Kim, *Interrogation Rooms of the Korean War*, 23–24.

27   Kraut, "Marathon Freedom of Information Fight."

28   Rosenfeld, "Activist Richard Aoki Named as Informant."

29   Ho, "Fred Ho Refutes the Claim That Richard Aoki Was an FBI Informant" and
      "Analysis of Seth Rosenfeld's FBI Files on Richard Aoki."

30   Ho, "Analysis of Seth Rosenfeld's FBI Files on Richard Aoki."

31   Gilbert, "Keeping Secrets"; Monahan and Fisher, "Strategies for Obtaining Ac-
      cess to Secretive or Guarded Organizations"; Baker, *Baseless*; Kim, "Intelligence
      of Fools"; Chard, "Teaching with the FBI's Science for the People File."

32   Browne, *Dark Matters*, 1–6. Notably, Browne also requested the CIA's file on
      Fanon, but received nothing.

33   Pratt, "Using FBI Records in Writing Regional Labor History," 481.

34   Cohn, "Sex and Death in the Rational World of Defense Intellectuals."

35   Latner, "'Agrarians or Anarchists?,'" 121–22.

36   Latner, "'Agrarians or Anarchists?,'" 128–32.

37   Maxwell, *F. B. Eyes*; Maxwell, "Ghostreaders and Diaspora-Writers," 23–38. Max-
      well's work offers a substantive reading of the FBI's attempts at literary criticism
      and readings of Black modernist writers. Interestingly, he places this read-
      ing in contrast with the kind of literary interpretation possible within the Ivy
      League–populated CIA. His readings of the FBI also suggest that the surveillance
      file provides an unexpected insight most profoundly on the bureau itself.

38   Burton, *Tip of the Spear*, 16.

39   Spencer, *The Revolution Has Come*. Spencer's work, for instance, illuminates the
      counterintelligence program and its intimate history within the Black Panther
      Party as lived, particularly by party women.

40   Burton, *Tip of the Spear*, 15–16. I reproduce Burton's discussion on archival war
      at length here to capture the revolutionary spirit that can be used to engage the
      carceral archive. He writes, "Just as the effective conduct of revolutionary war
      demands mobility, flexibility, and creativity, so too does its historical interpre-
      tation. I therefore deploy carceral sources — surveillance files, official investiga-
      tions, prison records, police reports, and mainstream journalism — in varied ways

depending on context. In some moments I cite them to corroborate what people have told me. In others, I invoke them to expose silences, distortions, and redactions in narratives of domination or to demystify the racist and patriarchal logics of the permanent war machine" (15–16).

41 Walby and Luscombe, "Freedom of Information Research"; Yaremko and Walby, "Social Movement Groups"; Luscombe et al., "Brokering Access Beyond the Border and in the Wild." Luscombe et al., argue for an idea of "feral lawyering" as an unruly way to account for the practical, structural antagonisms in utilizing freedom of information laws in the United States and Canada to gain access to police department files.

42 Nguyen, *Sympathizer*, 61.

43 Espada, "Who Burns for the Perfection of Paper."

44 Perry, *Vexy Thing*, 99. Though Perry's work isn't directly about the politics of paper, she uses Espada's poem as an entry to critique modes of subject formation under neoliberalism, thinking about entrepreneurialism, consumerism, and labor.

45 Stahl, "Dispatches from the Militainment Empire," 147–58; Birkhold, "Unclassified Fictions"; Berlin, "Let Freedom Ring"; Secker and Alford, "New Evidence for the Surprisingly Significant Propaganda Role." It should be noted that Tom Secker and Matthew Alford documented at least 1,947 film and television productions that were assisted in some way by the Department of Defense, though, as they note, the real number is likely much higher.

46 Gitelman, *Paper Knowledge*. Gitelman discusses the relationships between paper (as a material object) and the document (as a genre) and, importantly, argues that the idea of the document is an evidentiary genre that is fundamental to modernity and the knowledge regimes therein.

47 McKinney, *Information Activism*, 22.

48 Fraser, "Rethinking the Public Sphere."

49 Briet, *What Is Documentation?*, 16.

50 Briet, *What Is Documentation?*, 17.

51 Berland, *North of Empire*, 72–75.

52 Hayles, *Electronic Literature*; Gitelman, *Paper Knowledge*, 112–29; Bratich, "Adventures in the Public Secret Sphere," 1120. A significant and important body of work exists thinking through questions of documentation, papers, and files in the digital public sphere, the networks of circulation and dissemination, and the specificity of the electronic form. My argument, though related, traces a different current, in thinking about the longer history of archives in a racial capitalist context as they interface with forms of militarism, intelligence, and policing.

53 Gitelman, *Paper Knowledges*, 1–7.

54 Graeber, *Utopia of Rules*, 73.

55   Graeber, *Utopia of Rules*, 72–80. Though bureaucracy predates capitalism, Graeber notes it took on a uniquely important place in the social forms of the mid-twentieth century, and dually in the imagination of intellectuals and scholars. We might trace the rise of recordkeeping to the era of mass production, the moment of state secrecy, and the emergence of new possibilities of recordkeeping and administrative office work.

56   Azoulay, *Potential History*. I'm thinking alongside Azoulay's suggestions to imagine the originary moments of violence present in looted objects, nonconsensual images, and other imperial debris while raising about possibilities of repair, restitution, reparation, and transformation.

57   I want to note here that there is work on paperwork and paper as media that is in relation to yet distinct from sociological theories of bureaucracy. Whereas scholars working in the Weberian context have critically appraised the social meanings of bureaucracy and the techniques of bureaucratic governance, a concurrent line has emerged, primarily in media studies, that looks at the media histories of paper, the circulation of paper and its social meanings, technologies of reproduction, etc.

58   Robertson, *Filing Cabinet*.

59   Weld, *Paper Cadavers*, 90–93.

60   Glissant, *Poetics of Relation*.

61   Gómez-Barris, *Extractive Zone*; Blas and Gaboury, "Biometrics and Opacity"; Stanley, "Anti-Trans Optics"; Dark Opacity Lab, *Dark Opacities Lab*; N. Lee, "Fold of Undetectable"; Birchall, *Radical Secrecy*; Galloway, "Are Some Things Unrepresentable?"

62   Blas, "Opacities"; Davis, "Politics of Édouard Glissant's Right to Opacity"; McKittrick, "Dear April"; Monahan, *Crisis Vision*; Sharpe, *In the Wake*, 116–30.

63   Hetherington, *Guerrilla Auditors*; El Raggal, "Egyptian Revolution's Fatal Mistake."

64   Vismann, *Files*.

65   Mao, "U.S. Imperialism Is a Paper Tiger." The comment was among those collected in the widely circulated *Quotations from Chairman Mao Tse-tung* (*The Little Red Book*) and purportedly made during a conversation with two Latin American visitors to China.

66   Birchall, "Radical Transparency?"

67   Monahan, *Surveillance in the Time of Insecurity*; Cho, *Mass Capture*; Browne, *Dark Matters*; Singh, "Decoding Dress"; McCoy, "Policing the Imperial Periphery." Questions of countersurveillance are situated in relation to the racial and gendered politics of surveillance and the social histories of people who question, evade, and look back at the state. A partial genealogy can be gleaned from the above.

68   Goodnough and Sanger-Katz, "Medicaid Covers a Million Fewer Children";
       Spade, *Normal Life*, 137–62; Beauchamp, *Going Stealth*.
69   Nader, "Dossier Invades the Home."

01   SECRECY IS FOR LOSERS

Epigraph: Daniel P. Moynihan, *Secrecy*, 227.

1   Richardson, *Bomb in Every Issue*.

2   Richardson, "Perilous Fight."

3   Braden, "I'm Glad the C.I.A. Is 'Immoral.'"

4   Stonor Saunders, *Cultural Cold War*, 80–81, 335–36. Stonor Saunders points out
       that Braden's code name was not Warren Haskins but "Homer D. Hoskins," add-
       ing to the theory that Braden's revelations were actually done under the auspices
       of the CIA, for reasons still unknown.

5   Carew, *American Labour's Cold War Abroad*, 90–91.

6   Stonor Saunders, *Cultural Cold War*, 129–30.

7   Stonor Saunders, *Cultural Cold War*, 335–36; De Vries, "1967 Central Intelli-
       gence Agency Scandal." Stonor Saunders shows that Braden gave a very strange
       excuse for revealing these details: He claimed to have forgotten that he signed
       a secrecy agreement with the CIA, leading to some speculation that he drafted
       the account under the auspices of the CIA. De Vries shows that some of these
       details had already been circulating within the public sphere prior to the 1967
       revelations, arguing that the 1967 revelations were in fact more about the
       publicity.

8   Spillers, "Mama's Baby, Papa's Maybe," 67.

9   Browne, *Dark Matters*, 9.

10   Chow, "How (the) Inscrutable Chinese Led to Globalized Theory," 73.

11   Shils, "Color, the Universal Intellectual Community," 279.

12   Shils, "Color, the Universal Intellectual Community," 279–80.

13   Shils, "Culture of the Indian Intellectual," 402.

14   Harris, "Whiteness as Property," 1791.

15   Dyer, *White*, 47.

16   Gilman, *Mandarins of the Future*, 59–60.

17   Shils, "Prospect for Lebanese Civility." For a corrective to this view see U. Mak-
       disi, *Culture of Sectarianism*.

18   Hall, *Cultural Studies 1983*, 18.

19   Shils, *Torment of Secrecy*, 74–75, emphasis added.

20   Cheney-Lippold, "New Algorithmic Identity."

21   Shils, *Torment of Secrecy*, 77.

22   Shils, *Torment of Secrecy*, 77–81.

23   Lipsitz, *Possessive Investment in Whiteness*; Harris, "Whiteness as Property." It is

helpful here to draw from scholarship that understands whiteness not simply as a social identity but also as a structure of value and an infrastructure of valuation; by extension, transparency discourse, as forwarded by its elected protagonists, emerged from such valuations.

24   Shils and Coleman, "Remembering the Congress of Cultural Freedom."

25   Rogers, "Black Orpheus."

26   Shils and Coleman, "Remembering the Congress of Cultural Freedom." Though Shils maintained he did not know the CCF received CIA funding, and he argued toward the end of his life that the CIA funds didn't in fact make much of a difference in the way he saw or valued the work of CCF, in his view the CIA's imprint was unremarkable and did not taint the overall project he was trying to advance with his work in CCF.

27   Daniel Patrick Moynihan, "Introduction," in Shils, *Torment of Secrecy*, xviii, xix. Moynihan also goes into depth about the inspiration Shils drew from Richard Hofstadter, author of the famous 1964 essay "The Paranoid Style in American Politics." One of the arguments that Hofstadter concludes that the "paranoia" of an American populist and conspiratorial thinking emerges from nontranspraency, real or perceived: "They see only the consequences of power—and this through distorting lenses—and have no chance to observe its actual machinery." Hofstadter, "The Paranoid Style," 86.

28   Said, "Clash of Ignorance."

29   Huntington, *American Politics*, 79.

30   Kaiser and Wilson, "American Scientists as Public Citizens"; "The Atomic Scientists of Chicago," *Bulletin of the Atomic Scientists of Chicago* 1, no. 1 (1945): 1. In their inaugural issue the BAS wrote that their two aims of the organization are "1. To explore, clarify, and formulate the opinion and responsibilities of scientists in regard to the problems brought about by the release of nuclear energy, and 2. To Educate the public and to a full understanding of the scientific technological and social problems arising from the release of nuclear energy." We can see here that the emphasis on transparency, rather than on any particular outcome of nuclear science, reflects the broad aims of the *Bulletin*.

31   De Volpi, *Born Secret*.

32   Lippit, *Atomic Light (Shadow Optics)*, 82. Incidentally, Lippit notes that Japanese postbomb cinema took up and reimagined the figure of the "invisible man" from American film and literature, and significantly included the "translation of the word *invisibility* as *transparency* (*tōmei*) in the Japanese versions," rather than the word *fukashi*, which more closely approximates *invisible* (82–86).

33   Wang, *American Science*, 23–24. See Wang for the different versions of the Atomic Energy Act.

34   Wang, *American Science*.

35 Wang, *American Science*. Many scientists were troubled by the support of the largest figures in the field of this bill, including Oppenheimer and others.

36 *Bulletin of the Atomic Scientists* 8, no. 7 (1952).

37 Shils, "America's Paper Curtain," 210–11.

38 Shils, "America's Paper Curtain," 211.

39 Ngai, *Impossible Subjects*, 237–39.

40 Gerhardt, "Worlds Come Apart," 19.

41 Shils, "America's Paper Curtain," 210.

42 John Moss, "Is There a Paper Curtain in Washington," August 2, 1955, 84th Cong., 1st sess., *Congressional Record* 101, pt. 10:13246.

43 Schudson, *Rise of the Right to Know*, 48.

44 John E. Moss Jr., interview by Donald B. Seney, 1989, State Government Oral History Program, California State University, Sacramento, 183.

45 Foucault, *"Society Must Be Defended."*

46 Moss, interview, 187–88.

47 Lebovic, "How Administrative Opposition Shaped," 21–23. Kennedy, "Advocates of Openness," 29, 95–97. Lebovic expounds this point in his discussion of the way the national security exemptions and a logic of deference was baked into FOIA, in no small part due to the biases of Moss and other pro-transparency actors. Kennedy affirms the "ginger" treatment of national security exemptions in the transparency movement and reveals how Cross's desire to move the exemption from "national security" to "defense," presciently anticipated this broad application and calcification of withholding practices.

48 Cuillier, "People's Right to Know," 43; Kennedy, "Advocates of Openness," 42–45; Schudson, *Rise of the Right to Know*, 41–45.

49 Cross, *People's Right to Know*, 14.

50 Cuillier, "People's Right to Know," 440–41.

51 Cross, *People's Right to Know*, 3.

52 Cross, *People's Right to Know*, 12.

53 Grisinger, "Hearing Examiners."

54 Feinberg, "FOIA, Federal Information Policy," 440.

55 Cross, *People's Right to Know*, 227.

56 Mellinger, "Washington Confidential," 858.

57 Mellinger, "Washington Confidential," 872n4.

58 Roberts, *Blacked Out*, 51-54.

59 National Security Archive, "FOIA @ 50," last modified July 1, 2016, https://ns archive.gwu.edu/briefing-book/foia/2016-07-01/foia50. The National Security archive furthers this point by noting the signing of FOIA doesn't appear in LBJ's daily diary. They also point out that he had specifically written, "No Ceremony," by hand on a memo about the possible signing in the lead up to the actual day.

60 Vaughn, "Freedom of Information Act." Vaughn provides a detailed account of the legal cases preceding and just subsequent to *Vaughn v. Rosen* that contoured the implementation of eight out of nine FOIA exemptions, which were of course the years just after its passage.

61 Foucault, *Order of Things*, 158.

62 *Oxford English Dictionary*, "classified," accessed February 10, 2025, https://www.oed.com/search/dictionary/?scope=Entries&q=classified.

63 Gaddis, "Long Peace."

64 Vaughn, "Freedom of Information Act," 866–67.

65 Nader, "Freedom from Information," 2.

66 Nader, "Freedom from Information," 2–5; Bollier, *Citizen Action and Other Big Ideas*. Bolier notes the impact of Nader's Raiders on a variety of spheres, including the shaping of FOIA.

67 Kennedy, "Advocates of Openness," 140–46; Nader, "Freedom from Information," 2–3. Nader wrote, "Since the effective date of the FOIA on July 4, 1967, court records reveal that forty cases were brought under the FOIA through March, 1969. Thirty-seven of these cases involved actions by corporations or private parties seeking information relating to personal claims or benefits. In only three cases did the suits involve a clear challenge by or for the right of the public at large to information."

68 Vaughn, *Spoiled System*. Vaughn originally released his report in 1972, but it was published in 1975, and that version remains the most popular and accessible copy.

69 *University of Pennsylvania Law Review*, "Vaughn v. Rosen," 731–32.

70 *Vaughn v. Rosen*, 484 F.2s 820 (DC Circuit 1973), 827.

71 Aid et al., "Project Azorian."

72 Longworth, *Seduction*.

73 Central Intelligence Agency, "Project Azorian: The Story of the Hughes Glomar Explorer," Approved for release January 4, 2010, https://nsarchive2.gwu.edu/nukevault/ebb305/doc01.pdf. National Security Archive, "Project Azorian," last modified February 10, 2010, https://nsarchive2.gwu.edu/nukevault/ebb305/index.htm.

74 *Phillipi v. Central Intelligence Agency*, 546 F.2d 1009, 1012 (D.C. Cir. 1976).

75 Cohen, "Literary Studies on the Terraqueous Globe."

76 Central Intelligence Agency (@CIA), "We can neither confirm nor deny that this is our first tweet." Twitter, June 6, 2014, 1:49 p.m. https://x.com/CIA/status/474971393852182528?lang=en.

77 LaGrone, "Former CIA Spy Ship Hughes Glomar Explorer Sold for Scrap."

78 Dahlburg, "CIA's Raising of Soviet Sub Told."

79 Central Intelligence Agency, "Burial at Sea of Soviet Submariners from Hughes Glomar Explorer—September 4, 1974," posted August 21, 2020 by CT1660, YouTube, 14 min. 03 sec., https://youtu.be/TOypyBdVZhU?si=_-R1I3uVChcmolCM.

80 Kornbluh, "CIA: 'Pinochet Personally Ordered' Letelier Bombing."

81 "Moynihan Bill Would Abolish CIA, Shift Functions to State," *Washington Post*, January 23, 1991, https://www.washingtonpost.com/archive/politics/1991/01/23 /moynihan-bill-would-abolish-cia-shift-functions-to-state/3355e413-7b93-4bbc -bca5-305880f627c2/; US Congress, Senate, Statements on Introduced Bills and Joint Resolutions, 137th Cong., 1st sess., 1991, S979.

82 MacKenzie, *Secrets*, 183.

83 US Congress, Senate, Statements on Introduced Bills and Joint Resolutions, 137th Cong., 1st sess., 1991, S979.

84 Ferguson, *Aberrations in Black*, 110–37.

85 Spillers, "Mama's Baby, Papa's Maybe."

86 Crouse, "Daniel Patrick Moynihan." Crouse's article from 1976 points to Moynihan's defense of Nixon against bureaucratic leaks, arguing, "He accused bureaucratic leakers of 'disloyalty to the presidency.' 'Too much do they traffic in stolen goods,' he wrote, 'and they know it.'" The contradictions of this sentiment arise only after Moynihan's turn toward transparency legislation.

87 McGarr, "'Do We Still Need the CIA?'"

88 McGarr, "'Do We Still Need the CIA?,'" 280.

89 McGarr, "'Do We Still Need the CIA?,'" 281. McGarr details both the Indian press coverage of the CIA activities globally and the concerns about activities in India. He also discusses Indira Gandhi's concerns about the CIA and her criticism of the United States' policies of regime change and destabilization.

90 Moynihan and Weisman, *Daniel Patrick Moynihan*, 360.

91 Moynihan and Weisman, *Daniel Patrick Moynihan*, 361.

92 Moynihan, "United States in Opposition." India, in this essay, features a prime example of misguided modernity, in part because of the spirit of what he calls their "British Revolution." He can't bring himself to call this "decolonization"; instead he says that their desire for freedom and socialism should be chalked up to the British influence. See also Teltsch, "Moynihan Calls on U.S. to 'Start Raising Hell' in U.N."

93 McGarr, "'Do We Still Need the CIA?'"

94 Commission on Protecting and Reducing Government Secrecy, "Secrecy: A Brief Account of the American Experience," 105th Cong., 1st sess., 1997, S. Doc. 105-2.

95 Commission on Protecting and Reducing Government Secrecy, "Secrecy," A-1.

96 Commission on Protecting and Reducing Government Secrecy, "Secrecy," A-77.

97 Moynihan, *Secrecy*, xvii.

98 Commission on Protecting and Reducing Government Secrecy A-76.

99 Moynihan, *Secrecy*, 227.

100 Donald Rumsfeld, Letter to John Moss, March 17, 1982 [John Moss Papers, 788–19], FOIA, Member Mail, 1982 Member Mail Regarding President Reagan's Freedom of Information Policies.

02 HOW TO FREE INFORMATION

Epigraph: Grand Jury Project, "Part of a Threat to Liberation Struggles."

1   Campaign for Political Rights to Stansfield Turner, January 26, 1979, https://www.cia.gov/readingroom/docs/CIA-RDP88-01365R000300110005-0.pdf.

2   Campaign for Political Rights, Invite List, February 6, 1979, box 6, folder "Washington DC Opening," Campaign for Political Rights Records, Wisconsin Historical Society, Madison (hereafter cited as CPR Papers).

3   Allen, "Big Brother Network"; Guestbook, box 11, folder "The Intelligence Network Guestbook," CPR Papers. The guestbook from the premiere confirms the *Washington Post* story.

4   Campaign for Political Rights, "Materials List," December 1978, https://www.cia.gov/readingroom/docs/CIA-RDP88-01365R000300110005-0.pdf.

5   Saloschin, "Administering the Freedom of Infomration Act," 183-188. In this piece from 1974, Saloschin reflects on his experience with the emergent FOIA as at the time Chairman of the Justice Department's Freedom of Information Committee. Saloschin's essay illuminates how use and litigation shaped the meaning of the law in these early years of its existence.

6   Gitelman, *Paper Knowledge*, 83–86.

7   Medsger, *Burglary*, 99–101.

8   Foerstel, *Surveillance in the Stacks*.

9   Medsger, *Burglary*, 270–74.

10   *Win* 8, nos. 4–5 (March 1972).

11   Burton, *Tip of the Spear*, 13–17; Bonilla, "Latina/o Communists"; Phillips, "The Poswer of the First Person Narrative"; Churchhill and Vander Wall, *Agents of Repression*.

12   McKinney, *Information Activism*.

13   "Sabotage," *Jihad News* 1, no. 6 (1974): 4; Onaci, *Free The Land*, 39–40. See Onaci for political context for the Revolutionary Action Movement's reconstitution as the Afrikan People's Party within a broader liberation struggle.

14   "Sabotage," 4.

15   Treleven, "Interviewing a Close Friend." Wilkinson was one of the main figures in the housing authority in Los Angeles who pioneered the idea of seizing the land of Chavez Ravine from its eleven thousand inhabitants, most of whom were people of Mexican origin. Wilkinson, influenced by poverty alleviation and socialist programs, saw the opportunity to build public housing in order to diminish social inequity. But in doing so he pushed for the destruction of the lifeworlds of the vibrant Mexican neighborhood nestled in the mountains of East LA. Ultimately, on the day Wilkinson was supposed to present his eminent domain case, he was confronted about his connections to the Communist Party and subse-

quently harassed by HUAC and further surveilled. His place in the history of the American social movements is stained by his involvement in the Chavez Ravine case.

16 Wilkinson, "Why I Won," 40.

17 Miller, "Will Access Restrictions Hold Up in Court?" This case is detailed in articles written both by the director of the Wisconsin Historical Society at the time and by the oral historian who was, at the time, attempting to record Wilkinson's oral history. The oral history, as well, had to be suspended, because the FBI demanded that the oral history tapes be turned over.

18 "Finding Aid," Carl and Anne Braden Papers, 1928–2006, box 151, files 19–26, https://digicoll.library.wisc.edu/cgi/f/findaid/findaid-idx?c=wiarchives;cc=wiarchives;view=text;rgn=main;didno=uw-whs-mss00006.

19 McLuhan, *Understanding Media*; Sharma, "Introduction." I am especially thinking with Sarah Sharma's feminist rearticulations of McLuhan here as a way to think about method: "A feminist approach to 'the medium is the message' rejects the focus on the message as a singular change on a singular subject and instead locates the multiplicity of unaccounted changes ushered in by the media technology related but not limited to changes in pace, pattern, and scale. . . . Through McLuhan we can understand how the medium sets the parameters and possibilities for not only communicative action but political and social change" (6).

20 "Rosenbergs' Sons Lose an Appeal," *New York Times*, May 25, 1986.

21 Buitrago et al., *Getting FBI Files*.

22 Omatsu, "Book and Resource Notes," 187–88.

23 Ann Mari Buitrago, "Memo from the Desk of Ann Mari Buitrago," May 24, 1979, box 8, folder "FOIA Correspondence 1981 2," CPR Papers. Buitrago attaches an excerpt from the Federal Register to the correspondence and notes that the FOIA Inc. guides drew from "others reported by GAO + information we elicited in a) depositions and b) 'friendly' meetings with the FBI (e.g., the Abstract System. Therefore, I think our version of the CRS is more useful than the FR reprint." CRS refers to the central records system, i.e., the kinds of indexes that would be used to catalogue information.

24 Kimball, *File*, 5–6.

25 Center for National Security Studies, *Using the Freedom of Information Act: A Step by Step Guide* (Washington, DC: Center for National Security Studies, [1979]), 8, part 8 M92-045, box 4, folder "Campaign to Stop Government Spying, Lobbying and Organizing," National Committee Against Repressive Legislation Records, Wisconsin Historical Society, Madison (hereafter cited as NACRL Records).

26 *Organizing Notes* 2, no. 1 (January 1978): 3.

27 *Organizing Notes* 3, no. 1 (January 1979): 4; Mills, *CIA Off Campus*, 153.

28 Campaign for Democratic Freedoms, program for "Conspiracy in America," May

16, 17, 18, 1975, box 22, file [5, 6, or 22], Meeropol Papers, Boston University, Boston, MA.

29 Unknown author, "June 11 FOIA Conference Program Outline" and handwritten "FOIA Conference" notes, June 11, 1980, box 8, file "FOIA, Inc. Conference," CPR Papers.

30 *Organizing Notes* 1, no. 1 (March 1977): 1.

31 *Organizing Notes* 1, no. 1 (March 1977): 1.

32 Agee, *Inside the Company*.

33 "Advertisement for *Recon*," *Counterspy* 2, no. 4 (1976): 12.

34 *Counterspy* 1, no. 1 (March 1973): 1.

35 Kullman," Group 'Reveals' Network of Surveillance at KSU."

36 Olmstead, "Reclaiming Executive Power," 730–31.

37 Agee et al., "Who We Are," 3.

38 Kadonaga, "Anti–*Spy Magazine* Split."

39 "Do You Have Any Intelligence Agency Files?," *Organizing Notes* 2, no. 9 (1978): 4.

40 "Do You Have Any Intelligence Agency Files?," 4.

41 Macy and Kaplan, *Documents*, 139–55.

42 Fund for Open Information and Accountability, Inc., "Fact Sheet: The Freedom of Information Act and FOIA, Inc.," box 37, file "FOIA, Inc.," CPR Papers. The description of what the ability for an "In Camera" review of documents as part of the new 1974 FOIA amendment was reflects FOIA Inc.'s visual stakes. This document also provides a brilliant discussion of the 1974 FOIA amendment.

43 Fund for Open Information and Accountability, Inc. (FOIA Inc.), "FOIA, Inc., 'Save the Files' Project," 1979, box 37, file "FOIA, Inc.," CPR Papers.

44 FOIA Inc., "FOIA, Inc., 'Save the Files' Project."

45 "Correspondence," box 6, file "Film Festivals," CPR Papers.

46 "Hearings Document Past and Present FBI Abuse," *Organizing Notes* 1, no. 7 (November 1977): 4–5. This two-page spread gave account of similar efforts around the country by local antispying or community organizations to document FBI and intelligence abuses.

47 Campaign to Stop Government Spying, "CSGS Proposal for Organizing Film," 2, box 11, file "The Intelligence Network—Production," CPR Papers.

48 Campaign for Political Rights, "Materials List," December 1978, https://www.cia.gov/readingroom/docs/CIA-RDP88-01365R000300110005-0.pdf.

49 *Organizing Notes* 4, no. 7 (1980): 11.

50 "Prison Bars Film," *Organizing Notes* 1, no. 2 (1981): 6.

51 Linda Valentino to Susan Woods (Campaign for Political Rights), January 16, 1980, box 14, file "The Intelligence Network Correspondence and Reviews," CPR Papers.

52 Felker-Kantor, *Policing Los Angeles*, 152.

53 Linda Valentino to Susan Woods (Campaign for Political Rights), January 16, 1980, box 14, file "The Intelligence Network Correspondence and Reviews," CPR Papers.

54 "Public Deserves Full Truth on Government," *Sun-Times*, October 19, 1981, 37, M92-045, box 4, folder "FOIA," NACRL Records.

55 Grand Jury Project staff (Joan P. Gibbs, Lynora Williams, and Sarah Wolfe) to Peggy Shaker (Campaign for Political Rights), July 20, 1981, MAD 1057, box 17, file "Campaign for Political Rights, 1981–1984," Institute for Policy Studies Papers, Wisconsin Historical Society, Madison (hereafter cited as IPS Papers).

56 Lucius Walker to Peggy Shaker (Campaign for Political Rights), September 8, 1981, MAD 1057, box 17, file "Campaign for Political Rights, 1981–1984," IPS Papers.

57 Ken Lawrence, "Memorandum on Morton Halperin, Jerry Berman, the American Civil Liberties Union, and the Campaign for Political Rights," September 30–October 10, 1981, 5, MAD 1057, box 17, file "Campaign for Political Rights, 1981–1984," IPS Papers.

58 Ken Lawrence, Memorandum on Morton Halperin, Jerry Berman, the American Civil Liberties Union, and the Campaign for Political Rights, September 30–October 10, 1981, 5, MAD 1057, box 17. Lawrence goes on to argue, specifically, Morton Halperin's support of civil liberties is conditional, citing his written work promoting the idea that government spying is acceptable and his collaborative approach to the creation of FISA courts in 1978 and the Intelligence Agencies Identities Act of 1981.

59 Esther Herst to "Friends," October 27, 1981; Rick Gutman to Ken Lawrence, October 21, 1981, MAD 1057, box 17, file "Campaign for Political Rights, 1981–1984," IPS Papers.

60 Hendricks, *Former Secrets*.

61 Phone interview with Evan Hendricks, June 7, 2018.

62 Hendricks, *Former Secrets*, 161.

63 Royko, "Ask Not for Whom the Welcome Wagon Rolls." The resultant article in the *Los Angeles Times* provides a few interesting and chilling details of the encounter. The woman only vaguely remembered the Welcome Wagon representative but recalled that she'd been asked several questions about their former hometown and her partner's employment. The surveilled woman said of the brief encounter, "But it never occurred to me that I was really talking to J. E. Hoover. I would have told her to shove the tickets from the laundromat." The article also notes that the unnamed woman's request was one of many FOIAs sent to the government during the 1970s, writing, "They are curious about who was spying on them."

64 Grand Jury Project, "Part of a Threat to Liberation Struggles . . . ," in FOIA Inc.,

Our Right to Know! Endangered (FOIA Inc.: Brooklyn, 1981), M096-71, box 2, file "Intelligence Charter," NCARL Records.

65 Grand Jury Project, "Part of a Threat to Liberation Struggles . . . " in FOIA Inc., *Our Right to Know!*, M096-71 box 2, file "Intelligence Charter," NCARL Records.

66 Kwoka, "FOIA, Inc." Kwoka's legal article reveals in a more contemporary context how corporations have come to dominate the landscape of FOIA, using it to gather information meant to assure a competitive advantage in a profit-driven marketplace. Commercial requesters use, Kwoka argues, crowd out investigative journalists and others looking for actionable material that would impact the public good or connect with questions of civil liberties and civic society.

67 Middle East Studies Association Task Force on Civil and Human Rights, "Memo on Public Records Harassment and Defense," Middle East Studies Association, November 20, 2019, https://mesana.org/advocacy/task-force-on-civil-and-human-rights/2019/11/20/memo-on-public-records-harassment-and-defense.

03 ON REDACTED DOCUMENTS AND THE VISUAL POLITICS OF TRANSPARENCY

An earlier version of this chapter was published in *Cultural Studies Critical Methodologies* 14, no. 1 (2014).

Epigraph: CIA, "Inventory of Videotapes."

1 Rejali, *Torturing Democracy,* 458–66; Hajjar, *War in Court,* 288–89; McCoy, *A Question of Torture,* 158–59.

2 "The Vice President Appears on Meet the Press with Tim Russert," September 16, 2001, https://georgewbush-whitehouse.archives.gov/vicepresident/news-speeches/speeches/vp20010916.html.

3 Paglen, *Blank Spots on the Map.*

4 Said, *Culture and Imperialism,* 66–67.

5 Obama, "Freedom of Information Act Memorandum."

6 Feinberg, "FOIA, Federal Information Policy"; Caidi and Ross, "Information Rights and National Security."

7 Feinberg, "FOIA, Federal Information Policy," 442–45.

8 Masco, "'Sensitive but Unclassified.'" Masco cites examples from his own archival research and use of FOIA requests illustrating that what is considered "classified" and "unclassified" can vary between departments and change over time.

9 Feinberg, "FOIA, Federal Information Policy," 443.

10 Masco, "'Sensitive but Unclassified.'"

11 Feinberg, "FOIA Federal Information Policy," 445–46.

12 Benjamin, *Illuminations.*

13 Cole, *Torture Memos,* 19–25.

14 Scott-Clark and Levy, *Forever Prisoner,* 175–83.

15 Cole, *Torture Memos.*

16 Feinberg, "FOIA, Federal Information Policy."

17 Rose and Miller, "Political Power Beyond the State," 278.

18 Ouellette and Hay, *Living Better Through Reality TV*, 10.

19 M. Dean, *Governmentality*, 168–69.

20 Caidi and Ross, "Information Rights and National Security"; Feinberg, "FOIA, Federal Information Policy"; Masco, "'Sensitive but Unclassified.'" All elaborate on some of the competing tensions within the recent history of e-government acts, especially as the move toward digital open government has emerged in an era of greater secrecy around government actions.

21 Nichols, *Representing Reality*; Gaines, "Political Mimesis." Gaines and Nichols consider the relationship between images, the indexical bind, and political affect.

22 Haraway, "Situated Knowledges."

23 Sontag, "Regarding the Torture of Others."

24 Nath, "Toward the Dark Side."

25 Rejali, *Torture and Democracy*; Scarry, *Body in Pain*, 35–38; McCoy, *Question of Torture*.

26 Desai et al., "Torture at Times."

27 Mbembe, "Necropolitics," 21–26.

28 Gordon, "Prisoner's Curse"; James, *Resisting State Violence*, 24–42. James and Gordon similarly reveal the racialized life-negation unaccounted for in biopower.

29 Esposito, *Bios*, 9–10, 45–47.

30 Esposito, *Bios.*

31 Scott-Clark and Levy, *The Forever Prisoner*, 50.

32 Guh, "On Some Aspects of the Historiography of Colonial India," 37–43; Arondekar, *For the Record*; Chakrabarty, *Provincializing Europe*. The literature on postcolonial methods in the archive is vast. By recognizing history (as a discipline with a particular methodological form of inquiry) as a part of the colonial apparatus, scholars questioned what it means to write "history" when attempts to understand the past are filtered through archives written in the service of the imperial state.

33 Said, *Culture and Imperialism*, 67 (emphasis added).

34 Guha, "Prose of Counter-Insurgency," 48.

35 Guha, "Prose of Counter-Insurgency," 58–59.

36 Cole, *Torture Memos*, 20–21. Cole argues that the August 1, 2002, memos were primarily concerned with whether the CIA would be breaking federal criminal law, and not with international treaties against torture, as those had been dispensed with in previous OLC memos.

37 American Civil Liberties Union, "Documents Released by the CIA and Justice Department in Response to the ACLU's Torture FOIA," July 24, 2008. https://www.aclu.org/documents/documents-released-cia-and-justice-department-response-aclus-torture-foia.

38 US Department of Justice Office of Legal Council, "Memorandum for [redacted]" (Released July 24, 2008) August 1, 2002, https://www.aclu.org/files/pdfs/safefree /cia_3686_001.pdf.

39 US Department of Justice Office of Legal Council, "Memorandum for [redacted]," 18, https://www.aclu.org/files/pdfs/safefree/cia_3686_001.pdf.

40 American Civil Liberties Union, "Justice Department Releases Bush Administration Torture Memos," April 19, 2009, http://www.aclu.org/safefree/torture /39393prs20090416.html. Cole, *Torture Memos*, 108.

41 Ahuja, "Abu Zubaydah and the Caterpillar," 133–35; US Department of Justice "Memorandum for John Rizzo" (Released April 16, 2009) August 1, 2002 (14), https://web.archive.org/web/20090731132148/http://luxmedia.vo.llnwd.net /010/clients/aclu/olc_08012002_bybee.pdf.

42 Myers, "Knee-Jerk Redaction?"

43 White, *Body and the Screen*, 22–29; J. Dean, *Publicity's Secret*, 4, 42–46.

44 Caidi and Ross, "Information Rights and National Security."

45 Warner, *Publics and Counterpublics*, 161–63. J. Dean, *Publicity's Secret*, 5–17, 34–42.

46 Weiss, "Fifth Lawyer Said to Oppose Destruction of CIA Videotapes." CIA General Counsel informed the Congress House Intelligence Committee leaders of this investigation as well as the pending destruction of the tapes in question. Congresswoman Jane Harman responded to this assertion with a letter asking the agency to reconsider destroying these tapes, but to no end.

47 Siems, *Torture Report*, 75.

48 Siems, *Torture Report*, 85–87.

49 Michael Hayden quoted in Siems, *Torture Report*, 88.

50 Barthes, *Camera Lucida*, 26–28; 42–51.

51 American Civil Liberties Union, "CIA Confirms 12 Destroyed Videotapes Depicted 'Enhanced Interrogation Methods,'" March 6, 2009, https://www.aclu .org/press-releases/cia-confirms-12-destroyed-videotapes-depicted-enhanced -interrogation-methods.

52 Central Intelligence Agency, "Inventory of Videotapes," 1 [2002]. https://www .aclu.org/files/torturefoia/released/030609/videotape_inventory.pdf.

53 Lippit, *Atomic Light (Shadow Optics)*, 32.

54 Sturken, *Tangled Memories*, 38–42.

55 Sturken, *Tangled Memories*, 40.

56 Hilderbrand, "Grainy Days and Mondays"; Marks, *Touch*.

57 Siems, *Torture Report*, 74.

58 Denbeaux, Beroth, et al., "Death in Camp Delta," 4, 14–15.

59 Denbeaux, Beroth, et al., "Death in Camp Delta," 50.

60 Denbeaux, Beroth, et al., "Death in Camp Delta," 16, 33.

61 Denbeaux, Beroth, et al., "Death in Camp Delta," 33.

62 Rejali, *Torture and Democracy*, 35–44.

63 "Declaration of Leon E. Panetta," 8, https://sgp.fas.org/jud/aclu-panetta.pdf.

64 Denbeaux, Ghannam, and Zubaydah, "American Torturers."

65 Denbeaux, Ghannam, and Zubaydah, "American Torturers," 61.

66 Pilkington, "'The Forever Prisoner.'"

04 PAPER AND THE ART OF CENSORSHIP

Epigraph: SFMoMA. "Across Space and Time: An Interview with Sadie Barnette," August 2022.

1 Aranke, "Material Matters."

2 Sharpe, *In the Wake*, 114–17; Sharpe posits an aesthetic and aristic practice of Black annotation and Black redaction, extending beyond the document itself, which reimagines and repurposes these forms of erasure to critique the visual violence of the racial state and its attendant social forms.

3 Slaughter, "Vanishing Points," 208; Carroll and Gusejnova, "Malevich's Black Square Under X-Ray." Interestingly, the works also bear a resemblance to the pre-Revolutionary Russian Suprematist paintings of Kazimir Malevich, as some critics have noted.

4 Chave and Rothko, *Mark Rothko*, 77.

5 Guilbaut, *How New York Stole the Idea of Modern Art*.

6 Stonor Saunders, *Cultural Cold War*; Bennett, *Workshops of Empire*.

7 Corris, *Ad Reinhardt*. Corris notes discord between Reinhardt and Rothko, though they shared a similar color-field aesthetic.

8 Reinhardt, "War Chief." Interestingly, one of Reinhardt's late pieces right before he died in 1967, which coincided with the beginnings of the Vietnam War, was *No War*, a postcard with anti-imperialist, antimilitary messages written on one side, and addressed to a "War Chief" in Washington, DC.

9 Guilbaut, *How New York Stole the Idea of Modern Art*, 108. Guilbaut here quotes specifically from Robert Motherwell and Adolph Gottlieb.

10 Maxwell, FB *Eyes*. Another elaboration can be found in the literary world; as Maxwell details the way surveillance of Black writers in the Cold War shaped their writing, as they formed explicit responses and implicitly responded to a common sense shaped by the idioms of surveillance.

11 Alter, "At 17, She Fell in Love with a 47-Year-Old." As this manuscript was in its final stages, Mesches's widow published a memoir questioning consent in their early relationship, which began when she was seventeen and he was forty-seven. Her account is introspective and attempts to reconcile this predatory, inappropriate beginning with her appreciation and love for Mesches.

12 Mesches, "American Uncanny," 37.

13 Mesches, "American Uncanny," 36–37.

14 Mesches, "FBI Files," 292.

15 Currier, "Redaction Art."

16 Keenen, "Look Up."

17 BBC News, "Artist's Journey to Paint Watercolours of Guantánamo Bay."

18 Bogad, *Cointelshow*, 6.

19 Poniewozik, "Celebrities Read the Mueller Report." See also the cottage industry of mostly white artists taking redaction up in these very uninteresting ways.

20 Bailey, "Unknown Knowns," 144–47.

21 Lewine, "Art House." Holzer also notes that the Russian Supremacist painter Kazimir Malevich had an impact on these works. Kiki Smith, "Jenny Holzer," *Interview*, March 26, 2012, https://www.interviewmagazine.com/art/jenny-holzer.

22 Craze, "Can We See Torture?," 62.

23 P. M. Lee, *Think Tank Aesthetics*, 229–31.

24 Craze, "Can We See Torture?," 61; Craze, "In the Dead Letter Office."

25 National Gallery of Art, "Overview: DODDOACID, 2007."

26 Dorotheum, "Jenny Holzer Exhibit at Dorotheum London"; JC Reporter, "Holzer Offers Light Relief to Art Museum."

27 Slyomovics, *Object of Memory*, 29–41; Al-Hayia' and Jones, "Ayn Hawd and the 'Unrecognized Villages'"; Estefan, "When Artists Boycott"; Estefan et al., *Assuming Boycott*.

28 Abowd, "Politics and Poetics of Place."

29 S. Makdisi, "Architecture of Erasure," 554.

30 Museum on the Seam, "Right to Protest."

31 Bishara, "Unspoken Truths in Jenny Holzer's Truisms"; Greenberger, "Jenny Holzer's Facile Guggenheim Museum Show Fails to Meet Our Moment." As this book was going to press in 2024, Jenny Holzer's 2024 exhibition *Light Line* at the Guggenheim was met with underwhelm by art writers for the same political vacuousness and silence on the issue of Israel's continuing violence against Palestinians. Greenberger noted that Holzer exhibited a scrolling text LED installation, echoing almost exactly her exhibition there thirty-five years earlier. The work featured disembodied text, which in its 2024 incarnation drew from an Israeli poet, a survivor of the war in Ukraine, a Palestinian father from Gaza, and others disparately impacted by violence across space and time. Both Greenberger and Hakim note that the specificity and variation in these utterances was entirely elided, flattening out differences.

32 Jason Farago, "An Interview with Jenny Holzer," *Even Magazine*, Fall 2016, http://evenmagazine.com/jenny-holzer/; Stuart Jeffires, "Jenny Holzer: Drawn to the Dark Side [Interview]," *Guardian*, June 2, 2012, https://www.theguardian.com/artanddesign/2012/jun/04/jenny-holzer-interview.

33 MoMA, "Redaction: A Project by Titus Kaphar and Reginald Dwayne Betts," https://www.moma.org/calendar/exhibitions/5056.

34 Ebadolahi, "Did You Kiss the Dead Body?"

35 Kahlon, "Did You Kiss the Dead Body?"

36 Kapadia, *Insurgent Aesthetics*, 136–44.

37 Balaghi, "Silenced Histories and Sanitized Autobiographies," 72.

38 Behbahani and Balaghi, "Artist Talk with Bahar Behbahani and Dr. Shiva Balaghi," 30:00–30:45.

39 Balaghi, "Surrounded by Quiet Nothingness," 7.

40 Ganesh and Ghani, "Introduction to an Index," 111.

41 Gopinath, "Archive, Affect, and the Everyday," 181–87; Tang, "Persons and Profiles," 312–17; Kapadia, *Insurgent Aesthetics*, 125–33.

42 Sharpe, "Archive and Affective Memory in M. Nourbese Philip's *Zong!*," 472.

43 For instance, in 2016 artist Greg Mocilnikar exhibited a series of paintings and works on paper called *Redaction* at the Walter Maciel Gallery in Los Angeles. "Press Release for Greg Mocilnikar, *Redaction*," accessed February 10, 2025, http://www.waltermacielgallery.com/gmocilnikar/Mocilnikarpr16.doc.

44 Kumar, "Terrorcraft," 45.

45 Deutsch and Thompson, "Secrets and Lies (Part I)."

46 Kat Cizek, "Assia Boundaoui and Inverse Surveillance: Meet Co-Creation Studio's New Fellow—MIT CoCreate," MIT CoCreate, December 7, 2021, https://cocreationstudio.mit.edu/assia-boundaoui-and-inverse-surveillance-meet-co-creation-studios-new-fellow/.

47 Lippit, *Atomic Light (Shadow Optics)*; Nixon, *Slow Violence*.

48 SFMoMA, "Across Space and Time: An Interview with Sadie Barnette," August 2022, https://www.sfmoma.org/read/across-space-and-time-an-interview-with-sadie-barnette/.

49 Said, "Zionism from the Standpoint of Its Victims."

EPILOGUE

Epigraph: Mohamedou Ould Slahi, *Guantánamo Diary: Restored Edition*, 1.

1 Slahi and Siems, "Scribo Ergo Sum," 161. Slahi was also still writing in other languages, but it is striking that he perfected English and became a writer in this horrific context.

2 Hajjar, *War in Court*, 14. Guantánamo detainees were granted the right to file habeas cases only after the 2004 ruling in the *Rasul v. Bush* case.

3 Slahi and Siems, "Scribo Ergo Sum," 162–63. While Slahi makes clear that the letters were meant as a book, he doesn't indicate at what point in the process this became the clear intention.

4 Nancy Hollander, email to author and Robert Moeller, July 20, 2017.

5 Slahi and Siems, "Scribo Ergo Sum," 162.

6   Luk, *Life of Paper*, 194.
7   Siems, "Notes on the Text, Redactions, and Annotations," in Slahi, *Guantánamo Diary*, xii.
8   "Notes on the Text, Redactions, and Annotations," in Slahi, *Guantánamo Diary*, xiii.
9   Slahi, *Guantánamo Diary: Restored Edition*, l.
10 Coundouriotis, "Torture and Textuality"; Mcheimech, "Resisting Islamophobia"; Goyal, "The Genres of Guantánamo Diary"; Trapp, "Redacted Tears"; Swanson and Moore, "Indefinite Detention."
11 Adelman, "Fictive Intimacies of Detention."
12 Baik, *Reencounters*, 6. Baik's notion of the "reencounter" as a reckoning with—and refusal of—official narrative is particularly germane here, as she suggests multi-genre memory work as a form of redress.
13 Slahi, *Guantánamo Diary* (1st ed), 55–60.
14 See Slahi's interview at the International Journalism Festival: Slahi, "15 anni senza accuse."
15 Slahi and Siems, "Scribo Ergo Sum," 169.
16 Fenster, *Transparency Fix*. While Fenster does not grapple with the core political questions of an imperial state, his work points to the contradictions of transparency even within a liberal frame.
17 Abdur-Rahman and Browne, "Capture, Illegibility, Necessity"; Birchall, *Radical Secrecy*.
18 Hall, "Notes on Deconstructing 'the Popular,'" 443.
19 Hall, "Problem of Ideology." I'm deliberately summoning Hall's canonical essay on Marxism here (and the phrase with which it is associated, "without guarantees"). I do so not because "transparency" is an analogous ideology with Marxism but, rather, because he's inviting us to think about the social production of ideology as shaped by historical materialist forces. Transparency is neither a foregone conclusion as a method of imperial control nor a formed and self-explanatory tool of radical social movements—ideology without guarantee.
20 Genette and Maclean, "Introduction to the Paratext." I reproduce the beginnings of Genette's well-known essay on paratext here to think with it about how the question of paratext might relate to the appearance of Slahi's letters in the public sphere. Though Genette was writing in the universal, there is a specific resonance with Slahi's work: "One does not always know if one should consider that they belong to the text or not, but in any case they surround it and prolong it, precisely in order to present it, in the usual sense of this verb, but also in its strongest meaning: to *make it present*, to assure its presence in the world, its 'reception and consumption, in the form, nowadays at least, of a book. This accompaniment, of varying

size and style, constitutes what I once christened elsewhere, in conformity with the frequently ambiguous meaning of this prefix in French—consider, I said, adjectives *parafiscal* or *paramilitary*—the *paratext* of the work. Thus the paratext is for us the means by which a text makes a book of itself and proposes itself as such to its readers, and more generally to the public. Rather than with a limit or a sealed frontier, we are dealing in this case with a threshold, or—the term Borges used about a preface—with a 'vestibule' which offers to anyone and everyone the possibility either of entering or of turning back" (261).

21 Jurgenson and Rey, "WikiLeaks."
22 Roberts, *Blacked Out*, 201. It bears mentioning that Roberts notes in his 2006 publication the emergent relationships between FOIA requests and bulk data analysis.
23 Trouillot, *Silencing the Past*; Gordon, *Ghostly Matters*; Kelley, *Freedom Dreams*.

BIBLIOGRAPHY

Abdur-Rahman, Aliyyah, and Simone Browne. "Capture, Illegibility, Necessity: A Conversation on Black Privacy." *Black Scholar* 51, no. 1 (2021): 67–72.

Abowd, Thomas. "The Politics and Poetics of Place: The Baramki House." *Jerusalem Quarterly* 21 (2004): 49–58.

Adelman, Rebecca A. "Fictive Intimacies of Detention: Affect, Imagination, and Anger in Art from Guantánamo Bay." *Cultural Studies* 32, no. 1 (2018): 81–104.

Adelman, Rebecca A. "One Apostate Run Over, Hundreds Repented: Excess, Unthinkability, and Infographics from the War with ISIS." In *ISIS Beyond the Spectacle*, edited by Mehdi Semati, Piotr M. Szpunar, and Robert Alan Brookey. London: Routledge, 2020.

Agee, Philip. *Inside the Company: CIA Diary*. New York: Farrar, Straus and Giroux, 1975.

Agee, Philip, Ellen Ray, Bill Schaap, Elsie Wilcot, Jim Wilcott, and Lou Wolf. "Who We Are." *Covert Action Information Bulletin* 1, no. 1 (1978): 3.

Ahuja, Neel. "Abu Zubaydah and the Caterpillar." *Social Text* 29, no. 1 (2011): 127–49. https://doi.org/10.1215/01642472-1210292.

Aid, Matthew, William Burr, and Thomas Blanton. "Project Azorian: The CIA's Declassified History of the Glomar Explorer." National Security Archive, George Washington University, posted February 10, 2010. https://nsarchive2.gwu.edu/nukevault/ebb305/index.htm.

Al-Hayja', Muhammad Abu, and Rachel Leah Jones. "'Ayn Hawd and the 'Unrecognized Villages.'" *Journal of Palestine Studies* 31, no. 1 (2001): 39–49.

Allen, Henry. "Big Brother Network." *Washington Post*, February 14, 1979.

Alter, Alexandra. "At 17, She Fell in Love with a 47-Year-Old. Now She Questions the Story." *New York Times*, June 10, 2024. https://www.nytimes.com/2024/06/10/books/jill-ciment-memoir-consent.html.

Aranke, Sampada. "Material Matters: Black Radical Aesthetics and the Limits of Visi-

bility." *E-flux Journal* 79 (2017). https://www.e-flux.com/journal/79/94433
/material-matters-black-radical-aesthetics-and-the-limits-of-visibility/.

Arondekar, Anjali. *For the Record: On Sexuality and the Colonial Archive in India.*
Durham, NC: Duke University Press, 2009.

Azoulay, Ariella. *Potential History: Unlearning Imperialism.* London: Verso, 2019.

Baik, Crystal. *Reencounters: On the Korean War and Diasporic Memory Critique.* Philadelphia: Temple University Press, 2019.

Bailey, Robert. "Unknown Knowns: Jenny Holzer's Redaction Paintings and the History of the War on Terror." *October*, no. 142 (2012): 144–61.

Baker, Nicholson. *Baseless: My Search for Secrets in the Ruins of the Freedom of Information Act.* New York: Penguin, 2021.

Balaghi, Shiva. "Silenced Histories and Sanitized Autobiographies: The 1953 CIA Coup
in Iran." *Biography* 36, no. 1 (2013): 71–96.

Balaghi, Shiva. "Surrounded by Quiet Nothingness: On Behar Behbahani's Paintings."
In *Let the Garden Eram Flourish* (exhibition catalog), edited by John R. Stomberg.
Hanover, NH: Hood Museum of Art, Dartmouth College, 2018.

Barthes, Roland. *Camera Lucida: Reflections on Photography.* New York: Hill and Wang,
1982.

BBC News. "An Artist's Journey to Paint Watercolours of Guantánamo Bay." November
11, 2013. https://www.bbc.com/news/av/magazine-24824275.

Beauchamp, Toby. *Going Stealth: Transgender Politics and U.S. Surveillance Practices.*
Durham, NC: Duke University Press, 2018.

Behbahani, Bahar, and Shiva Balaghi. "Artist Talk with Bahar Behbahani and Dr. Shiva
Balaghi." Video posted by Thomas Erben Gallery, New York City, June 2, 2016, Vi-
meo, 42 min., 15 sec. https://vimeo.com/169640204.

Benjamin, Walter, *Illuminations.* New York: Schocken Books, 1986.

Bennett, Eric. *Workshops of Empire: Stegner, Engle, and American Creative Writing During
the Cold War.* Iowa City: University of Iowa Press, 2015.

Berland, Jody. *North of Empire: Essays on the Cultural Technologies of Space.* Durham,
NC: Duke University Press, 2009.

Berlin, Kayla. "Let Freedom Ring: Broadening FOIA's Public Domain and the Applica-
bility of the Waiver Doctrine." *Loyola of Los Angeles Entertainment Law Review* 35
(2014): 63–94.

Birchall, C. "Radical Transparency?" *Cultural Studies Critical Methodologies* 14, no. 1
(2014): 77–88.

Birchall, Clare. *Radical Secrecy: The Ends of Transparency in Datafied America.* Minneapolis: University of Minnesota Press, 2021.

Birkhold, Matthew H. "Unclassified Fictions: The CIA, Secrecy Law, and the Dangerous Rhetoric of Authenticity." *Berkeley Journal of Entertainment and Sports Law* 3,
no. 1 (2014): 17–71.

Bishara, Hakim. "The Unspoken Truths in Jenny Holzer's Truisms." *Hyperallergic*, June 7, 2024. http://hyperallergic.com/916808/unspoken-truths-jenny-holzer -truisms-light-line-guggenheim-museum/.

Blas, Zach. "Opacities: An Introduction." *Camera Obscura* 31, no. 2 (2016): 149–53.

Blas, Zach, and Jacob Gaboury. "Biometrics and Opacity: A Conversation." *Camera Obscura* 31, no. 2 (2016): 155–65.

Bogad, L. M. *Cointelshow: A Patriot Act*. Oakland: PM Press, 2018.

Bollier, David. *Citizen Action and Other Big Ideas*. Washington, DC: Center for Study of Responsive Law, 1991.

Bonilla, Eddie. "Latina/o Communists, Activism, and the FBI During the Chicana/o and New Communist Movements." *Southern California Quarterly* 104, no. 1 (2022): 83–127.

Braden, Thomas W. "I'm Glad the C.I.A. Is 'Immoral.'" *Saturday Evening Post*, May 20, 1967, 10–14.

Bratich, Jack Z. "Adventures in the Public Secret Sphere: Police Sovereign Networks and Communications Warfare." *Cultural Studies Critical Methodologies* 14, no. 1 (2014): 11–20.

Briet, Suzanne. *What Is Documentation? English Translation of the Classic French Text*. Translated by Ronald E. Day and Laurent Martinet, with Hermina G. B. Anghelescu. Lanham, MD: Scarecrow Press, 2006.

Browne, Simone. *Dark Matters: On the Surveillance of Blackness*. Durham, NC: Duke University Press, 2015.

Browne, Simone. "Digital Epidermalization: Race, Identity and Biometrics." *Critical Sociology* 36, no. 1 (2010): 131–50.

Buitrago, Ann Mari, Leon Andrew Immerman, and Bonnie Brower. *Getting FBI Files: An Activist's Handbook*. New York: FOIA Inc., 1981.

Burton, Orisanmi. *Tip of the Spear: Black Radicalism, Prison Repression, and the Long Attica Revolt*. Berkeley: University of California Press, 2023.

Caidi, Nadia, and Anthony Ross. "Information Rights and National Security." *Government Information Quarterly* 22, no. 4 (2005): 663–84.

Carew, Anthony. *American Labour's Cold War Abroad: From Deep Freeze to Détente, 1945–1970*. Edmonton: Athabasca University Press, 2018.

Carroll, Khadija von Zinnenburg, and Dina Gusejnova. "Malevich's Black Square Under X-Ray: A Dialogue on Race, Revolution and Art History." *Third Text Online Forum*, September 9, 2019. http://www.thirdtext.org/anielh-blacksquare.

Carson, Clayborne. *Malcolm X: The FBI File*. New York: Skyhorse Publishing, 2012.

Chakrabarty, Dipesh. *Provincializing Europe: Postcolonial Thought and Historical Difference*. Princeton, NJ: Princeton University Press, 2000.

Chard, Daniel S. "Teaching with the FBI's Science for the People File." *Radical History Review* 2017, no. 127 (2017): 180–85.

Chave, Anna, and Mark Rothko. *Mark Rothko: Subjects in Abstraction*. New Haven, CT: Yale University Press, 1989.

Cheney-Lippold, John. "A New Algorithmic Identity: Soft Biopolitics and the Modulation of Control." *Theory, Culture and Society* 28, no. 6 (2011): 164–81.

Cho, Lily. *Mass Capture: Chinese Head Tax and the Making of Non-Citizens*. Montreal: McGill-Queen's Press-MQUP, 2021.

Chow, Rey. "How (the) Inscrutable Chinese Led to Globalized Theory." *PMLA* 116, no. 1 (2001): 69–74.

Churchill, Ward, and Jim Vander Wall. *Agents of Repression: The FBI's Secret Wars Against the Black Panther Party and the American Indian Movement*. Vol. 7. Cambridge, MA: South End Press, 2002.

Churchill, Ward, and Jim Vander Wall. *The COINTELPRO Papers*. Boston: South End, 1990.

Cohen, Margaret. "Literary Studies on the Terraqueous Globe." *PMLA* 125, no. 3 (2010): 657–62.

Cohn, Carol. "Sex and Death in the Rational World of Defense Intellectuals." *Signs: Journal of Women in Culture and Society* 12, no. 4 (1987): 687–718.

Cole, David. *The Torture Memos*. New York: New Press, 2009.

Color of Change and Center for Constitutional Rights. "DHS 'Race Paper' Briefing Guide." Color of Change. Accessed February 2, 2025. https://ccrjustice.org/sites/default/files/attach/2018/03/COC%20FOIA%20-%20Race%20Paper%20Briefing%20Guide%20031918.pdf.

Color of Change and Center for Constitutional Rights. "FOIA to DHS and FBI Letter." Color of Change, July 5, 2016. https://ccrjustice.org/sites/default/files/attach/2019/04/COC_FOIA.pdf.

Cook, Blanche Wiesen, and Gerald Markowitz. "History in Shreds: The Fate of the Freedom of Information Act." *Radical History Review* 26 (1982): 173–78.

Corris, Michael. *Ad Reinhardt*. London: Reaktion Books, 2008.

Coundouriotis, Eleni. "Torture and Textuality: Guantánamo Diary as Postcolonial Text." *Textual Practice* 34, no. 7 (2020): 1061–80. https://doi.org/10.1080/0950236X.2019.1580216.

Craze, Joshua. "Can We See Torture?" In *Evidentiary Realism: Investigative, Forensic, Documentary Art*, edited by Paolo Cirio. Berlin: Nome, 2019.

Craze, Joshua. "In the Dead Letter Office." In *Jenny Holzer: War Paintings*, edited by Jenny Holzer and Kristen Asp. Cologne: König, 2015.

Cross, Harold L. *The People's Right to Know: Legal Access to Public Records and Proceedings*. New York: Columbia University Press, 1953.

Crouse, Timothy. "Daniel Patrick Moynihan: Ruling Class Hero." *Rolling Stone*, August 12, 1976. https://www.rollingstone.com/politics/politics-news/aniel-patrick-moynihan-ruling-class-hero-228185/.

Cuillier, David. "The People's Right to Know: Comparing Harold L. Cross' Pre-FOIA World to Post-FOIA Today." In *The US Freedom of Information Act at 50*, edited by W. Wat Hopkins. London: Routledge, 2019.

Currier, Cora. "Redaction Art: How Secrets Are Made Visible." *Intercept*, March 5, 2016. https://theintercept.com/2016/03/05/redaction-art-how-secrets-are -made-visible/.

Dahlburg, John-Thor. "CIA's Raising of Soviet Sub Told: Diplomacy: Agency Chief Robert Gates Tells Russian President About 1974 U.S. Intelligence Coup." *Los Angeles Times*, October 17, 1992.

Dark Opacities Lab. *Dark Opacities Lab: A Manifesto on the Evasion of Racial and Colonial Capture*. Vol. 1. Montreal: B&D Press, 2023.

Davis, Benjamin P. "The Politics of Édouard Glissant's Right to Opacity." *C. L. R. James Journal* 25, nos. 1–2 (2019): 59–70.

Dean, Jodi. *Publicity's Secret: How Technoculture Capitalizes on Democracy*. Ithaca, NY: Cornell University Press, 2002.

Dean, Mitchell. *Governmentality: Power and Rule in Modern Society*. London: Sage, 1999.

Denbeaux, Mark, Brian Beroth, et al. "Death in Camp Delta." Seton Hall Law School Legal Studies Research Paper No. 2010–37, December 12, 2009. http://dx.doi.org /10.2139/ssrn.1582658.

Denbeaux, Mark, Jess Ghannam, and Abu Zubaydah. "American Torturers: FBI and CIA Abuses at Dark Sites and Guantánamo." Seton Hall Law School Legal Studies Research Paper, May 9, 2023. http://dx.doi.org/10.2139/ssrn.4443310.

Desai, Neal, et al. "Torture at Times: Waterboarding in the Media." Student paper, Joan Shorenstein Center on the Press, Politics, and Public Policy, Harvard University, 2010.

Deutsch, Michael E., and Erica Thompson. "Secrets and Lies: The Persecution of Muhammad Salah (Part I)." *Journal of Palestine Studies* 37, no. 4 (2008): 38–58.

De Volpi, Alexander. *Born Secret: The H-Bomb, the Progressive Case and National Security*. New York: Pergamon, 1981.

De Vries, Tity. "The 1967 Central Intelligence Agency Scandal: Catalyst in a Transforming Relationship Between State and People." *Journal of American History* 98, no. 4 (2012): 1075–92.

Diamond, Sigmund. *Compromised Campus: The Collaboration of Universities with the Intelligence Community, 1945–1955*. New York: Oxford University Press, 1992.

Dorotheum. "Jenny Holzer Exhibit at Dorotheum London." *Dorotheum Blog*, June 2, 2017. https://blog.dorotheum.com/en/jenny-holzer-dorotheum-london/.

Dyer, Richard. *White: Essays on Race and Culture*. New York: Routledge, 1997.

Ebadolahi, Mitra. "Did You Kiss the Dead Body? Artist's Work Keeps Human Realities of Torture Alive." *ACLU Blog*, February 22, 2013. https://www.aclu.org/blog

/national-security/torture/did-you-kiss-dead-body?redirect=blog/content
/did-you-kiss-dead-body.

El Raggal, Aly. "The Egyptian Revolution's Fatal Mistake." *Middle East Report* 291
(2019). https://merip.org/2019/09/the-egyptian-revolutions-fatal-mistake/.

Espada, Martin. "Who Burns for the Perfection of Paper." *Ploughshares* 19, no. 1 (1993):
80–81.

Esposito, Roberto. *Bios: Biopolitics and Philosophy*. Minneapolis: University of Minnesota Press, 2008.

Estefan, Kareem. "When Artists Boycott." *Art in America* 102, no. 11 (2014): 37–38.

Estefan, Kareem, Carin Kuoni, and Laura Raicovich, eds. *Assuming Boycott: Resistance, Agency and Cultural Production*. New York: OR Books, 2017.

Feinberg, Lotte E. "FOIA, Federal Information Policy, and Information Availability in a Post-9/11 World." *Government Information Quarterly* 21, no. 4 (2004): 439–60.

Feldman, Allen. "On the Actuarial Gaze: From 9/11 to Abu Ghraib." *Cultural Studies* 19, no. 2 (2005): 203–26.

Felker-Kantor, Max. *Policing Los Angeles: Race, Resistance, and the Rise of the LAPD*. Chapel Hill: University of North Carolina Press, 2018.

Fenster, Mark. *The Transparency Fix: Secrets, Leaks, and Uncontrollable Government Information*. Stanford, CA: Stanford University Press, 2017.

Ferguson, Roderick. *Aberrations in Black: Toward a Queer of Color Critique*. Minneapolis: University of Minnesota Press, 2004.

Foerstel, Herbert N. *Surveillance in the Stacks: The FBI's Library Awareness Program*. Westport, CT: Greenwood, 1991.

Foucault, Michel. *The Order of Things: An Archaeology of the Human Sciences*. Translated by Alan Sheridan. New York: Random House, 1970.

Foucault, Michel. *"Society Must Be Defended": Lectures at the College de France, 1975–1976*. Translated by David Macy. New York: Picador, 2003.

Fraser, Nancy. "Rethinking the Public Sphere: A Contribution to the Critique of Actually Existing Democracy." *Social Text* nos. 25–26 (1990): 56–80.

Friedly, Michael and David Gallen, *Martin Luther King Jr.: The FBI File*. New York: Carrol and Graff Publishers, 1993.

Gaddis, John Lewis. "The Long Peace: Elements of Stability in the Postwar International System." *International Security* 10, no. 4 (1986): 99–142.

Gaines, Jane. "Political Mimesis." In *Collecting Visible Evidence*, edited by Jane Gaines and Michael Renov. Minneapolis: University of Minnesota Press, 1999.

Galloway, Alexander. "Are Some Things Unrepresentable?" *Theory, Culture and Society* 28, nos. 7–8 (2011): 85–102.

Ganesh, Chitra, and Mariam Ghani. "Introduction to an Index." *Radical History Review* 2011, no. 111 (2011): 110–29. https://doi.org/10.1215/01636545-1268740.

Gates, Kelly. "Policing as Digital Platform." *Surveillance and Society* 17, nos. 1–2 (2019): 63–68.

Genette, Gérard, and Marie Maclean. "Introduction to the Paratext." *New Literary History* 22, no. 2 (1991): 261–72. https://doi.org/10.2307/469037.

Gerhardt, Uta. "Worlds Come Apart: Systems Theory Versus Critical Theory: Drama in the History of Sociology in the Twentieth Century." *American Sociologist* 33, no. 2 (2002): 5–39.

Gilbert, Emily. "Keeping Secrets: Freedom of Information Requests and Critical Security Studies." In *Research Methods in Critical Security Studies*, edited by Mark B. Salter, Can E. Mutlu, and Philippe M. Frowd. London: Routledge, 2023.

Gilman, Nils. *Mandarins of the Future: Modernization Theory in Cold War America*. Baltimore: Johns Hopkins University Press, 2003.

Gitelman, Lisa. *Paper Knowledge: Toward a Media History of Documents*. Durham, NC: Duke University Press, 2014.

Glissant, Édouard. *Poetics of Relation*. Translated by Betsy Wing. Ann Arbor: University of Michigan Press, 1997.

Gómez-Barris, Macarena. *The Extractive Zone: Social Ecologies and Decolonial Perspectives*. Durham, NC: Duke University Press, 2017.

Goodnough, Abby, and Margot Sanger-Katz. "Number of Uninsured Children Rose 400,000, Eroding Gains." *New York Times*, October 23, 2019.

Goodnough, Abby, and Margot Sanger-Katz. "Medicaid Covers a Million Fewer Children: Baby Elijah Was One of Them." *New York Times*, October 22, 2019. https://www.nytimes.com/2019/10/22/upshot/medicaid-uninsured-children .html.

Gopinath, Gayatri. "Archive, Affect, and the Everyday: Queer Diasporic Re-Visions." In *Political Emotions*, edited by Janet Staiger, Ann Cvetkovich, and Ann Reynolds. London: Routledge, 2010. https://doi.org/10.4324/9780203849538–15.

Gordon, Avery. *Ghostly Matters: Haunting and the Sociological Imagination*. Minneapolis: University of Minnesota Press, 1997.

Gordon, Avery. "The Prisoner's Curse." In *Toward a Sociology of the Trace*, edited by Herman Gray and Macarena Gómez-Barris. Minneapolis: University of Minnesota Press, 2010.

Goyal, Yogita. "The Genres of Guantánamo Diary: Postcolonial Reading and the War on Terror." *Cambridge Journal of Postcolonial Literary Inquiry* 4, no. 1 (2017): 69–87.

Graeber, David. *The Utopia of Rules: On Technology, Stupidity, and the Secret Joys of Bureaucracy*. Brooklyn, NY: Melville House, 2015.

Greenberger, Alex. "Jenny Holzer's Facile Guggenheim Museum Show Fails to Meet Our Moment." *ARTnews* (blog), May 16, 2024. https://www.artnews.com/art -news/reviews/jenny-holzer-guggenheim-museum-review-1234707322/.

Grisinger, Joanna L. "The Hearing Examiners and the Administrative Procedure Act, 1937–1960." *Journal of the National Association of Administrative Law Judiciary* 34 (2014): 1–46.

Guha, Ranajit. "On Some Aspects of the Historiography of Colonial India." In *Selected Subaltern Studies*, edited by Ranajit Guha and Gayatri Spivak. Oxford: Oxford University Press, 1988.

Guha, Ranajit. "The Prose of Counter-Insurgency." In *Selected Subaltern Studies*, edited by Ranajit Guha and Gayatri Spivak. Oxford: Oxford University Press, 1988.

Guilbaut, Serge. *How New York Stole the Idea of Modern Art: Abstract Expressionism, Freedom and the Cold War*. Chicago: University of Chicago Press, 1983.

Hajjar, Lisa. *The War in Court: Inside the Long Fight Against Torture*. Oakland: University of California Press, 2022.

Hall, Stuart. *Cultural Studies 1983: A Theoretical History*. Durham, NC: Duke University Press, 2020.

Hall, Stuart. "Notes on Deconstructing 'the Popular'" (1981). In *Essential Essays*, vol. 1, edited by David Morley. Durham, NC: Duke University Press, 2020.

Hall, Stuart. "The Problem of Ideology: Marxism Without Guarantees." *Journal of Communication Inquiry* 10, no. 2 (1986): 28–44.

Haraway, Donna. "Situated Knowledges: The Science Question in Feminism and the Privilege of Partial Perspective." *Feminist Studies* 14, no. 3 (1988): 575–99.

Harris, Caroline, and Cristina Chan. "Across Space and Time: An Interview with Sadie Barnette." SFMoMA. Accessed November 19, 2024. https://www.sfmoma.org /read/across-space-and-time-an-interview-with-sadie-barnette/.

Harris, Cheryl I. "Whiteness as Property." *Harvard Law Review* (1993): 1707–91.

Hayles, N. Katherine. *Electronic Literature: New Horizons for the Literary United States*. Notre Dame, IN: University of Notre Dame Press, 2008.

Hendricks, Evan. *Former Secrets: Government Records Made Public Through the Freedom of Information Act*. Washington, DC: Campaign for Political Rights, 1982.

Hetherington, Kregg. *Guerrilla Auditors: The Politics of Transparency in Neoliberal Paraguay*. Durham, NC: Duke University Press, 2011.

Hilderbrand, Lucas. "Grainy Days and Mondays: Superstar and Bootleg Aesthetics." *Camera Obscura* 19, no. 3 (2004): 57–91.

Ho, Fred. "An Analysis of Seth Rosenfeld's FBI Files on Richard Aoki." *San Francisco Bay View*, September 8, 2021. https://sfbayview.com/2012/09/an-analysis-of -seth-rosenfelds-fbi-files-on-richard-aoki/.

Ho, Fred. "Fred Ho Refutes the Claim That Richard Aoki Was an FBI Informant." *San Francisco Bay View*, August 21, 2012. https://sfbayview.com/2012/08/fred-ho- refutes-the-claim-that-richard-aoki-was-an-fbi-informant/.

Hofstadter, Richard. "The Paranoid Style in American Politics" *Harpers Magazine*. November 1964: 77–86.

Huntington, Samuel P. *American Politics: The Promise of Disharmony*. Cambridge, MA: Belknap Press of Harvard University Press, 1981.

James, Joy. *Resisting State Violence: Radicalism, Gender, and Race in US Culture*. Minneapolis: University of Minnesota Press, 1996.

JC Reporter. "Holzer Offers Light Relief to Art Museum." June 30, 2017. https://www.thejc.com/community/community-news/holzer-offers-light-relief-to-art-museum-supporters-1.440773.

Jones, Nate. "Statement of Nate Jones, Director of the Freedom of Information Act Project of the National Security Archive, George Washington University Before the United States House of Representatives Committee on Oversight and Government Reform on 'Ensuring Transparency Through the Freedom of Information Act.'" US House Committee on Oversight and Government Reform, June 2, 2015. https://oversight.house.gov/wp-content/uploads/2015/06/Jones-GW-Statement-6-2-FOIA.pdf.

Jurgenson, Nathan, and P. J. Rey. "WikiLeaks: Liquid Information Leaks." *International Journal of Communication* 8 (2014): 2651–65.

Kadonaga, Cynthia. "Anti–*Spy Magazine* Split." *Washington Post*, July 8, 1976. https://www.cia.gov/library/readingroom/docs/CIA-RDP88–01314R000100360014–1.pdf.

Kafka, Ben. *The Demon of Writing: Powers and Failures of Paperwork*. New York: Zone Books, 2012.

Kafka, Ben. "Paperwork: The State of the Discipline." *Book History* 12, no. 1 (2009): 340–53.

Kaiser, David, and Benjamin Wilson. "American Scientists as Public Citizens: 70 Years of the *Bulletin of the Atomic Scientists*." *Bulletin of the Atomic Scientists* 71, no. 1 (2015): 13–25.

Kahlon, Rajkamal. "Did You Kiss the Dead Body?: Visualizing Absence in the Archive of War." *Comparative Studies of South Asia, Africa, and the Middle East* 34, no. 2 (2014): 336–63. https://doi.org/10.1215/1089201X-2773887.

Kapadia, Ronak K. *Insurgent Aesthetics: Security and the Queer Life of the Forever War*. Durham, NC: Duke University Press, 2020.

Kaplan, Caren. *Aerial Aftermaths: Wartime from Above*. Durham, NC: Duke University Press, 2017.

Keenen, Katherine. "Look Up: Trevor Paglen's Work on Government Surveillance." *Art Critique*, December 26, 2018. https://www.art-critique.com/en/2018/12/look-up-trevor-paglens-work-on-government-surveillance/.

Kennedy, George Penn. "Advocates of Openness: The Freedom of Information Movement." PhD diss., University of Missouri-Columbia, 1978.

Kelley, Robin D. G. *Freedom Dreams: The Black Radical Imagination*. Boston: Beacon, 2002.

Kim, Monica. "The Intelligence of Fools: Reading the US Military Archive of the Korean War." *positions: east asia cultures critique* 23, no. 4 (2015): 695–728.

Kim, Monica. *Interrogation Rooms of the Korean War: The Untold History*. Princeton, NJ: Princeton University Press, 2019.

Kimball, Penn. *The File*. New York: Harcourt, 1983.

Klein, Naomi. *The Shock Doctrine: The Rise of Disaster Capitalism*. New York: Picador, 2007.

Kullman, Joe. "Group 'Reveals' Network of Surveillance at KSU." *Daily Kent Stater*, May 3, 1974.

Kornbluh, Peter. "CIA: 'Pinochet Personally Ordered' Letelier Bombing." *National Security Archive*, October 8, 2015. https://nsarchive.gwu.edu/briefing-book/chile/2016-09-23/cia-pinochet-personally-ordered-letelier-bombing.

Kraut, Sarah. "A Marathon Freedom of Information Fight." *American Journalism Review*, December 13, 2012. https://ajr.org/2013/11/09/freedom-information-act-rosenfeld-2/.

Kumar, Deepa. "Terrorcraft: Empire and the Making of the Racialised Terrorist Threat." *Race and Class* 62, no. 2 (2020): 34–60. https://doi.org/10.1177/0306396820930523.

Kwoka, Margaret B. "FOIA, Inc." *Duke Law Journal* 65, no. 7 (2016): 1361–1437.

LaGrone, Sam. "Former CIA Spy Ship Hughes Glomar Explorer Sold for Scrap." *USNI News*, September 9, 2015. https://news.usni.org/2015/09/09/former-cia-spy-ship-hughes-glomar-explorer-sold-for-scrap.

Latner, Teishan A. "'Agrarians or Anarchists?': The Venceremos Brigades to Cuba, State Surveillance, and the FBI as Biographer and Archivist." *Journal of Transnational American Studies* 9, no. 1 (2018). https://doi.org/10.5070/T891034678.

Lebovic, Sam. "How Administrative Opposition Shaped the Freedom of Information Act." In *Troubling Transparency: The History and Future of Freedom of Information*, edited by David Pozen and Michael Schudson, 13–33. New York: Columbia University Press, 2018.

Lee, Nathan. "The Fold of Undetectable." *Camera Obscura* 31, no. 2 (2016): 167–73.

Lee, Pamela M. *Think Tank Aesthetics: Midcentury Modernism, the Cold War, and the Neoliberal Present*. Cambridge, MA: MIT Press, 2020. https://doi.org/10.7551/mitpress/12139.001.0001.

Lewine, Edward. "Art House." *New York Times Magazine*, December 16, 2009. https://www.nytimes.com/2009/12/20/magazine/20fob-domains-t.html?_r=0.

Lippit, Akira. *Atomic Light (Shadow Optics)*. Minneapolis: University of Minnesota Press, 2005.

Lipsitz, George. *The Possessive Investment in Whiteness: How White People Profit from Identity Politics*. Philadelphia: Temple University Press, 2006.

Longworth, Karina. *Seduction: Sex, Lies, and Stardom in Howard Hughes's Hollywood*. New York: HarperCollins, 2018.

Luk, Sharon. *The Life of Paper: A Poetics*. Berkeley: University of California Press, 2018.

Luscombe, Alex, Kevin Walby, and Randy K. Lippert. "Brokering Access Beyond the Border and in the Wild: Comparing Freedom of Information Law and Policy in Canada and the United States." *Law and Policy* 39, no. 3 (2017): 259–79.

MacKenzie, Angus. *Secrets: The CIA's War at Home*. Berkeley: University of California Press, 1999.

Macy, Christy, and Susan Kaplan. *Documents*. New York: Penguin Books and the Center for National Security Studies, 1980.

Makdisi, Saree. "The Architecture of Erasure." *Critical Inquiry* 36, no. 3 (2010): 519–59.

Makdisi, Ussama. *The Culture of Sectarianism: Community, History, and Violence in Nineteenth-Century Ottoman Lebanon*. Berkeley: University of California Press, 2000.

Mao Tse-tung. "U.S. Imperialism Is a Paper Tiger" (July 14, 1956). *Selected Works of Mao Tse-tung*, vol. 5. https://www.marxists.org/reference/archive/mao/selected-works/volume-5/mswv5_52.htm.

Marks, Laura U. *Touch: Sensuous Theory and Multisensory Media*. Minneapolis: University of Minnesota Press, 2002.

Masco, Joseph. "'Sensitive but Unclassified': Secrecy and the Counterterrorist State." *Public Culture* 22, no. 3 (2010): 433–63.

Maxwell, William J. *F.B. Eyes: How J. Edgar Hoover's Ghostreaders Framed African American Literature*. Princeton, NJ: Princeton University Press, 2015.

Maxwell, William J. *James Baldwin: The FBI File*. New York: Arcade Publishing, 2017.

Maxwell, William J. "Ghostreaders and Diaspora-Writers: Four Theses on the FBI and African American Modernism." In *Modernism on File: Writers, Artists, and the FBI, 1920–1950*, edited by Claire A. Culleton and Karen Leick. New York: Palgrave Macmillan, 2008.

Mbembe, Achille. "Necropolitics." *Public Culture* 15, no. 1 (2003): 11–40.

McCoy, Alfred. "Policing the Imperial Periphery: The Philippine-American War and the Origins of U.S. Global Surveillance." *Surveillance and Society* 13, no. 1 (2015): 4–26. https://doi.org/10.24908/ss.v13i1.5161.

McCoy, Alfred. *A Question of Torture: CIA Interrogation, from the Cold War to the War on Terror*. London: Henry Holt and Company, 2007.

McGarr, Paul. "'Do We Still Need the CIA?': Daniel Patrick Moynihan, the Central Intelligence Agency and US Foreign Policy." *History* 100, no. 340 (2015): 275–92.

Mcheimech, Zeinab. "Resisting Islamophobia via [Redacted] Prayers in the Handwritten Autobiographies of 'Umar ibn Sayyid and Mohamedou Ould Slahi." *Journal of Africana Religions* 7, no. 1 (2019): 163–71. https://muse.jhu.edu/article/715873.

McKinney, Cait. *Information Activism: A Queer History of Lesbian Media Technologies*. Durham, NC: Duke University Press, 2020.

McKittrick, Katherine. "Dear April: The Aesthetics of Black Miscellanea." *Antipode* 54, no. 1 (2022): 3–18.

McLuhan, Marshall. *Understanding Media: The Extensions of Man*. 1st ed. New York: McGraw-Hill, 1964.

Medsger, Betty. *The Burglary: The Discovery of J. Edgar Hoover's Secret FBI*. New York: Vintage, 2014.

Mellinger, Gwyneth. "Washington Confidential: A Double Standard Gives Way to the People's Right to Know." *Journalism and Mass Communication Quarterly* 92, no. 4 (2015): 857–76. https://doi.org/10.1177/1077699015596340.

Mesches, Arnold. "American Uncanny." *Cultural Politics* 11, no. 1 (2015): 36–52.

Mesches, Arnold. "The FBI Files." *Public Culture* 15, no. 2 (2003): 287–94.

Miller, Harold L. "Will Access Restrictions Hold Up in Court? The FBI's Attempt to Use the Braden Papers at the State Historical Society of Wisconsin." *American Archivist* 52, no. 2 (1989): 180–90. https://doi.org/10.17723/aarc.52.2.57607558u7j70177.

Mills, Ami Chen. *CIA off Campus: Building the Movement Against Agency Recruitment and Research*. Boston: South End Press, 1991.

Mirzoeff, Nicholas. *The Right to Look: A Counterhistory of Visuality*. Durham, NC: Duke University Press, 2011.

Monahan, Torin. *Crisis Vision: Race and the Cultural Production of Surveillance*. Durham, NC: Duke University Press, 2022.

Monahan, Torin. *Surveillance in the Time of Insecurity*. New Brunswick, NJ: Rutgers University Press, 2010.

Monahan, Torin, and Jill A. Fisher. "Strategies for Obtaining Access to Secretive or Guarded Organizations." *Journal of Contemporary Ethnography* 44, no. 6 (2015): 709–36.

Moss, John. 'Is There a Paper Curtain in Washington," August 2, 1955, 84th Cong., 1st sess., *Congressional Record* 101, prt. 10: 13246.

Moynihan, Daniel P. *Secrecy: The American Experience*. New Haven, CT: Yale University Press, 1998.

Moynihan, Daniel P. "The United States in Opposition." *Commentary* 59, no. 3 (1975): 31–44.

Moynihan, Daniel P., and Steven R. Weisman. *Daniel Patrick Moynihan: A Portrait in Letters of an American Visionary*. New York: PublicAffairs, 2010.

Museum on the Seam. "The Right to Protest." Accessed February 3, 2025. https://www.mots.org.il/en/all-exhibitions/the-right-to-protest.

Myers, Rachel. "Knee-Jerk Redaction?" *ACLU Blog of Rights*, May 28, 2008. http://www.aclu.org/blog/national-security/knee-jerk-redaction.

Nader, Ralph. "The Dossier Invades the Home." In *The Ralph Nader Reader*. New York: Seven Stories, 2000.

Nader, Ralph. "Freedom from Information: The Act and the Agencies." *Harvard Civil Rights–Civil Liberties Law Review* 5 (1970): 1–15.

Nath, Anjali. "Beyond the Public Eye: On FOIA Documents and the Visual Politics of Redaction." *Cultural Studies Critical Methodologies* 14, no. 1 (2014): 21–28.

Nath, Anjali. "Toward the Dark Side: Seeing Detainee Bodies in Documentary Film." In *A Companion to Contemporary Documentary Film*, edited by Alexandra Juhasz and Alisa Lebow. Malden, MA: John Wiley & Sons, 2015.

National Gallery of Art. "Overview: DODDOACID, 2007." Accessed February 3, 2025. https://www.nga.gov/collection/art-object-page.152280.html#overview.

Ngai, Mae. *Impossible Subjects: Illegal Aliens and the Making of Modern America*. Princeton, NJ: Princeton University Press, 2004.

Nguyen, Viet Thanh. *The Sympathizer*. New York: Grove, 2015.

Nichols, Bill. *Representing Reality: Issues and Concepts in Documentary*. Bloomington: Indiana University Press, 1991.

Nixon, Rob. *Slow Violence and the Environmentalism of the Poor*. Cambridge, MA: Harvard University Press, 2011.

Obama, Barack H. "Freedom of Information Act Memorandum for the Heads of Executive Departments and Agencies." White House Office of Press Secretary, January 21, 2009. http://www.dol.gov/dol/foia/2009_FOIA_memo.pdf.

Olmsted, Kathryn. "Reclaiming Executive Power: The Ford Administration's Response to the Intelligence Investigations." *Presidential Studies Quarterly* 26, no. 3 (1996): 725–37. http://www.jstor.org/stable/27551628.

Omatsu, Glenn. "Book and Resource Notes." *Amerasia Journal* 14, no. 1 (1988): 187–89.

Onaci, Edward. *Free the Land: The Republic of New Afrika and the Pursuit of a Black Nation-State*. Chapel Hill: University of North Carolina Press, 2020

Ouellette, Laurie, and James Hay. *Better Living Through Reality TV: Television and Post-Welfare Citizenship*. Malden, MA: Blackwell, 2008.

Paglen, Trevor. *Blank Spots on the Map: The Dark Geography of the Pentagon's Secret World*. New York: Dutton, 2009.

Panetta, Leon. "Declaration of Leon E. Panetta." *ACLU et al. v. Department of Defense*. https://sgp.fas.org/jud/aclu-panetta.pdf.

Perry, Imani. *Vexy Thing: On Gender and Liberation*. Durham, NC: Duke University Press, 2020.

Phillips, Mary. "The Power of the First-Person Narrative: Ericka Huggins and the Black Panther Party." *WSQ: Women's Studies Quarterly* 43, no. 3 (2015): 33–51. https://dx.doi.org/10.1353/wsq.2015.0060.

Pilkington, Ed. "'The Forever Prisoner': Abu Zubaydah's Drawings Expose the US's Depraved Torture Policy." *Guardian*, May 11, 2023. https://www.theguardian.com/law/2023/may/11/abu-zubaydah-drawings-guantanamo-bay-us-torture-policy.

Poniewozik, James. "Celebrities Read the Mueller Report, and It's a Dark Comedy." *New York Times*, June 25, 2019.

Pratt, William C. "Using FBI Records in Writing Regional Labor History." *Labor History* 33, no. 4 (1992): 470–82.

Price, David. "On Using Archives and Freedom of Information Act for Anthropological Research." *Anthrodendum*, October 7, 2018. https://anthrodendum.org/2018/10/07/on-using-archives-and-freedom-of-information-act-for-anthropological-research/.

Price, David H. *Cold War anthropology: The CIA, the Pentagon, and the Growth of Dual Use Anthropology*. Durham, NC: Duke University Press, 2016.

Price, David H. *Threatening Anthropology: McCarthyism and the FBI's Surveillance of Activist Anthropologists*. Durham, NC: Duke University Press, 2004.

Price, David H. *Weaponizing Anthropology: Social Science in Service of the Militarized State*. Chico, CA: AK Press, 2011.

Ratner, Michael, and Michael Steven Smith, eds. *Che Guevara and the FBI: The US Political Police Dossier on the Latin American Revolutionary*. New York: Ocean Press, 1997.

Rault, Jas. "Window Walls and Other Tricks of Transparency: Digital, Colonial, and Architectural Modernity." *American Quarterly* 72, no. 4 (2020): 937–60.

Reddy, Chandan. *Freedom with Violence: Race, Sexuality, and the US State*. Durham, NC: Duke University Press, 2011.

Reinhardt, Ad. "War Chief." Whitney Museum. Accessed February 3, 2025. https://whitney.org/collection/works/28109.

Rejali, Darius. *Torture and Democracy*. Princeton, NJ: Princeton University Press, 2007.

Report of the Commission on Protecting and Reducing Government Secrecy: Pursuant to Public Law 236, 103rd Congress. Vol. 105–2. Washington, DC: U.S. G.P.O., 1997.

Richardson, Peter. *A Bomb in Every Issue: How the Short, Unruly Life of* Ramparts Magazine *Changed America*. New York: New Press, 2009.

Richardson, Peter. "The Perilous Fight: The Rise of *Ramparts Magazine*, 1965–1966." *California History* 86, no. 3 (2009): 22–69. https://doi.org/10.2307/40495218.

Roberts, Alasdair. *Blacked Out: Government Secrecy in the Information Age*. Cambridge: Cambridge University Press, 2006.

Robertson, Craig. *The Filing Cabinet: A Vertical History of Information*. Minneapolis: University of Minnesota Press, 2021.

Rogers, Asha. "Black Orpheus and the African Magazines of the Congress for Cultural Freedom." In *Campaigning Culture and the Global Cold War: The Journals of the Congress for Cultural Freedom*, edited by Giles Scott-Smith and Charlotte A. Lerg. London: Palgrave Macmillan, 2017. https://doi.org/10.1057/978-1-137-59867-7_13.

Rose, Nikolas, and Peter Miller. "Political Power Beyond the State: Problematics of Government." In *Foucault and Law*, edited by Ben Golder and Peter Fitzpatrick. London: Routledge, 2017.

Rosenfeld, Seth. "Activist Richard Aoki Named as Informant." *SFGATE*, August 20, 2012. https://www.sfgate.com/crime/article/Activist-Richard-Aoki-named-as -informant-3800133.php.

Royko, Mike. "Ask Not for Whom the Welcome Wagon Rolls." *Los Angeles Times*, April 3, 1977.

Saloschin, Robert L. "Administering the Freedom of Information Act: An Insider's View." In *None of Your Business: Government Secrecy in America*, edited by Norman Dorsen and Stephen Gillers, 183–94.

Said, Edward W. "The Clash of Ignorance." *Nation*, October 4, 2001.

Said, Edward W. *Culture and Imperialism*. New York: Vintage, 1993.

Said, Edward W. "Zionism from the Standpoint of Its Victims." *Social Text* 1 (1979): 7–58.

Scarry, Elaine. *The Body in Pain: The Making and Unmaking of the World*. New York: Oxford University Press, 1985.

Schudson, Michael. *The Rise of the Right to Know: Politics and the Culture of Transparency, 1945–1975*. Cambridge, MA: Harvard University Press, 2015.

Schwellenbach, Nick, and Sean Moulton. "The 'Most Abused' Freedom of Information Act Exemption Still Needs to Be Reined In." Project on Government Oversight, February 6, 2020. https://www.pogo.org/analysis/2020/02/the-most-abused -foia-exemption-still-needs-to-be-reined-in/.

Scott-Clark, Cathy, and Adrian Levy. *The Forever Prisoner: The Full and Searing Account of the CIA's Most Controversial Covert Program*. New York: Atlantic Monthly Press, 2022.

Secker, Tom, and Matthew Alford. "New Evidence for the Surprisingly Significant Propaganda Role of the Central Intelligence Agency and Department of Defense in the Screen Entertainment Industry." *Critical Sociology* 45, no. 3 (2019): 347–59.

Sharma, Sarah. "Introduction: A Feminist Medium Is the Message." In *Re-Understanding Media*, edited by Rianka Singh and Sarah Sharma. Durham, NC: Duke University Press, 2022.

Sharpe, Christina Elizabeth. *In the Wake: On Blackness and Being*. Durham, NC: Duke University Press, 2016.

Sharpe, Jenny. "The Archive and Affective Memory in M. Nourbese Philip's *Zong!*" *Interventions* 16, no. 4 (2014): 465–82.

Shils, Edward. "America's Paper Curtain." *Bulletin of the Atomic Scientists* 8, no. 7 (1952): 210–17. https://doi.org/10.1080/00963402.1952.11457325.

Shils, Edward. "Color, the Universal Intellectual Community, and the Afro-Asian Intellectual." *Daedalus* 96, no. 2 (1967): 279–95.

Shils, Edward. "The Culture of the Indian Intellectual." *Sewanee Review* 67, no. 2 (1959): 239–61.

Shils, Edward. "The Prospect for Lebanese Civility." In *Politics in Lebanon*, edited by Leonard Binder. New York: John Wiley and Sons, 1966.

Shils, Edward. *The Torment of Secrecy: The Background and Consequences of American Se-curity Policies.* Glencoe, IL: Free Press, 1956. Reprint. Chicago: Ivan R. Dee, 1996.

Shils, Edward, and Peter Coleman. "Remembering the Congress of Cultural Freedom." *Society (New Brunswick)* 46, no. 5 (2009): 437–44.

Siems, Larry. *The Torture Report.* New York: OR Books, 2011.

Singh, Balbir K. "Decoding Dress: Countersurveillance Poetics and Practices Under Permanent War." *Surveillance and Society* 17, no. 5 (2019): 662–80. https://doi.org/10.24908/ss.v17i5.12935.

Slahi, Mohamedou Ould. "15 Anni Senza Accuse: Mohamedou Slahi Racconta l'In-ferno di Guantánamo." Posted April 8, 2017, YouTube, 47 min., 11 sec. https://www.youtube.com/watch?v=XuvnSgQKEoo&t=3s.

Slahi, Mohamedou Ould. *Guantánamo Diary.* Edited by Larry Siems. New York: Little, Brown, 2015.

Slahi, Mohamedou Ould. *Guantánamo Diary: Restored Edition.* Edited by Larry Siems. Restored ed. New York: Back Bay Books, 2017.

Slahi, Mohamedou Ould, and Larry Siems. "Scribo Ergo Sum: Creating and Publishing *Guantánamo Diary.*" In *Prison Writing and the Literary World,* edited by Michelle Kelly and Claire Westall. London: Routledge, 2020.

Slaughter, Joseph R. "Vanishing Points: When Narrative Is Not Simply There." *Journal of Human Rights* 9, no. 2 (2010): 207–23.

Slyomovics, Susan. *The Object of Memory: Arab and Jew Narrate the Palestinian Village.* Philadelphia: University of Pennsylvania Press, 1998.

Smith, Christina M., and Kelly M. McDonald. "The Mundane to the Memorial: Cir-culating and Deliberating the War in Iraq Through Vernacular Soldier-Produced Videos." *Critical Studies in Media Communication* 28, no. 4 (2011): 292–313. https://doi.org/10.1080/15295036.2011.589031.

Sontag, Susan. *On Photography.* New York: Farrar, Straus and Giroux, 1977.

Sontag, Susan. "Regarding the Torture of Others." *New York Times Magazine* 23, no. 5 (2004): 4. http://www.nytimes.com/2004/05/23/magazine/regarding-the -torture-of-others.html.

Spade, Dean. *Normal Life: Administrative Violence, Critical Trans Politics, and the Limits of Law.* Brooklyn: South End, 2011.

Spencer, Robyn C. "Black Identity Extremists: COINTELPRO 2017." *Black Perspectives,* November 13, 2017. https://www.aaihs.org/black-identity-extremists -cointelpro-2017/.

Spencer, Robyn C. *The Revolution Has Come: Black Power, Gender, and the Black Panther Party in Oakland.* Durham, NC: Duke University Press, 2016.

Spillers, Hortense J. "Mama's Baby, Papa's Maybe: An American Grammar Book." *Dia-critics* 17, no. 2 (1987): 65–81.

Stahl, Roger. "Dispatches from the Militainment Empire." In *Media Imperialism: Con-*

tinuity and Change, edited by Oliver Boyd-Barrett and Tanner Mirrlees. Lanham, MD: Rowman and Littlefield, 2019.

Stanley, Eric A. "Anti-Trans Optics: Recognition, Opacity, and the Image of Force." *South Atlantic Quarterly* 116, no. 3 (2017): 612–20.

Stonor Saunders, Frances. *The Cultural Cold War: The CIA and the World of Arts and Letters.* New York: New Press, 1999.

Sturken, Marita. *Tangled Memories: The Vietnam War, the AIDS Epidemic, and the Politics of Remembering.* Berkeley: University of California Press, 1997.

Swanson, Elizabeth, and Alexandra S. Moore. "Indefinite Detention: Chronotopes of Unfreedom in Mohamedou Ould Slahi's Guantánamo Diary." *Ariel: A Review of International English Literature* 52, no. 1 (2021): 33–60.

Tang, Jeannine. "Persons and Profiles: Chitra Ganesh and Mariam Ghani's Index of the Disappeared (2004–)." *Women and Performance* 30, no. 3 (2020): 307–30.

Teltsch, Kathleen. "Moynihan Calls on U.S. to 'Start Raising Hell' in U.N." *New York Times*, February 26, 1975.

Theoharis, Athan. *From the Secret Files of J. Edgar Hoover.* Chicago: Ivan R. Dee, 1993.

Theoharis, Athan G. "FBI Surveillance During the Cold War years: A Constitutional Crisis." *Public Historian* 3, no. 1 (1981): 4–14.

Theoharis, Athan G. "The FBI and the FOIA: Problems of Access and Destruction." *Midwestern Archivist* 5, no. 2 (1981): 61–74.

Theoharis, Athan G. "Researching the Intelligence Agencies: The Problem of Covert Activities." *Public Historian* 6, no. 2 (1984): 67–76.

Trapp, Erin. "Redacted Tears, Aesthetics of Alterity: Mohamedou Ould Slahi's Guantánamo Diary." *Terror in Global Narrative: Representations of 9/11 in the Age of Late-Late Capitalism* (2016): 55–76.

Treleven, Dale E. "Interviewing a Close Friend, First Amendment Activist Frank Wilkinson." *Journal of American History* 85, no. 2 (1998): 611–19.

Trouillot, Michel-Rolph. *Silencing the Past: Power and the Production of History.* Boston: Beacon, 2015.

University of Pennsylvania Law Review Editors. "*Vaughn v. Rosen*: Toward True Freedom of Information." *University of Pennsylvania Law Review* 122 (1973–74): 731–44.

Vang, Ma. *History on the Run: Secrecy, Fugitivity, and Hmong Refugee Epistemologies.* Durham, NC: Duke University Press, 2021.

Vaughn, Robert G. "The Freedom of Information Act and 'Vaughn v. Rosen': Some Personal Comments." *American University Law Review* 23 (1973): 865–79.

Vaughn, Robert G. *The Spoiled System: A Call for Civil Service Reform.* New York: Charterhouse, 1975.

Vismann, Cornelia. *Files: Law and Media Technology.* Stanford, CA: Stanford University Press, 2008.

Walby, Kevin, and Alex Luscombe. "Freedom of Information Research and Cultural Studies: A Subterranean Affinity." *Cultural Studies* ↔ *Critical Methodologies* 21, no. 1 (2021): 70–79.

Wang, Jessica. *American Science in an Age of Anxiety: Scientists, Anticommunism, and the Cold War*. Chapel Hill: University of North Carolina Press, 1999.

Warner, Michael. *Publics and Counterpublics*. Brooklyn: Zone Books, 2002.

Weiss, Debra. "Fifth Lawyer Said to Oppose Destruction of CIA Videotapes." *ABA Journal*, December 21, 2007. http://www.abajournal.com/news/article/fifth_lawyer_said_to_oppose_destruction_of_cia_videotapes/.

Weld, Kirsten. *Paper Cadavers: The Archives of Dictatorship in Guatemala*. Durham, NC: Duke University Press, 2014.

White, Michele. *The Body and the Screen: Theories of Internet Spectatorship*. Cambridge, MA: MIT Press, 2006.

Wilkinson, Frank. "Why I Won My Case Against the FBI" *Human Rights* 15, no. 2 (1988): 38–55.

Wittner, Lawrence S. "Blanche Weisen Cook and World Peace." *Meridians: Feminism, Race, Transnationalism* 10, no. 2 (2010): 86–95.

Yaremko, Jeff, and Kevin Walby. "Social Movement Groups and Freedom of Information: Frames, Techniques, and Networks." *Interface: A Journal on Social Movements* 13, no. 2 (2021): 489–513.

INDEX

Page references in *italics* refer to figures

film as medium, 77
fingerprints, 62
FOIA (Freedom of Information Act), 1, 3–4,
    5; activism and, 20–21, 63; amendments,
    7, 44–45, 62, 63; authority of, 96; cases,
    84; categorization and, 96; changes to,
    85–86; Cold War and, 6, 32; court cases,
    11; cultural history of, 23–24; debates
    around (mainstream), 60; defenses of,
    86; denial, 47; digitization and, 110;
    documentation, 43; exemptions, 7, 70,
    96, 119, 120, 134; *Former Secrets: Gov-
    ernment Records Made Public Through
    the Freedom of Information Act*, 84–85;
    guides, 63, 68–69, 73; how-to pamphlets,
    63, 68–69, 70, 71; ideology of, 55; impe-
    rialism and, 6–15; implementation, 32,
    45, 47, 55, 56; improper functioning, 56;
    key figures, 32, 175n5; laws and, 60; liti-
    gation, 18, 46, 47, 48, 76–77, 120; materi-
    ality and, 56; 9/11 and, 96; origins, 6, 30,
    44, 92; other legislation and, 6–7; peo-
    ple of color and, 64; as a people's tool,
    70; Reagan administration and, 81–86;
    reform, 60; requests, 2–3, 8–10, 13, 17, 49,
    63, 84, 87, 98, 100, 103, 113, 145, 146, 147,
    154, 179n9; social justice work and, 84,
    87; sorting tools, 69–70; transparency
    and, 45; utopia of, 63; Vietnam War and,
    63; violence of state and, 8; visibility
    and, 34; whiteness and, 66; Wilkinson's
    file and, 68
FOIA Inc. (Fund for Open Access and Ac-
    countability, Inc.), 8, 24, 66–67
FOIA Inc. (Fund for Open Information and
    Accountability, Inc.), 8, 66, 68–69, 72,
    76, 85
"FOIA: Uncovering Racism, Repression in
    the Black Community," 65
FOIA Digest (publication), 74
The Forever Prisoner (Gibney), 91
*Former Secrets: Government Records Made
    Public Through the Freedom of Informa-
    tion Act*, 84–85
Foucault, Michel, 42, 45, 46, 98

Fraser, Nancy, 18
Frazier, Joe, 60
freedom and intimacies, 7
Fukuyama, Francis, 56

Gandhi, Indira, 53
Ganesh, Chitra, 140–42
Garden Coup (Behbahani), 26, 139–40, *141*
gardens, 139
gaze: of countersurveillance, 60; punitive,
    158; of state, 80; of surveillance, 75, 87
Genette, Gérard, 185n17
Ghadar Party, 54
Ghani, Mariam, 140–42
Ghannam, Jess, 121
Gitelman, Lisa, 60, 168n46
Glissant, Édouard, 21, 67
Global Marine, Inc., 49
Glomar denial, 50, 104
Glomar exemption, 49–50
Gómez-Barris, Macarena, 21
Gonzales, Alberto, 103
Gordon, Avery, 159
government: e-government discourses, 110;
    governmentality, 98
Goyal, Yogita, 155
Graeber, David, 19–20, 169n55
Grambo, Norris A., 29
Grand Jury Project, 59, 82, 85–86
Greenberger, Alex, 183n31
Guantanamo Bay Museum of Art and History
    (Paul), 131
Guantánamo Bay Naval Base (GTMO), 26,
    119, 184n2; art on, 131; deaths at, 118; lan-
    guage at, 157; living conditions, 154; pris-
    oner abuse at, 89, 91, 92, 99–100, 118. *See
    also* Slahi, Mohamedou Ould
Guantánamo Diary (Slahi), 26, 154, 155–56, 158
Guatemala, 21
Guevara, Che, 10
Guha, Ranajit, 102
Guilbaut, Serge, 128, 129
Gun, Katherine, 17
Gutman, Rick, 83
Guzmán, Jacobo Arbenz, 21

Habermas, Jürgen, 110
Hall, Stuart, 35, 158, 185n16
Halperin, Morton, 59, 83
Hampton, Fred, 59
Harman, Jane, 181n46
Harris, Cheryl, 35
Haskins, Warren G., 29
Hatch, Orrin, 81
Hawai'i, 48–49
Hayden, Michael, 112
Hearst, Esther, 83
Helgerson, John, 112
Hellerstein, Alvin, 25, 111, 113
Hendricks, Evan, 74, 84
heteronormativity, 42
Hilderbrand, Lucas, 116
hipster culture, 39
Hiroshima, 39
Ho, Fred, 12
Hofstadter, Richard, 171n27
Holliday, George, 115
Holzer, Jenny: DODDOACID, 134–35, 136, 137; Light Line (exhibition), 183n31; Redaction Paintings, 26, 132, 133, 134–35, 136, 137, 143
Hood, Gavin, Official Secrets, 16–17
Hoover, J. Edgar, 64, 75, 124, 150, 166n18
Hopscotch (Neame), 80
House Government Information Subcommittee, 44
House Un-American Activities Committee (HUAC), 67
how-to pamphlets, 63, 68–69, 70, 71
HRW (Human Rights Watch), 93
Hughes, Howard, 49
Hughes Glomar Explorer, 49, 50, 50–51
Huntington, Samuel, 38, 54, 56

ideology: art and, 143; assimilation of, 36; of freedom of information, 55; of transparency, 60
immigration, 39
imperialism: anti-, 54, 82, 83, 93, 100–101; critiques of, 53; Freedom of Information Act and, 6–15; reproduction and, 34;

transparency and, 30; unlearning (Azoulay), 20; visuality and, 129
incomprehensibility, 33
indexes, 18, 69, 70, 72, 84
Index of the Disappeared (Ghani, Ganesh), 140
India, 52–53, 174n89, 174n92
individualism, 37
information: activism, 10–11, 63, 77, 80, 93; censored documents as, 5; classification of, 44; management, 21; work (counterpublics and), 18
Innis, Harold, 19
Institute for Policy Studies (IPS), 59, 67
intelligence abuses, 62–63
The Intelligence Network (documentary), 17, 58–60, 66, 68, 85, 146; debut of and invites to, 58, 59–60, 79–80; diagram for, 79; marketing, 82; multimedia mobilizing with, 77–81
Internal Security Act (1950), 39
Internal Threats Division (Office of Intelligence and Analysis), 1, 2
Interrogation of al Qaeda Operative (Kuzmich), 131
interrogations, 90, 103–4, 105–9, 121–22; videos, 25, 48, 95, 111–13, 114, 116, 118–19. See also torture
intimacies and freedom, 7
Inverse Surveillance Project (Boundaoui), 145, 146–47
invisibility, 39, 157–58
Iran, 138–39
Iraqi people, 116
Iraq war, 17
Israel, 53, 101, 135–37, 146, 183n31
Ito, Suzanne, 103–4

Japanese Americans, 69
Jarpa, Voluspa, 140–42, 144, 150; En nuestra pequeña región de por acá, 140, 142
Jessen, Bruce, 97, 105
Jihad News (publication), 64
Johnson, Lyndon, 30, 44
Jones, Nate, 7

148, 169n57; capitalism and, 16; Cold
War and, 16, 22–23, 92; cuts, 15, 16; decolonization and, 62; digital and, 159;
documents and, 168n46; feeling of, 156;
lawfare through, 92, 120; life of, 144,
153; management, 98; as media, 19, 20;
neoliberalism and, 62; ownership and,
159; police work and, 19–20; politics of,
15–16, 23, 26; power and, 15–22; as proof,
30; public sphere and, 32; securitization
of, 36; state (importance for), 22; violence and, 19; weaponization of, 11
Paraguay, 22
Patriot Act, 132
Paul, Ian Allen, *Guantanamo Bay Museum of
Art and History*, 131
Pentagon Papers, 17, 60
perception, 99
performance of redactions, 132–33
Perlin, Marshall, 72
Perry, Imani, 16, 168n44
Philip, M. NourbeSe: *Zong!*, 143
Phillippi, Harriet Ann, 49
Phillippi v. the C.I.A., 49
photocopying, 17
photography, 99, 123
physical binding, 97
Pinochet, Augusto, 59
poetry, erasure, 142–43
Polanyi, Michael, 39
policing: bureaucracy and, 19–20; information management and, 21; organizing
against, 80; paper and, 19–20; spying
by, 81; state and, 72, 144; videos and,
111, 115
politics of paper, 15–16, 23, 26
Pollock, Jackson, 128
populations, management of, 98
The Post (Spielberg), 17
Pratt, William, 13
Price, David, 10
primary discourse, 102
prisoners, abuse of, 89, 90–91, 92, 99–100,
118
prisons, film screenings at, 80

Privacy Act, exemptions to, 70
progress, narratives of, 34
Project Azorian, 49, *50*
property, 60
propriety, 60
protests, 93
psychological torture tactics, 97
the public, creation of, 110–11
publications, 10–11
Public Citizen (organization), 47
Public Eye (magazine), 71, 75
The Public Eye (newsletter), 74
Public Interest Research Group, 48
public record requests, 1, 2. *See also* FOIA
(Freedom of Information Act):
requests
Puerto Rican Socialist Party, 58

queer media practices, 63

race: capitalism, 19; deconstruction and, 33;
documents and, 150; formations, 34;
government responses to, 2; language
and, 44; Moynihan on, 54; the other
and, 54–55; politics of, 33; racism, 33,
36–37, 52, 81–83; state and, 34, 36, 67,
68, 145; transparency and, 33, 83; United
States and, 37
"Race Paper," 1–3, *3*, 15
Ramparts (magazine), 28–30, *31*, 53
RAND Corporation, 60
rationalism, 32
Ratner, Michael, 10
Rault, Jas, 166n15
RDI (Rendition, Detention, and Interrogation) program, 25, 91–92, 93, 154
reading: contrapuntal, 94, 101–2, 143, 148; redacted documents (experience of), 109
Reagan, Ronald and administration, 57, 66,
81–86
"Reckoning with Torture" (performance),
132
Recon: Keeping an Eye on the Pentagon (news-
letter), 74
Redaction (exhibition), 138

www.ingramcontent.com/pod-product-compliance
Lightning Source LLC
Chambersburg PA
CBHW020531270326
41927CB00006B/532